RELIGIOUS UPBRINGING AND THE COSTS OF FREEDOM

Edited by **PETER CAWS AND STEFANI JONES**

RELIGIOUS UPBRINGING AND THE COSTS OF FREEDOM

Personal and Philosophical Essays

The Pennsylvania State University Press
University Park, Pennsylvania

Library of Congress Cataloging-in-Publication Data

Religious upbringing and the costs of freedom :
personal and philosophical essays / edited by Peter Caws
and Stefani Jones.
      p.   cm.
Includes bibliographical references and index.
Summary: "Brings together autobiographical narratives
and reflections by philosophers who were brought up in
strict religious environments"—Provided by publisher.
ISBN 978-0-271-03679-3 (cloth : alk. paper)
ISBN 978-0-271-03680-9 (pbk. : alk. paper)
1. Religious biography.
I. Caws, Peter.
II. Jones, Stefani, 1971– .

BL72.R48 2010
200.92'2—dc22
[B]
2009046588

Copyright © 2010 The Pennsylvania State University
All rights reserved
Printed in the United States of America
Published by The Pennsylvania State University Press,
University Park, PA 16802-1003

It is the policy of The Pennsylvania State University Press
to use acid-free paper. Publications on uncoated stock
satisfy the minimum requirements of American National
Standard for Information Sciences—Permanence of Paper
for Printed Library Material, ANSI Z39.48–1992.

Contents

Acknowledgments vii

Introduction: The Indoctrination Project 1
   Peter Caws and Stefani Jones

PART 1: CHILDHOOD VULNERABILITY AND INTERNALIZED BELIEF

1 Indirect Indoctrination, Internalized Religion, and
   Parental Responsibility 11
   Christine Overall
2 Religious Indoctrination and the Wish for the Irrevocable:
   Reflections on a Muslim Upbringing 27
   Irfan Khawaja
3 From Fundamentalist to Freethinker (It All Began with Santa) 50
   Raymond D. Bradley
4 Growing Up to Question Catholicism: Emotional Suffering,
   the *Euthyphro*, and the Life of the Mind 73
   Damien Alexander Dupont

PART 2: RECONFIGURING THE MORALITY OF INDOCTRINATION

5 Biting into the Hermeneutical Apple: Biblical Literalism
   and the Lure of Uncertainty 97
   Amalia Jiva
6 Autonomy and Indoctrination in Evangelical Christianity 111
   Tasia Persson
7 Indoctrination, Autonomy, and Authenticity 134
   Glen Pettigrove

PART 3: EMBODIMENT, FAMILY, AND CONFLICT

8 From Revelation and Faith to Reason and Agnosticism 155
   Paul H. Hirst

9 For the Love of Paradox: Mennonite Morality and Philosophy   176
   Diane Enns
10 Finding My Voice   192
   Stefani Jones
11 Tragedies of Belief   214
   Peter Caws

About the Contributors   237

Index   241

Acknowledgments

Getting free of doctrinal entrapment is in many ways a lonely and difficult business. The hold doctrine has on the involuntary believer (because belief is coerced as a condition of family and social acceptance) operates at a deep level, dating from earliest childhood conditioning. It does not let go easily, and it may never let go entirely. One of the most potent helps along the way can be the double realization that nonbelievers can be as humane and compassionate as believers—far more so in fact—and that there may be others out there who have escaped from the same or similar constraints. Such personal reinforcement comes in diverse forms, as the various chapters of this book suggest, but for ourselves we would like to acknowledge at this point a few people who by friendship and example, or by encouragement and practical support, have contributed directly or indirectly to its making.

To begin with the practical: we would like to thank Jennifer Sieck, research assistant to the University Professor of Philosophy at the George Washington University, for her unfailing and good-humored reliability, and for her sharp eye in matters both of form and of content. The doctoral program in the Human Sciences at George Washington provided the interdisciplinary environment in which the project took shape. Professor Lewis Gordon of Temple University and an anonymous reader for the Pennsylvania State University Press offered valuable advice and encouragement.

Speaking now individually rather than jointly:

(SJ) I would like to thank Leslie Francis and Bridget Newell, who, unknowingly, changed my life by giving me a gift that I can never repay—the encouragement and support I needed to believe in myself and to forge a life of my own. I am especially grateful to my coeditor, Peter Caws, for being a mentor and friend. This book would never have been written without his passion for the topic and kind patience and persistence with me. Finally, I thank my daughters, Uma and Laila, who remind me on a daily basis that children deserve the opportunity to make and live futures of their own.

(PC) Among the many individuals who deserve my thanks, whose wisdom and warmth have (often unawares) marked stages on the way from indoctrination to freedom or provided stability and reassurance, I mention just a few—it would be impossible to list them all: the late C. G. Vernon,

Tony and Marjorie DeReuck, Thomas Pinney, Molly Donovan, Reed Whittemore, my cherished friends in the "Thursday group," Richard Wyman, Jill Mytton and the worldwide forum she founded and nurtures, and Lisa DeLeonardo; among my family, my sister, Jean Caws, my children, Hilary Caws-Elwitt and Matthew Rorison Caws and Elisabeth Breslin Caws, and above all my wife, Nancy Breslin, whose strength and love and understanding continue to anchor my life.

Finally we join once more in thanking all of our contributors for sharing their stories with us and for their responsiveness and patience along the way from first contact to publication.

Washington, D.C.
February 2010

INTRODUCTION: THE INDOCTRINATION PROJECT

Peter Caws and Stefani Jones

The essays in this book belong to two genres at once: they are memoirs, and they are philosophical analyses; they tell stories, and they make arguments. The stories are personal, the arguments more general. Their authors have two things in common: they have been trained in philosophy, but they were brought up religiously, in various strict versions of more or less familiar doctrines: Baptist, Catholic, Mormon, Mennonite, and Muslim. Each of them has had to break free, in one way or another, from restraint and oppression. Each has come to a mature view that rejects some or all of the teachings that were imposed upon them as children.

Everyone has to come to terms with a few basic conditions: embodiment, family, sexuality, interpersonal relations, the expectation of death. Many people deal with these things in ways accepted uncritically from their cultures of origin and do not consider them exceptionally problematic or stressful. A small minority think seriously about them and come to conclusions at odds with the culture, adopting new ways of life accordingly, and many of these remain on good terms with the unthinkingly orthodox. But some of the orthodox who are fanatically attached to their principles insist on conformity, exacting penalties for thought or behavior outside cultural norms— in some cases extreme penalties, as, for example, death for women who offend the supposed honor of their faith or family by marrying outsiders. Groups whose members behave in this way have come to be called "high demand organizations."

This clash of rebels and fanatics plays itself out continuously in less dramatic forms. Fierce Muslim youth in madrasas and ecstatic Christian youth in Sunday Schools and summer Bible study camps help to keep ideological oppositions (and their deadly political consequences) alive, but we hear less about the independent young people who resist their indoctrination and break away. What enables them to see past the official stories and strike out for understandings of their own? What forms of coercion and rejection are they subjected to—how costly is the freedom they achieve in terms of family affection and social acceptance?

It is hard to get good evidence on these points. People do not advertise their histories, so it is not usually obvious which of us have passed this way. The editors of this book did not initially know this about each other. In the course of working together in the Ph.D. program in the Human Sciences at the George Washington University we discovered (in the context of a small reading group on feminist ethics) a community of personal interest in the fact that under different regimes, at different times, and in different places, we had been subjected to similar ordeals—the frequent and all too familiar ordeals of children brought up by stubbornly religious parents. We came respectively from the Exclusive Brethren in England in the 1930s and 1940s, and from the Church of Jesus Christ of Latter-day Saints in Utah in the 1970s and 1980s. It was not surprising that the dissertation topic we agreed on should reflect an interest in parental influences on the potential autonomy of their children.

When that work was finished and defended,[1] we reopened a discussion that had begun along the way about the possibility of writing a joint article on the specific moral issues that arise when the convictions of one generation have a determining effect on the freedom of the next. But a scholarly article would capture only part of what concerned us; it would not convey a sense of the lived experience of indoctrination and of the work involved in achieving liberation from it. Here already our histories diverged, the details of the religious background and the reaction of the faithful to our apostasy (a term fraught with significance for believers) being quite different in the two cases. Mormons tend to be inclusive—those who lapse are still considered members and would no doubt be welcomed back at any time. But Exclusives are true to their name, and cut off those who lapse as rapidly and definitively as possible. So the vivid autobiographical parts of each story would not be easy to incorporate smoothly into the same text.

The project therefore remained tentative until it occurred to us that since presumably not too many people in the field were aware of our own intellectual origins, there were probably others out there of whose origins we and the rest of the profession were similarly unaware, even though they might have be as difficult and as interesting as ours. The idea of an article therefore metamorphosed into the idea of a book—this book.

Our suspicions about others having similar experiences were confirmed by the number of enthusiastic responses we received to our call for papers. There were not just a few people whose interest in philosophy helped them come to terms with their own childhood religious indoctrination, but dozens scattered around the world. And their personal stories differed, at times drastically. We eventually selected what we think to be a good representation of the variety of personal experiences, philosophical analyses, and religious orientations we encountered. The autobiographical components of the chapters reflect the nature of each writer's childhood community of belief and the price that had to be paid to escape from it. Most, though not all, of these histories involved some degree of personal stress. The professional components look at the moral issues that arise when caregivers try to coerce the beliefs of those entrusted to them, particularly when this involves restricting opportunities for personal development, the withholding of love, and so on.

The testimonies and reflections collected here are diverse, but their common theme gives them a striking unity. Their importance goes far beyond the bounds of professional philosophy—the fates of nations hang on the conflicting views with which each new generation of citizens is indoctrinated. If the world is to be really free, the chains of belief that seem to descend inexorably from parents to children, from religious and political leaders to their followers, have to be broken—in our own culture no less than in alien ones. We want to draw attention, through concrete examples, to the moral responsibilities of those who influence the young—responsibilities not only to those who resist, but even more to those who do not. While our examples are drawn from contexts in which there are overt religious agendas, the issues they raise are no less important in education generally, with its burden of unstated ideological and even theological assumptions.

While all our authors were brought up in religious familial or community contexts, the reactions of their coreligionists to their apostasies varied. For some, the break was painful and included varying degrees of estrangement from family. Others had the comparative luxury of calmly sorting through what is objectionable about inculcating a belief system and what is not. Their conclusions do not always agree. One source of disagreement is the concept of "indoctrination" itself. Is indoctrination necessarily coercive, or can it be benign? It seems inevitable that young children should be "indoctrinated" in the sense of being constrained to certain sorts of behavior, and beliefs about that behavior, while still too young to understand and appreciate the reasons why the behavior and the beliefs are desirable. But up to what age is it permissible to impose these things without explanation? or without consent? (note that explanation and consent do not necessarily come into play at the same age). Limited indoctrination does not necessarily pose a moral problem, provided that children are also taught the skills to critically examine the rules, principles, and beliefs that were indoctrinated and then encouraged to use those skills as soon as they are able to act responsibly on their own. Learning to act responsibly and autonomously has less to do with acquiring a belief system or framework than it has to do with developing the ability to decipher for oneself what one should do. Abuses of parental authority tend to result in diminished space for the child to practice freedom. When the initiative is not eventually handed over to the children, when indoctrination offers no space for them to become free and autonomous, parents are abusing their authority.

A central theme of this book, then, is an exploration into the ways that religious indoctrination interferes with a child's discovery of freedom. It is through other people, most often parents, that children are first introduced to the world and are provided with or inhibited from access to it. Children are always born into specific situations, into particular social and cultural contexts with already established moral and value systems, within which they become adults. In coming to terms with their freedom, they need the opportunity to deconstruct these systems and then to reconstruct them in ways they can call their own. For them to have the best chances of developing the self-esteem and confidence required to strike out for an autonomous understanding takes parental recognition and support.

Young people who are not offered such recognition and support may find the strength to embark on this voyage alone, but they often bear emotional scars from abandoning internalized systems of belief and coming to terms with rejection from family and community. Several of our contributors fit this description. Their stories reveal that the costs of autonomy are lived both internally and externally—in psychological upheaval, and in estrangement from loved ones and the communities that provided their first introduction to the world. Others, though, while undergoing changes no less radical, went through the process with less overt interference from without. Our first chapter, by Christine Overall, represents such a case. It describes an upbringing in the Anglican Church in Canada—not a setting normally associated with rigidity in doctrine. But as the author points out, indoctrination can happen indirectly, simply from the immersion of an impressionable child in a culture of belief, even belief not especially strongly held by the adult members of the relevant community. It can take hold just as effectively, if the child is serious and thoughtful, as in more coercive cases, and getting free of it may be just as distressing and require just as much work (if less family trauma).

The second chapter, by Irfan Khawaja, echoes Overall's experience in a starkly different cultural setting, that of a Sunni Muslim community in New Jersey. Rather than "indirect indoctrination," Khawaja speaks of "self-indoctrination," which follows again from the child's immersion in a belief system, in this case an absolutist system that leaves virtually no room for nuance, let alone dissent. The apparently cast-iron completeness of the doctrine answers to a human "wish for the irrevocable," so that lesser certainties seem unreal by comparison. Yet this unreality may in fact be the reality of the world we live in, which must be reappropriated by a process of "counter-indoctrination."

Chapter 3 takes us to a Baptist childhood and upbringing in New Zealand. Raymond Bradley's family came well connected in the Baptist hierarchy, from his missionary grandfather to the renowned theologian E. M. Blaiklock, an avuncular figure who eventually became an opponent in debate. Bradley's evolution into a freethinker went through family violence to professional maturity, leaving him with the conviction, shared by many of our contributors, that fundamentalist belief is "the most dangerous phenomenon of our times."

Chapter 4, the last in the first section of the book, begins with an account of growing up Catholic in the American Bible Belt. The Catholic Church had the kind of grip on Damien Dupont that Islam had on Irfan Khawaja, with some psychological complications that make his story compelling in a different way. But Dupont performs a similar deconstruction of the absolutist doctrines of the church. He concludes that all indoctrination is abusive, particularly of vulnerable children. Indoctrination may occur in nonreligious contexts; this too is contingently abusive, but religious indoctrination is constitutively so.

The next three chapters take a gentler approach. Amalia Jiva (Chapter 5) was a Romanian Baptist who on resettlement in the United States found herself a student at Jerry Falwell's Liberty University. She is critical of fundamentalist indoctrination and has rejected its literalism, but that rejection was experienced less as an opening out into freedom than as an introduction to a productive uncertainty, which she treasures. In Chapter 6 Tasia Persson, raised a conservative evangelical, undertakes a careful critique of the moral risks and consequences of indoctrination, and wonders whether evangelical parents might find ways of teaching their children that are not coercive and manipulative. And in Chapter 7 Glen Pettigrove, son of a Wesleyan pastor, describes a gradual and relatively stress-free transition from fundamentalism to a more liberal position, not involving the wholesale rejection of belief at which some of our contributors have arrived, and offers what he calls a "qualified defense of religious indoctrination," which need not as he sees it involve coercion or irrationality, or be inconsistent with autonomy and authenticity. It becomes morally objectionable only when it compromises autonomy or violates trust. Pettigrove's chapter takes a more benign view than that of some other chapters as to the possibility of avoiding these outcomes, and recommends a presumption of innocence with respect to indoctrination rather than one of suspicion.

The final section of the book comprises four accounts of upbringings in radically doctrinaire sects. Paul Hirst and Peter Caws come from different parts of England and different offshoots of the Plymouth Brethren, a loose grouping which was itself an offshoot from the Church of England in the 1830s—in Caws's case the suburbs of London and the Taylorite Exclusive Brethren, in Hirst's the industrial north and the Glanton Brethren (named for a village in Northumberland where a tempest in a doctrinal teapot led to a split in the Exclusives in 1908). Diane Enns grew up among Russian Mennonites in Ontario, and Stefani Jones as part of a Mormon family in Utah. In Chapter 8 Hirst recounts his spare, strict, and affectively bleak life as the child of an all too spiritual father and the opening up of perspective provided, among other things, by an exposure to mathematics and sex. But he was able to find his way to Cambridge and philosophy without making a complete break with his family—his slow, but final departure from belief tracked his career as a professional philosopher.

In Chapter 9 Enns describes the constricted life of immigrant fundamentalists, its grip on her—its inculcation of mistrust of the physical, mental, and emotional aspects of human life—but also its inconsistencies and moral flaws, and traces the path that led her to feminism and phenomenology. Jones too, in Chapter 10, comes to feminism, in part as a reaction to the situation of women in the Mormon Church, but helped by the liberating influence of some significant women with whom she was fortunate enough to study as an undergraduate. In her case the suppression of women's voices leads her to stress the importance of finding her own. Finally in Chapter 11 Caws places his main emphasis on the doubly tragic conflict between a son who cannot maintain belief and parents who cannot imagine life or salvation without it.

These thumbnail sketches of the chapters that follow stress their diversity, but for the most part overlook an important component that in different forms is present in all. The authors, as remarked at the beginning, are professional philosophers, and each refers in one way or another to his or her intellectual formation, reading, and experiences of the academy. Some of them give striking insights into specific university settings, notably Paul Hirst's account of the philosophical life of Oxford and Cambridge at critical moments in his history. And as professional philosophers most of them engage in serious conceptual and analytical work on the leading topics of the book—indoctrination itself and its moral status, freedom of thought and the human price it sometimes exacts. It can safely be said that none of them would be willing to go back to their points of departure; what they all would wish, we think, is that their experiences might serve as encouragement to others who may have to follow similar personal and philosophical trajectories.

NOTE

1. Stefani Jones, "The Becoming of a Moral Agent: Autonomy, Recognition, and the Parent-Child Relation" (Ph.D. diss., The George Washington University, 2004).

PART 1

CHILDHOOD VULNERABILITY AND
INTERNALIZED BELIEF

1

INDIRECT INDOCTRINATION, INTERNALIZED RELIGION, AND PARENTAL RESPONSIBILITY

Christine Overall

In this paper I present and defend three main claims, which I illustrate by means of my own experiences with religious indoctrination:

1. Parents may have a variety of reasons for supporting the religious indoctrination of their children. Despite the inadequacies of those reasons, the parents may not be morally culpable for the indoctrination of their children if they (the parents) lack the background, education, and cultural context that would enable them to evaluate the justifications for their actions.
2. There is such a thing as *indirect* indoctrination—the inculcation of religion that results not only from direct teaching and propaganda, but also indirectly, from what is missing from an upbringing, from the absence of alternatives, and from the absence of ways of thinking critically. This form of indirect indoctrination can be as effective as direct indoctrination in ensuring that a young child adopts a deeply religious worldview, particularly if the child internalizes the worldview and makes it a part of her self-understanding.
3. Leaving a religious institution after a process of indoctrination, whether direct or indirect, can be a distressing experience *even if* there are no direct external consequences for leaving the faith. If the doctrine is sufficiently internalized, the individual's entanglement within the religious system becomes its own source of negative consequences when she abandons her faith.

I wish to acknowledge and thank my family, especially my mother, Dorothy Overall, my husband, Ted Worth, and my children, Devon Worth and Narnia Worth, who in various ways enabled me to write this chapter. I am also grateful to Peter Caws and Stefani Jones for the opportunity to contribute to their anthology.

Nonculpable Indoctrination

I received a formal religious upbringing and was baptized and confirmed as an Anglican (a faith called Episcopalianism in the United States and the Church of England in Britain). My godmother gave me one of my first books, a children's collection of Bible stories, which I still possess today. Some of my earliest memories are of attending Sunday School while my mother was at church services. I learned the usual Bible stories and ended up with a narrative understanding of some of the key figures in the Old Testament—Adam and Eve, Moses, David, Solomon, Samson—and Jesus and his disciples in the New Testament. I also learned children's hymns:

> Jesus loves me, this I know,
> For the Bible tells me so.
> Little ones to him belong.
> They are weak but he is strong.[1]

By the age of eight I was known to be a good reader, and so for a couple of years I was chosen to read the Christmas story in church. But it was evident to me that real maturity would come when I was finally allowed to attend church services regularly. On the rare occasions when I was permitted to do so, I felt that the minister was preaching directly to me.

Every year for four summers in a row, starting when I was nine, I was sent to an Anglican church camp for two weeks. The original impulse to send me was not religious but pragmatic. The third child in the family, my baby brother, was born the summer I turned nine. My parents thought it would be good to have at least one child out of the way for part of the summer. And church camp was relatively inexpensive. For me, the camp experience was a mixed bag. I loved some aspects of it—especially the opportunity to sing together after every meal, to play games, and to put on skits. But I was also deeply homesick, scared by some of the leaders, and very afraid of the immense darkness of the rural location.

Religious instruction was an important part of the camp experience. We had religious teaching every day and church services at an outdoor "chapel" on Sundays. The instructors were dull and lifeless. They faced an uphill struggle to communicate with pubescent girls who were more preoccupied with sex and romance than with religion. Attempts to make us feel sinful for talking about sex were mostly unsuccessful, and I suspect that few new church teachings penetrated our preoccupied minds. Perhaps more effective, however, were the spirituals we sang each day. Although the Anglican Church itself was sedate and self-contained, the spirituals we were taught were fervent and highly emotional. They conveyed a deep sense of faith. We sang,

> Ezekiel saw a wheel a'rollin', way in the middle of the air.
> A wheel within a wheel a'rollin', way in the middle of the air.
> And the big wheel ran by faith, and the little wheel ran by the grace of God.
> A wheel within a wheel a'rollin', way in the middle of the air.

and

> I've got a home in glory land that outshines the sun, oh Lordy,
> I've got a home in glory land that outshines the sun.
> I've got a home in glory land that outshines the sun,
> Look away beyond the blue horizon.[2]

I was thrilled and inspired by the sound of a hundred young girls, their counselors, and their leaders singing these songs with spirit, enthusiasm, and even occasional harmonization. I still remember and love the melodies today.

At the age of twelve I was confirmed in the Anglican Church. Confirmation training was a dull process. For a couple of hours each week the group of boys and girls who were candidates had to sit in the church pews to be instructed by the minister. The other kids fooled around a lot, behavior that scandalized me. I was bored but I took the instruction seriously. I remember little about the minister's instruction, except for his explanation that "atonement" should be understood as "at one-ment," a process of being reunited with God.

On my confirmation day my gifts included a copy of the King James Bible and an Anglican prayer book. I felt grown up as I took my first communion, savoring the sip of holy wine. The host, which I could not quite bring myself to think of as Jesus's body, rested flavorlessly on my tongue and then stuck to the roof of my mouth.

The *Concise Oxford Dictionary* defines the verb "indoctrinate" as "teach (a person or group) systematically or for a long period to accept (esp. partisan or tendentious) ideas uncritically."[3] By this definition there is no doubt that I was successfully indoctrinated into the Anglican faith. I was deeply convinced that prayer was both important and powerful. As an eight-year-old I had experienced an attempted abduction by a stranger, which continued to worry me for years. I was afraid of everything from housefires and burglaries to bombs and nuclear war. There was no space in my family for talking about our fears or receiving reassurance, so I turned to God for comfort.

My parents had taught me to pray before bedtime. I had to kneel at the bedside with my hands pressed together and my elbows resting on the mattress. The family prayer was:

> Jesus, tender shepherd, hear me.
> Bless thy little lamb tonight.
> Through the darkness be thou near me.
> Keep me safe till morning light.[4]

It was a verse guaranteed to make a sensitive child even more aware of possible dangers. Since I was deeply afraid of the dark—a fear I did not get over until I was twenty—I had a genuine sense of needing protection at night. After saying the verse, I had to add the God blesses: "God bless Mummy, Daddy, Johnny, Davey, and Tiger [our cat]. And God bless me and make me a good girl. Aaahmen!"

When I outgrew that ritual and was no longer required to pray in front of my parents, I continued to pray silently in bed after the lights were out. My parents believed in putting children to bed early. I was an insomniac and lay awake for at least an hour, often two, before falling asleep. Some of that time was taken up with praying. In the spirit of "making me a good girl," I talked with God about my various failings—not only those frequently picked out by my parents and teachers (in particular, the crime of "talking back"), but also some I had spotted in myself, such as envy and jealousy. I continued to ask God to "keep me safe" both night and day. When I was at church camp praying seemed especially apropos, and it was my only recourse in dealing with my fear of the dark.

Although I had been successfully indoctrinated, neither of my parents, oddly enough, was particularly committed to the Anglican Church. I knew my father did not go to services, but that was normal gender behavior for almost all the men in my family and my neighborhood. What I did not know was that my father had returned from a stint in the Canadian Air Force during World War II that had pretty well taken the moral and spiritual stuffing out of him. Meanwhile my mother, apparently an observant Christian and definitely the more active of the two, privately entertained doubts about the truth of religious belief—although I did not find out about her skepticism until I was an adult.

To analyze my parents' approach to religious education, I need to distinguish between reasons and causes. Reasons are the ideas, evidence, and arguments that are used to support and defend beliefs. Causes are the factors—physical, social, or psychological, conscious or not—that produce actions, including human behavior.

In retrospect, I now understand that my parents had several reasons for encouraging in their children a faith about which they themselves were somewhat skeptical, even cynical. Partly it was a matter of adhering to tradition, a tradition strongly upheld in both my mother's middle-class family and my father's working-class family. Both families were Anglican; everyone in both families was baptized, confirmed, and married, and had been or would eventually be buried within the rituals of the Anglican Church.[5] Another reason my mother apparently experienced no discomfort in indoctrinating me and my brothers in the church was that she herself sought solace in the history and beauty of Anglicanism. She loved the traditional music and prayers and enjoyed the splendor of old churches. She appreciated good sermons and treasured the language of the King James Bible. But neither tradition nor beauty and solace would seem to be sufficient moral justification for teaching children beliefs that one does not regard as true.

My parents also saw religious indoctrination as a straightforward way of teaching morality. This is the attitude of many people, including, to my dismay, some parents of my own Baby Boomer generation. They think that religious teachings are the soundest method for inculcating solid values into their children. There is no need to think through a list of rights and wrongs, puzzling about moral quandaries, if the Bible already purports to do that for you, and if the church and Sunday School teachers reinforce the religious code. It might seem that allocating moral instruction to religion is the abdication of responsibility for teaching one's children to be good people. But most people, and my parents were among them, have never thought about the foundations of morality. If asked, most people would probably be comfortable with the idea that moral values come from God. That answer would have been a little more difficult for my parents, given their skepticism. But neither one of them had attended university. They graduated from high schools that relied on memorization and required little in the way of original or creative thought (exactly my own situation in high school twenty-five years later). There was no encouragement to think about theoretical issues such as the origin and foundation of morals.

But perhaps the most important reason for indoctrinating us, as my mother now, in her eighties, will admit, was her engagement in a kind of

Pascalian wager.[6] Pascal argued that one cannot know whether or not God exists; hence one should treat the issue as a wager. If God exists, the consequence of religious belief is positive ("infinitely happy life"), whereas the consequence of disbelief is negative (the loss of infinitely happy life). Therefore, reason bids you to believe that God exists.[7] My mother applied the wager in particular to my youngest sibling David, who was born with serious health problems. My mother felt we might lose him, and so she hastened to have him baptized, even though her faith was weaker than it had been when I was baptized. She admits now that she did it as a kind of insurance: Just in case Christianity was correct, my brother would have a hope of heavenly life if he were to die in childhood. And if he was baptized, then God (if he existed) might even be moved to save his life.

In the end my brother did not die; in fact, he recovered completely. I doubt that his recovery was the result of divine intervention. Nonetheless, my parents had ensured that all three of their children were protected, *in case* Christianity should turn out to be correct, by making us members of the Anglican Church. I believe their wager is neither morally nor epistemically justified. Among its many flaws, the wager assumes that Christianity is the only viable form of religion; that if God exists he punishes unbelievers; and that there is no other choice than belief or disbelief. But understandably, my parents never engaged in a systematic critical evaluation of their bet.

Prima facie, parents should be held morally culpable for the religious indoctrination of their children if they have reasons to know better. But I do not hold my parents culpable for the religious indoctrination that I received. Although their reasons for doing so were inadequate, they could not have known better. And here I turn to the main *causes* of their practice of indoctrination, the forces that prevented them from doing anything else.

My parents grew up in Anglo-Saxon urban Toronto during the Great Depression. Virtually everyone was religiously observant. Adopting any religion other than Christianity was unthinkable. In addition to the absence of alternatives, my parents and their friends and neighbors acquired no tools for thinking critically about religion and its place in society. None of them had studied philosophy or any of the other humanities at the university level. None of them had any familiarity with social sciences. My parents each completed high school, but many of their generation did not. In the first half of the twentieth century, behavioral and ideological conformity was a norm so compelling that it could not even be recognized. Within this context, religious indoctrination was an unquestioned practice, and it is this milieu that caused my parents to indoctrinate my brothers and me—very much as they themselves had been indoctrinated—and to regard it as the enactment of their parental duty.

Direct and Indirect Indoctrination

I was directly and actively indoctrinated by means of church doctrines, prayers, hymns, and Bible stories—at home, to a small extent, but even more in Sunday School, church, church camp, and even my ostensibly "public" school, which offered compulsory religious teachings given by an Anglican minister when I was in grade eight. There was little that was profound or complex about anything I learned. The main idea that I extracted from the teachings was the fundamental and unreflective belief that there is a God; that he (most definitely he) created the world; and that he loved me. Despite being a confirmed Christian, I thought very little about Jesus, who appeared to be simply a stand-in for the most important personage, his father, who was also the father of us all.

But the kind of indoctrination I received was at least as much passive and indirect as it was active and direct. Here's what I mean.

First, within the neighborhood where I grew up, I knew only Roman Catholics and Protestants. We Protestants were aware of some divisions among us—as well as the Anglicans, there were Baptists and members of the United Church (a Canadian combination of Methodist and Presbyterian). But these versions of Christianity were not sufficiently different from the Anglican to provoke thought or provide a real alternative. Indeed, I was subtly encouraged to think of "my" religion as superior, since on the one hand it was not "watered down" like the United Church's doctrines, and on the other hand not socially highly conservative like the Baptist Church, which, to our amazement, forbade dancing, card-playing, and the consumption of alcohol. Jehovah's Witnesses occasionally attempted to proselytize at our door, but my mother felt a real vitriol for them; their faith was never seen as any competition to our own.[8]

The other religious possibility evident in my childhood world was Roman Catholicism. Catholic children attended their own religious schools; the rest of us went to the public schools. Because immigration had not yet produced the multicultural environment that now defines most large Canadian cities, the differences between Protestants and Catholics were the defining schism in my neighborhood. Nonetheless, Catholics and Protestants could become friends. On one occasion when I was about fourteen, a few of us attempted our own little entente across the Catholic/Protestant divide. I had occasionally been attending the Catholic Church, since my boyfriend was an altar boy there. (He was the main attraction as far as I was concerned.) In reciprocity, a few of my Catholic friends came to my own church. Unsurprisingly, we found relatively few differences between the Mother Church, Catholicism, and Anglicanism, the wayward offspring created as a result of Henry VIII's desire for a divorce centuries ago. Yet my friends and I had further ambitions. We wanted to investigate other religions, of whose existence we were just barely cognizant, but we could see no evidence of any, anywhere. There were no Jews, Muslims, Buddhists, Hindus, Taoists, Sikhs, or Jains in our district. I did not meet Jewish people until I was sixteen and was introduced to a group of students from another part of the city. I did not encounter Muslims until I was in my twenties, although in high school I was moved to do a project on Islam for a history course.[9]

As a result, my religious indoctrination was indirect in the sense that there was no opportunity or encouragement to experience or even imagine an alternative to the belief system in which I was raised. Moreover, not being religious at all was literally unthinkable. There was simply no alternative to belief. There were also no role models. Growing up in a postwar working-class suburb, I don't ever remember meeting a self-declared agnostic or atheist. Nonbelievers, if there were any, must have been closeted. Despite being a voracious reader, I never encountered agnostics or atheists in my books.

In addition, there was no explicit training in critical thinking. This weakness was perhaps not surprising at my home, since neither of my parents had gone to university. But there was also no such training in primary school or high school. No one whom I encountered before going to university myself ever suggested that religious faiths might be critically examined. Indeed, there was little or no critical thinking encouraged about anything, except (and only by the most creative of our English teachers) with respect to works of literature that we studied in English class.

As a result of all these factors, direct and indirect, my religious indoctrination was highly successful. It was not painful, seldom intrusive, and apparently benign. It worked not just because of what it was, but because of the absence of any countervailing factors that might have created skepticism in my mind. The only possible source of skepticism would have been my parents—and for my first two decades, they kept their thoughts to themselves.

Internalized Religion and the Pain of Leaving the Faith

I lost my faith in my late teens. Although in high school we were not encouraged to engage in independent thinking, I began to see that there was something inherently improbable in many of the stories taken to be the word of God. The sheer physical impossibility of many events struck me, especially the creation of the universe in six days and the resurrection of Jesus after his crucifixion. Around seventeen I actually took out a philosophy book from the local library. It was an introductory text on Descartes, Locke, Berkeley, and Hume. I could make very little of it, but the fact that I borrowed it indicates, I think, that my mind was struggling to wake up. At the same time, church services began to seem tiresome, mostly just an imposition on an adolescent whose life was divided between studying and going on dates. I stopped attending.

My journey to atheism was greatly accelerated when I took my first philosophy course at the University of Toronto. I was eighteen, and dazzled by the subject—as well as amazed that grown men (of course they were all men) could earn a living talking about the kinds of difficult issues of which I had heretofore gotten only a glimpse. Over six hundred students were packed into the "Introduction to Philosophy" course held in the university's Convocation Hall. Every few weeks we had a different professor, chosen from among the most senior in the department, to introduce a new topic to us. We worked our way through baby logic and Plato's *Meno* in the first term. In the second term we were confronted with *a priori* knowledge, ethics, political philosophy, and philosophy of religion. The latter consisted primarily of arguments for and against the existence of God, sympathetically taught by a philosophy professor who had a positive attitude toward spiritual matters. His teaching was fair and judicious. Within days of thinking about his lectures I could clearly see that none of the standard arguments—cosmological, teleological, or ontological—could possibly support belief in God. Then the argument from evil dealt a deathblow to my theism. I could not reconcile the existence of an omnipotent and omnibenevolent God with the existence of enormous amounts of suffering by human and nonhuman animals.

The foundation of my religious commitment had been exploded—exploded via philosophical examination. The new critical thinking to which I was introduced also made it impossible for me any longer to rely on authority or popular opinion as a prop for my faith. So philosophy freed me, in what appeared to be a straightforward triumph of the inculcation of critical thinking via higher education. But it also freed me into anomie and terror. Losing my faith created a serious crisis for me.

The crisis was not occasioned by any external consequences. There were no negative consequences from the church itself or my community, neither of which had any way of punishing me. My parents had been equanimous when I stopped attending Sunday services. By that time, my mother must have concluded I was safe enough: I knew Christianity; I was a permanent member of the Anglican Church. Moreover, having never attended university themselves, my parents were almost in awe of my university training. Believing that they lacked the skills, they would not engage in philosophical debate with me, and expressed nothing but bemusement when I tried to describe the ideas I was learning.

Instead of coming upon me from without, the negative consequences of losing my faith were generated from within, for I had actively incorporated my religion into my sense of self. My faith had played an important role in supporting me, as the eldest daughter of an alcoholic father, during an upbringing that was often bewildering and filled with physical punishments. I was very accustomed to talking to the great Father in the sky. Most of all, my religious beliefs were tied to my sense of purpose and meaning in life. I had wholly accepted the idea that all values come from and are justified by a divine source. No other possible sources had occurred or been presented to me.

So when I lost God, I immediately concluded that there could be no meaning in life and no point to my own continued existence. I seemed to have been tossed into this huge universe, finding myself to be not a child of God but an organism with no more significance than an ant or a worm. Moreover, if there is no God, I reasoned, there could also be no life after death. I was stuck with the skimpy few decades on earth allotted to every human being. And after our deaths I would never be reunited with my grandparents and parents in heaven.

I did not actively plan suicide, but I thought about death a lot. I could see no other alternative. Any way of life, any plan or activity, looked like nothing more than make-work with no intrinsic value. I discussed my loss of faith with almost no one, having come to believe that my crisis was unique and I must handle it on my own. Even now, it is hard to see who might have helped me. Not my family, who had no apparent interest in discussing questions of life's meaning; they were too busy just getting by. Not my friends. I was close to very few of them, and none of them was capable of understanding and responding to the existential dread that was enveloping me.

Not my professors. At that time, the 1960s, one did not discuss one's life crises with a professor, even if that life crisis had been partly engendered by intellectual material. In my second year of university, feeling desperate, I made an appointment with a psychiatrist at the university's student services department. He saw me twice, then sent me away, saying I didn't need help. I was more disoriented than ever, for now I had been told that the problem that consumed me was of no real significance.

It took me a couple of years to work my way out of this despair, although its aftereffects lingered for some time. Three factors helped me to make the transition: the excitement and inspiration of my philosophy courses; feminism, which I discovered around that time; and my relationship with my Catholic boyfriend, who, as he became closer to me, gradually withdrew from his own church.

My studies in philosophy helped for two reasons. First, they gave me a way to identify difficult moral and metaphysical problems and methods for creating and evaluating possible solutions to them. Second, the particularity of the problems I was considering provided a focus for my thinking and a distraction from what I believed to be the biggest question, What are we here for? It is perhaps not surprising that I became especially interested in epistemological questions about the reliability of sense perception and the challenges posed to it by experiences that were what I called "non-normal": drug experiences, mysticism, and trance experiences.[10] I had no particular confidence in religious experiences, but I was struck by what seemed to be the universality of mystical experiences and wondered if, by providing insight into another and greater reality, they could offer an alternate source of meaning, one that would be nontheistic—or at least non-monotheistic—in nature.

Feminism also helped save me. I had previously overlooked, ignored, rationalized, or resigned myself to gender inequities. Now, by developing my political sensibility, feminism enabled me to identify and explain the sexist and misogynist behavior I witnessed almost everywhere. It helped me to recognize sexual harassment, reject sexist messages in the media, and challenge social policies and practices that disadvantaged women. It attuned me, in ways I had never been before, to the culture in which I was living and its subtle and implicit ideology. Perhaps most important, however, it gave me a new sense of self, as a person who could make a life out of intellectual pursuits, and who, even while being a sexual being, need not become the appendage of a man. As a result, my deep yet inchoate search for capital-M Meaning in human life became a more manageable search for purpose and direction in my own life.

Perhaps surprisingly, it was also my Catholic boyfriend who helped me to recover from my helpless dark night of the soul. He had been, as far as I can tell, as thoroughly indoctrinated in the Catholic faith as I in the Anglican faith. Yet his break from Catholicism was gradual and, from what he says, painless. Religion just came to seem irrelevant to his life, and having a skeptical girlfriend did not encourage him to stick with it. He also made it evident that he would love me whatever my religious beliefs might be. At one point, briefly, we made plans to marry within the Catholic Church. Ironically, it was not my burgeoning atheism that eventually caused me to reject that plan. It was my feminism, which balked at the idea of a sexist institution's forcing me to raise my children (not that I planned to have any, at that point) as Roman Catholics.

I can now say that despite the short-term pain, over the much longer term there has been no negative aftermath of my break from my religious upbringing. There were no repercussions within my family of origin. Not only were my parents neutral about my rejection of religion; my mother in some ways admired my strident atheism. I married my Catholic boyfriend in a brief civil ceremony at Toronto city hall. We have now been married for thirty-six years. We raised our two children openly and honestly to know that their mother is an atheist and their father an agnostic.

Still, I find it a little surprising that neither child is now a believer, since their father's side of the family consists of a number of practicing Catholics, including the children's favorite aunts and cousins. When he was three, our son went through a brief period of interest in religion, and we encouraged him to talk with his Catholic aunts and with friends of ours who are progressive Protestants. There were lively discussions around the dinner table as our children grew up. At about the age of about five, our daughter staked her claim as the only believer in the family (influenced, apparently, by the teachers at her day care center). In the end our son settled for outspoken atheism, like his mother, while his sister became a more laid-back agnostic like her father.

Religious believers are sometimes inclined to say that nonbelievers have their own religion, the religion of unbelief. Similarly, it might be argued that my spouse and I indoctrinated our children into skepticism. I think that charge would be unfounded. Unlike my parents, we were not motivated by any Pascalian wager. Nor did we use religion as an easy route to the teaching of morality, but instead indicated clearly what our values are, putting forward honesty, love, kindness, and loyalty as virtues that are essential simply to being a good person.

In addition, by interaction and example, we sought to teach our children the tools of critical thinking. Our success was mixed at first. I once heard my five-year-old son arguing with his friend, who was Jewish. My son insisted, over his friend's objections, that there was no God. The friend insisted, over my son's objections, that there was no Santa Claus. I don't know which one was more shocked.[11]

Our children, now adults, seem to have experienced no untoward effects from their upbringing—except that they are regrettably ignorant of both the Old and New Testaments. However, so is my husband, since Roman Catholics of his generation were not encouraged to study the Bible. By contrast, I have a fund not only of religious stories but of direct quotations in my head, all from the beautiful King James Version. When I finally recognized this cultural liability in my children, I attempted to set it right, but by then they were beyond the point of being willing to listen to Bible stories and hymns.

As for myself, I have retained a lingering fascination with religion. Perhaps a part of me wants to believe, even though it cannot, in good faith—so to speak—do so. Although I was a highly indignant atheist at first (much as those who quit smoking are most critical of the habit), my militancy gradually diminished. When I undertook doctoral training in philosophy, I wrote a doctoral thesis on mystical experiences, focusing on the work of W. T. Stace, an Anglo-American philosopher who was the first person within the analytic tradition to treat mysticism seriously.[12]

Now, as a tenured professor, I occasionally teach the philosophy of religion, although my main fields are feminist philosophy, applied ethics, and social philosophy. My perspective in philosophy of religion is atheistic, at least with respect to Western theism. I have published a number of papers arguing that if miracles were to occur, they would be *prima facie* evidence against the existence of God.[13] Most recently, I have written about feminist arguments for atheism.[14] Although I reject those forms of theism that involve a separation between God and the universe, and that require acceptance of a hierarchy of beings, I remain interested in, although still not convinced by, forms of pantheism that emphasize the oneness of reality and its purported divinity.[15]

Conclusion

There are many kinds of consequences of leaving a religious faith. Most social scientific discussions focus on the external consequences: ostracism, expulsion, and the loss of property, status, and community. But my experience suggests that there may also be internal consequences, and they can be painful. When one has been raised to suppose that all value rests upon divine fiat, the loss of faith produces anomie, an absence of meaning, and the disappearance of goals and groundedness. I am glad I survived the experience.

I have no doubt that I was indoctrinated into the Anglican faith. The reasons for which my parents initiated and supported that indoctrination—tradition, beauty, and history; moral instruction; wagering on God's existence—are not adequate to justify it. Yet I do not hold them culpable because they were nonetheless *caused* to indoctrinate their children by the sheer absence of any other choice. My parents grew up and lived within a relatively impoverished, monolithic cultural environment that failed to offer any alternative, whether religious or nonreligious, to Christianity. As a consequence, like them I was the target not only of direct indoctrination, but of indirect indoctrination, which is just as effective.

Thanks both to my education and to the gradual but profound enrichment of Canadian urban culture, primarily as a result of new immigrants from all over the world, I do not exist within the homogeneous society that defined my parents' lives. In Canada, I suggest, religious indoctrination remains morally unjustified and is now much harder to excuse. The void that surrounded Christianity—the absence of alternatives that my parents and I experienced—disappeared in late twentieth-century Canada. As a result, parents like me had and continue to have a responsibility to raise their children differently than we were raised. I am fortunate that it has been possible for me to make reasoned choices about my own beliefs and about educating my children.

I still think about my old question: If there is no God, how can life have a meaning? On the one hand, we all belong to the same species. On the other hand, we're all different, both as individuals and as communities. So maybe it's a mistake to think in terms of *the* meaning of life. Perhaps the answer is that there are multiple meanings.

An understanding of the meaning of my life came to me over the course of many dinner table discussions with my husband and children. What could be more necessary than human understanding? What could be more important than human connections? For me, the meaning of life is to know what is true and to love and be loved. My religion of upbringing gave me glimpses of the importance of those goals, but I could fully comprehend them only once I had stepped outside religion's boundaries.

Moreover, I would argue that knowing what is true and loving and being loved are incompatible with religious indoctrination. Indoctrination makes it more difficult for us to understand the world and our place in it. And it thereby also makes love more difficult. For when parenting includes indoctrination, there is a risk that the offspring may one day learn that their beliefs have been manipulated and their trust is misplaced. So, indoctrination also compromises the creation of loving relationships in which all persons flourish.

NOTES

1. Words by Anna B. Warner, 1860.
2. I've been unable to find the authors of these two songs, although various Web references confirm that they are common camp songs and that both may be African American spirituals.
3. *The Concise Oxford Dictionary of Current English*, 9th ed., s.v. "indoctrinate."
4. The verse comes from a hymn created by Mary Duncan in 1839.
5. My mother's own mother, although outwardly a progressive and even at times unorthodox woman, was very "high church." After her death I found two rosaries among her possessions, although to my knowledge the Anglican Church, unlike the Roman Catholic Church, does not advocate the use of rosaries.
6. Blaise Pascal, *Pensées*, trans. A. J. Krailsheimer (Harmondsworth, U.K.: Penguin Books, 1966), 149–52.
7. Pascal also assumed that if there is no God, then one has still lost nothing from a lifetime of belief. This assumption appears to be unfounded, since one might have made sacrifices for nothing and engaged in pointless behavior.
8. One Sunday a pair of Jehovah's Witnesses showed up at our door just as my mother was trying to get her three young children ready for church. "I'm going to *my* church," proclaimed my mother to their startled faces. "Why don't you go to *yours?*"
9. I think my choice of the topic was related both to my strong interest in religion and my later attraction to philosophy. However, the "research" for the project (in books from the school and community libraries) encouraged me to think of Islam as an exotic set of beliefs and rituals utterly foreign to my own life and religious faith.
10. Two of the most important books I read at the time are Charles T. Tart, ed., *Altered States of Consciousness* (Garden City, N.Y.: Anchor Books, 1972), and John White, ed., *The Highest State of Consciousness* (Garden City, N.Y.: Anchor Books, 1972).
11. My son had already decided against God, but Santa Claus was more difficult for him to give up. I had not wanted to encourage him to believe in Santa, but early in his life my spouse persuaded me to permit it. For family reasons we were, after all, raising our children as "cultural Christians"—that is, they were being taught some of the cultural customs of the faith (primarily centered around holidays), although not the religious ideology associated with those customs.
12. His most important work on the philosophy of mysticism is W. T. Stace, *Mysticism and Philosophy* (London: Macmillan, 1961). Also see Christine Overall, "The Nature of Mystical Experience," *Religious Studies* 18 (1982): 47–54; Overall, "Mysticism, Phenomenalism, and W. T. Stace," *Transactions of the Charles S. Peirce Society* 18 (1982): 177–90; and Overall, "Walter Terence Stace," in the *Dictionary of Twentieth Century British Philosophers*, ed. Stuart Brown (Bristol: Thoemmes Press, 2005), 990–94.
13. See Christine Overall, "Miracles as Evidence Against the Existence of God," *Southern Journal of Philosophy* 23, no. 3 (1985): 347–53; Overall, "Miracles and God: A Reply to Robert A. H. Larmer," *Dialogue* 36 (1997): 741–52; Overall, "Miracles and Larmer," *Dialogue* 42 (2003): 123–35; and Overall, "Miracles, Evidence, Evil, and God," *Dialogue* 45 (2006): 355–66.

14. See Overall, "Feminism and Atheism," in *The Cambridge Companion to Atheism*, ed. Michael Martin and Ricki Monnier (Cambridge: Cambridge University Press, 2006), 233–49.

15. See, for example, Grace M. Jantzen, *Becoming Divine: Towards a Feminist Philosophy of Religion* (Manchester: Manchester University Press, 1998), and Carol P. Christ, *She Who Changes: Re-Imagining the Divine in the World* (New York: Palgrave Macmillan, 2003).

2

RELIGIOUS INDOCTRINATION AND THE WISH FOR THE IRREVOCABLE: REFLECTIONS ON A MUSLIM UPBRINGING

Irfan Khawaja

I was born in Jersey City in 1969 into a middle-class family of Pakistani origin and indoctrinated into the orthodox Sunni Muslim faith literally from birth: Muslim fathers traditionally whisper the "Fatiha" or Exordium of the Qur'an into the ear of a newborn child, and my father was no exception.[1]

That, I suppose, is indoctrination if anything is, but in its ordinary connotations, the term "indoctrination" misses what I take to be one of the most morally salient features of the phenomenon. In one sense, "indoctrination" is a relatively innocuous practice. Taken literally, to indoctrinate is simply to teach a doctrine, and since parents impart moral education of some sort to their children, and any principled moral teaching is in some weak sense a doctrine, indoctrination would seem to be an unavoidable feature of child-rearing. In another sense, however, indoctrination is taken to be something sinister—the impartation of a doctrine by methods that undercut autonomy, like brainwashing or coercion. In this sense, indoctrination is typically associated with crime, terrorism, and fanaticism: images readily spring to mind of the brainwashing of the Jim Jones, Branch Davidian, or Heaven's Gate cults, or of the mindless chanting and head-bobbing of the stereotypical Islamic madrasa.

Without denying either the benign or the sinister interpretations of indoctrination, there is in my view a subtler story to be told about it, one that I know from decades of personal experience. Though my religious upbringing put me on the receiving end of some (relatively mild) coercion, the real threat to autonomy in it had its source in an apparently paradoxical sort of *self*-indoctrination—a sort more sinister than the mere impartation of moral education, but less dramatic than any legally adjudicable crime. My aim here is to describe the nature of self-indoctrination in a fairly typical Muslim-American setting and offer an assessment of it that applies specifically to Islam, and more broadly to religious indoctrination as such.

A Muslim Upbringing

A discussion of indoctrination into the "orthodox Sunni Muslim faith" presupposes at least a rudimentary knowledge of Muslim doctrine, as well as the form that that doctrine characteristically takes in middle-class Pakistani-American families like my own. I begin, then, by describing the essential features of Muslim doctrine as I learned and practiced them, and the way in which I was indoctrinated into them.

Though the 9/11 attacks (and Islamic terrorism generally) have made Islam seem an exorbitantly alien or exotic religion, in fact, orthodox Islam differs very little in its essential features from orthodox Judaism or Christianity. The basic creed of Islam is the *shehada*, affirmation of which is the necessary and sufficient condition of membership in the Islamic faith: "There is no deity but God and Muhammad is the messenger [or 'prophet'] of God." Anyone who calls himself a Muslim must recite and wholeheartedly believe the *shehada*; by the same token anyone who *does* believe the *shehada* is by definition a Muslim, whatever else may be said about him. Contrary to many writers on the subject—including some experts in Islamic Studies[2]—this fact by itself implies that Islam is as much an ortho*doxy* as it is an ortho*praxy*. What matters is *both* what a Muslim believes and what he does: ritual without correct belief is by Islamic strictures aimless and valueless.[3] The *shehada* is thus the crux of Muslim belief, and wholehearted doxastic commitment is the crux of the *shehada*. It follows, trivially, that to successfully indoctrinate someone into Islam, you must induce him to believe wholeheartedly in the *shehada*. Ideally, one induces belief in a self-reinforcing manner, so that the believer actively seeks out confirmation of the *shehada*, and actively stifles his own doubts in it.

The content of the *shehada* is deceptively simple. To believe it, one has to believe the conjunction of two propositions, along with what they imply:

1. A single God exists.
2. Muhammad is the messenger of the God mentioned in (1).

The content of these claims turns in large part on the content of the "message" implicit in (2), and the message comes to us by way of the Qur'an, which in its standard edition is thought by Muslims to contain a direct, accurate, and verbatim transcription of the word of God as dictated to the Prophet Muhammad. Implicit in affirming the *shehada*, then, is an affirmation of the Qur'an as the eternal and infallible repository of Islamic doctrine. Understood in this way, its claims bind every Muslim in every applicable dimension of life: the Qur'an tells a Muslim what to believe, what to desire, what to do, and why. Given the Qur'an's description of the Prophet Muhammad as an exemplary figure (and given its commands to emulate and obey him),[4] the Qur'an indirectly suggests another relatively autonomous source of Muslim belief, known as the *sunnah*, or the "way" of the Prophet as expressed in his words and actions.

Thus the implicit content of the *shehada*, when made explicit, can be described as follows:

1. Affirm the existence of a single God.
2. Affirm that Muhammad is God's messenger.
3. Affirm that the Qur'an is the (fundamental) statement of God's message to Muhammad.
4. Affirm that every claim of the Qur'an is indubitably true.
5. Strive to the utmost to put the Qur'an's precepts into practice.
6. Seek out reliable accounts of the life of Muhammad, and emulate his example in all respects consistent with (1) through (5).

A life *fully* devoted to these six propositions is a *fully Muslim* life, literally the life of one who has fully submitted to the will of God (and secondarily to the will of Muhammad insofar as that accords with God's will). In practice, this requires extensive study of the text of the Qur'an; five daily prayers, intended to remind one of God's presence in one's life (including communal worship for the Friday afternoon prayer); an annual month of fasting during Ramadan; prohibitions on the consumption of pork, alcohol, and nonmedicinal drugs; almsgiving; pilgrimage to Mecca; abstention from extramarital sex; and *jihad*, or holy struggle in the cause of Islam, understood as a lifelong struggle against evil and injustice, both in oneself and in the external world, whether by peaceful means or by force.

In short, affirmation of the *shehada* is the very epitome of a package deal: accept one deceptively simple proposition, and you are committed to an all-embracing and fully regulated way of life. To paraphrase Salman Rushdie, this is a doctrine with rules for every damn thing:[5] it dictates what you may say; what you eat and drink; how you may spend your free time; how, when, where, and with whom you have sex; how you conduct yourself while engaging in excretion; your career and its purpose; the structure and terms of family life; the nature of economic, criminal, and political justice; and by implication, the terms of trade, punishment, and warfare. In principle, no part of life gets a waiver from regulation. Indeed, the subsumption of desire to doctrine is the mark of virtue: the *more* of one's life one submits to God, the morally *better* one is.

It is an astonishing fact, but a fact just the same, that I do not remember how I initially came to believe as momentous a thing as the *shehada*. What I remember are biographical bits and pieces.[6] I don't remember a time in childhood when I *didn't* believe the *shehada*, but I do remember times in childhood when it is questionable whether or not I did. I remember being obliged at age five or so by my mother and maternal grandmother to memorize and recite various elaborations on the *shehada* (called *kalimas*), and, obviously, to believe the message they conveyed. I remember my mother's teaching me Qur'anic Arabic around age five, and being beaten around that age (though not very severely) for failures of memory, inattentiveness, or sheer lassitude in doing my lessons. I was homeschooled from that age in Islamic doctrine (supplementing, not replacing, my normal schooling), and made my way through various hagiographies designed to teach the biography of the Prophet. In a happier vein, I remember spending hours with my grandmother (who lived with us), listening to her pious Qur'anic stories about the prophets Adam, Noah, Moses, Jonah, and Joseph.

By age nine, I had finished my first Arabic reading of the Qur'an, and I think it's safe to say that by that age I had fully accepted Islamic belief, and had begun to live a scripturally based life. At that age, at any rate, I recall that my mother was able to use the Qur'an as a handy polygraph to test the excuses and alibis I'd invented to avoid parental discipline. Since false witness with one's hand on the Qur'an is punishable by eternal damnation, the truth was easily extorted by the demand that I "take the oath." By age thirteen or fourteen, I had begun to regard the existence of God as being on a par with the existence of the "theoretical entities" I had encountered in science classes (and in the science fiction I had read)—atoms, electrons, gravity, quasars, black holes. Meanwhile, I'd come to wonder whether the sexism, anti-Semitism, and reactionary political attitudes in the Muslim community around me were endemic to Islam or were instead purely sociological aspects of the community, and thus separable from doctrine. The latter puzzle was, of course, motivated by a commitment to doctrine and a rejection of the relevant (unpalatable) attitudes. It mattered to me at an early age that Islam should stand vindicated, whatever the vices of its practitioners.

For all its lacunae, this brief description makes clear that I was force-fed a diet of theism at an early age, and in a fairly uncontroversial sense coerced into belief. I was made to believe without the slightest effort at argumentation that God existed, that Muhammad was his prophet, that the Qur'an contained God's message, and that God's commandments as expressed in the Qur'an were binding obligations. I was too young in early childhood to know that this story might be dubious or dubitable, so I didn't think of doubting it until late into my teenage years—and even then in a halting, tepid way. If one assumes, as I have, that the story is false through and through, then I was deceived into believing something that required me, late into my teenage years, to structure my life around a delusion. Considering the demands exerted by the commitment, considering that the demands were supposed to extend across my lifespan, and considering the use of force (however mild) to create the commitment, I would conclude that my initial belief in Islam was a matter of literal coercion.

And yet there is a mild paradox here. The coercion I've described lasted maybe five years, from age five until age ten. After that, my commitment to Islam looks to all outward appearances *voluntary*. I was indoctrinated in early childhood, but not in any obviously Branch Davidian or madrasa fashion. I've said that I was beaten to make sure that I recited the Qur'an accurately, but the beatings were never severe and had almost certainly stopped by age ten. In any case, after age twelve, I confronted robust alternatives to my Islamic faith. I went to a secular prep school where I encountered all sorts of un-Islamic ideas—in classes (principally literature classes) and from nonreligious friends. My parents never inquired into what I was learning at school, and never stopped me from learning anything for fear of its incompatibility with religion. Apart from the brief time I spent at the home of a close Muslim friend in a proselytizing family (a few weeks a year for about twelve years), I spent none of my time in communal prayer or in a traditional madrasa. And my friend's house was in any case *not* a traditional madrasa; it merely resembled one in certain limited respects. The bottom line is that I was essentially allowed throughout high school to read whatever I wanted.[7] Perhaps my parents didn't know well enough to discern the threat to faith posed by a good high school education, intellectually curious friends, and easy access to the public library, but the fact is that they didn't.

Despite that, I would insist that my faith *was* in fact coerced. For suppose (as for purposes of this essay I shall) that God doesn't exist. If so, my initial belief in God was, as I've suggested, initially induced by coercion. What then sustained my belief *after* the initial indoctrination? In one sense, *I* did: I read the Qur'an, giving it the initial credibility I was taught to give it; it told me to believe; and so I did. But in a deeper sense, I was coerced and defrauded into it on absolutely literal interpretations of those terms.

This becomes clear if one reflects a bit on the process by which belief is inculcated in a Muslim childhood. One comes to believe, say, the *shehada* in early childhood by force and/or deception imposed by parents who put belief in it on a par with ordinary moral duties, from truth-telling to obedience. In the nature of the case, this initial impetus to belief gives initial credibility to the proposition that God exists, that His messenger tells the truth, and that His message is true. Bearing this in mind, one then reads Scripture and confronts two things there: a *coercive ultimatum to believe*, and a *promise of reward for believing*. The ultimatum says (in apocalyptic language): "Banish all doubt and believe—or burn forever in Hell." The promise says (in evocatively poetic language): "Banish all doubt and believe— and you shall be repaid forever in Heaven." A child who is initially deceived into taking God to exist will regard the "person" making both the threat and the promise to be perfectly real. Such a child gradually becomes an adult who takes the threat and the promise literally. But taken literally, the threat meets the standard legal definition of assault, and (assuming God's nonexistence) the promise meets the standard legal definition of fraud.

We might then fairly describe religious indoctrination—certainly in the Muslim tradition, and very likely throughout the monotheistic tradition— as *a threat of violence embellished with fraud, induced by deception*. The key to understanding it, however, is to see that it relies heavily on norms and attitudes that a child internalizes at a very early age. The more trusting the child, the more vulnerable to the initial deception. The more fearful (or docile or acquiescent), the more vulnerable to a coercive ultimatum. The more desirous a child is of reward, the more vulnerable to a promise of reward. And of course, the more invested in morality, the more vulnerable to the whole setup. This is what I mean by "self-indoctrination." Ideally, I said, a Muslim's belief in the *shehada* is self-reinforcing. The Qur'anic ultimatum and promise line up with a believer's trust, fear, and desire so as to provide the mechanism of reinforcement.

Self-indoctrination is a real, powerful, but relatively invisible form of indoctrination. It is also a remarkably complex one, involving subtle issues in ethics, epistemology, and psychology. In the next two sections, I single out each element of specifically Islamic indoctrination—the Qur'anic ultimatum and its promise—and describe what we might call its "psycho-epistemological" structure, that is to say, the interaction between the believer's conscious confrontation with the text of Scripture and the subconscious reactions that arise in consequence.[8]

The Qur'anic Ultimatum: Faith, Fallacy, and Force

The Qur'an presents its readers with the coercive ultimatum of believing in God or being punished for not believing. In one sense, this ultimatum works like any other threat: the victim is presented with two exclusive and exhaustive options, one of which leads to harm, the other of which does not (or at least leads to less harm than the first option), and the demand is made to choose between them. In this sense, the Qur'anic ultimatum is just as coercive as any ordinary criminal ultimatum. But in another sense, the Qur'anic ultimatum is unlike any ordinary criminal act. For one thing, the *stakes* differ: criminals inflict merely finite harm, but God's damnation is infinite in duration. And then there is the fact that criminals seldom seek lifelong allegiance in the way that the Islamic God does. But at a deeper level, the point is that few criminal ultimatums are *doxastic or attitudinal* in character: the average criminal is not interested in what you think of him, but God surely is. In this respect, the Qur'anic ultimatum is more like the demand of a totalitarian government than that of a criminal: it demands both compliance *and* recognition. But governments have what a religious doctrine (at least in a liberal regime) lacks, namely, an external mechanism of enforcement. What a doctrine needs, then, is an *internal* enforcement mechanism. In the Islamic case, this mechanism has three aspects: the appeal to faith, the use of fallacy, and the appeal to (cosmic) force. I take these in turn.

Recall that one comes to the study of Scripture having been inculcated in the view that faith is a virtue, whereas doubt, questioning, and contention are cardinal vices. The initial impetus to belief is inculcated by way of a conjunction that I will call the *fideist's conjunction*, which consists of the following claims:

1. God exists.
2. It is morally good to believe and morally bad to doubt that God exists.

This conjunction of beliefs has several important consequences. To the extent that a child or teenager accepts the conjunction at face value, he will have to surrender cognitive autonomy to the person bequeathing the belief:

he will have to depend, uncritically, on that person for his beliefs. The implicit lesson is that credulity is a virtue and independence a vice, at least with respect to a delimited class of beliefs. It is, in short, virtuous to think that justification ends where talk of God begins, and with it, one's moral and epistemic right to ask why.[9]

So conceived, faith is a necessary condition for being able to take seriously the embarrassingly feeble "arguments" that the Qur'an offers for the existence of God. And so we are led from the appeal to faith to the use of fallacy. A typical "argument" in the Qur'an consists of a poetic recounting of various natural phenomena, along with the suggestion that the phenomena so described could *only* have been brought into existence by the Muslim God:

> This Scripture is sent down from God, the Mighty, the Wise. There are signs in the heavens and the earth for those who believe: in the creation of you, in the creatures God scattered on earth, there are signs for people of sure faith; in the alternation of night and day, in the rain God provides, sending it down from the sky and reviving the dead earth with it, and in His shifting of the winds there are signs for those who use their reason. These are God's signs that We recount to you [Prophet, to show] the Truth. (Qur'an 45:2–6)

> It is God who subjected the sea for you—ships sail on it by His command so that you may seek His bounty and give Him thanks—He has subjected all that is in the heavens and the earth for your benefit, as a gift from Him. There truly are signs in this for those who reflect. (45:12–13)

> But the disbelievers deny the truth when it comes to them; they are in a state of confusion. Do they not see the sky above them—how We have built and adorned it, with no rifts in it, how We spread out the earth and put solid mountains on it, and caused every kind of joyous plant to grow in it, as a lesson and reminder for every servant who turns to God; and how We send blessed water down from the sky and grow with it gardens, the harvest grain, and tall palm trees laden with clusters of dates, as a provision for everyone; how with water We give [new] life to land that is dead? This is how the dead will emerge [from their graves]. (50:5–11)

And so on. On this view, almost anything counts as a "sign" from God: testimony about prophets and prophecies from the distant and now unverifiable past (Qur'an 3:97); esoteric metaphors, typically of a horticultural variety (2:265–266); trivial zoological, botanical, and meteorological facts, tendentiously described (such as the water cycle, the existence of livestock, the potability of milk and honey, the edibility of dates, mortality, the fact that birds can fly, and so on, 16:65–80). Indeed, human activity and accomplishment turn out to be nothing but "signs" of God's existence: it is God who has "given" us homes, light, furniture, and garments, so that these things constitute "clear evidence" of his existence (16:80–82, with sura 98).

To add insult to epistemic injury, the Qur'an manages to couch its fallacious arguments for God's existence in two near paradoxes about the very point of the revelation itself. The Qur'an describes this life as a "test" designed to determine moral agents' doxastic and moral virtue, and describes itself as "indubitable" evidence of God's existence. A virtuous person is one who truly grasps the nature and significance of the evidence offered; a vicious person fails to. And yet the more one reflects on the "test" in question, the less sense it makes.[10]

There is first the problem that the Qur'an evinces an uncertain attitude toward doxastic voluntarism.[11] On the one hand, the Qur'an tells us that what we believe is up to us. Indeed, we are explicitly told that ought implies can: every divine command is within our capacities. On the other hand, there is a recurrent theme in the Qur'an to the effect that God loads the doxastic dice by guiding His favored persons to belief and facilitating the nonbelief of those He disfavors. We are thus given a test of whether or not to believe in God while being told that the result is simultaneously up to us *and* a foregone conclusion—fully in our capacities, *and* fully in God's. A sophisticated philosopher could *perhaps* reconcile these two claims, but *prima facie* they seem inconsistent, and one wonders why a just God would insist on belief while presenting the demand for it in the form of a paradox.

Second, even if one manages to read the relevant texts in a manner consistent with doxastic voluntarism, one faces the complication that while life is described as a "test" of one's doxastic virtue, no effort is made to guarantee (or even promote) workable or minimally fair test conditions. Generally speaking, a test is only fair if everyone taking the test takes the same test under the same conditions, and the test and conditions are designed to give an accurate assessment of the test-takers. But God's test is nothing like this. Some people hear God's message, some don't; some are taught it ineptly, some well; some have the leisure, comfort, and aptitude to contemplate it, some don't; and so on. Indeed, as we've seen, God guides some, refuses to guide others, and deliberately sends still others astray. It is, on the face of it, unclear what a test given under such variable conditions is supposed to reveal. Nor is the apparent unfairness of the test ever acknowledged or discussed.

Granted, given divine omniscience, God might be able to appraise everyone's doxastic virtue by applying universal moral principles to the most wildly divergent circumstances. So, we might think, a divine mind could in principle abstract away the differences in circumstance (however disparate) and focus on the similarity common to all cases of affirmation or disbelief. Perhaps; but this merely draws attention to the paradox of an omniscient being's needing to test His creation in the first place. Why would an omniscient being need to fashion creatures and design a test for them when He created their capacities in the full knowledge of their nature and foreknowledge of their future operations? And how could—as the Qur'an admits—*deception* figure among the designer's conception of the test conditions?

In the face of such obstacles to belief, one might imagine disbelief to be an obvious default position. But this is the point at which it is crucial to recall that the choice of belief or disbelief operates in the context of a coercive ultimatum involving eternal punishment: the reader of the Qur'an is presented with the alternative of believing in God or being destroyed in this life and damned for eternity in the next. The ultimatum is repeated dozens of times throughout the text and is one of three basic reasons given for belief in God (the other two being the design-based arguments just discussed and the promise discussed in the next section).[12] This passage states the ultimatum succinctly:

> If people do not believe in God's revelation, God does not guide them, and a painful punishment awaits them. Falsehood is fabricated only by those who do not believe in God's revelation: they are the liars. With the exception of those who are forced to say they do not believe, although their hearts remain firm in faith, those who reject God after believing in Him and open their hearts to disbelief have the wrath of God upon them and a grievous punishment awaiting them. This is because they love the life of this world more than the one to come, and God does not guide those who reject Him. (Qur'an 16:104–107)

A series of verses describing the Day of Judgment make the point yet more evocatively. On that day, we are told, "The Trumpet will be sounded," and disbelievers will be addressed as follows by God Himself:

> "This is the Day [you were] warned of." Each person will arrive attended by an [angel] to drive him on and another to bear witness: "You

paid no attention to this [Day]; but today We have removed your veil and your sight is sharp." The person's attendant will say, "Here is what I have prepared"—"Hurl every obstinate disbeliever into Hell, everyone who hindered good, was aggressive, caused others to doubt, and set up other gods alongside God. Hurl him into severe punishment!"—and his [evil] companion will say, "Lord, I did not make him transgress; he had already gone far astray himself." God will say, "Do not argue in My presence. I sent you a warning and My word cannot be changed: I am not unjust to any creature." We shall say to Hell on that day, "Are you full?" and it will reply, "Are there no more?" (Qur'an 50:20–30)

Woe on that Day to those who deny the Truth, who amuse themselves with idle chatter: on that Day they will be thrust into the Fire of Hell. "This is the Fire you used to deny. So is this sorcery? Do you still not see it? Burn in it—it makes no difference whether you bear it patiently or not—you are only being repaid for what you have done." (52:11–16)

For those who defy their Lord We have prepared the torment of Hell: an evil destination. They will hear it drawing in its breath when they are thrown in. It blazes forth, almost bursting with rage. Its keepers will ask every group that is thrown in, "Did no one come to warn you?" They will reply, "Yes a warner did come to us, but we did not believe him. We said, 'God has revealed nothing: you are greatly misguided.'" They will say, "If only we had listened, or reasoned, we would not be inhabitants of the blazing fire," and they will confess their sins. Away with the inhabitants of the blazing fire! (67:5–11)

As for the precise nature and degree of punishment for disbelief, it gets no less vivid a description:

We shall send those who reject our revelations to the Fire. When their skins have been burned away, We shall replace them with new ones so that they may continue to feel the pain: God is mighty and wise. (Qur'an 4:56).

The tree of Zaqqum will be food for the sinners: [hot] as molten metal, it boils in their bellies like seething water. "Take him! Thrust him into the depths of Hell! Pour scalding water over his head as punishment!" "Taste this, you powerful, respected man! This is what you doubted." (44:43–50).

> On the Day when God's enemies are gathered up for the Fire and driven onward, their ears, eyes, and skins will, when they reach it, testify against them for their misdeeds. They will say to their skins, "Why did you testify against us?" and their skins will reply, "God who gave speech to everything, has given us speech—it was He who created you the first time and to Him you have been returned—yet you did not try to hide yourselves from your ears, eyes and skin to prevent them from testifying against you. You thought that God did not know much about what you were doing, so it was the thoughts you entertained about your Lord that led to your ruin, and you became losers." The Fire will still be their home, even if they resign themselves to patience, and if they pray to be allowed to make amends, they will not be given permission to do so. (41:19–24).

My characterization of the Islamic demand for belief in God as coercion and assault may initially have sounded overblown, but in fact, I think these passages suggest that I considerably understated matters. Legally and morally, an act qualifies as assault even if it threatens little physical harm. If I threaten to punch you, I have assaulted you. But consider the sheer diminutiveness of ordinary assault with the threats made in the Qur'an. The most evil *Godfather*-like Mafioso typically threatens to torture you, kill you, and then kill your family if you don't do his bidding. But even *he* doesn't promise to torture you for eternity for failing to believe this or that metaphysical proposition. As far as I can see, the God of Abraham is unique in His guilt in this matter, as are the parents who suborn belief in His ultimatum.

Now consider the situation from the first-person perspective of the putative believer. On the one hand, I face a high-stakes coercive ultimatum that, *ex hypothesi*, has initial credibility. I come to the table, so to speak, believing it initially plausible that there is some such person as God, and that He is speaking to me through the Qur'an. So my doxastic default position inclines (for no very good reason) toward belief. On the other hand, it's obvious that the demand itself is an act of coercion (indeed, an instance of the *ad baculum* fallacy), that no genuine reasons have been given for belief, and that the context and content of the demand being made of me are simply absurd. I am to believe in something utterly implausible simply because I am told that I must believe, that I will be punished if I don't believe, and because certain commonplace phenomena can (tendentiously) be described in such a way as to cohere with belief in God. Those considerations push me from belief toward disbelief or at least doubt. And yet recall the fideist's conjunction:

I come to the situation with the conviction that faith is the epitome of virtue and that if I feel doubt or an inclination to disbelief, I must somehow be guilty of a hidden moral failing.

There are broadly speaking two doxastic possibilities at this point. If I come to the issue holding the fideist's conjunction with a high degree of confidence, I will welcome the Qur'anic ultimatum while ignoring the fact that it is an ultimatum. It will seem obvious to me which option to take: if it is obvious that God exists, and obvious that it is good to believe in His existence, and that He is now asking me to believe in Him, it is equally obvious that I should believe. Notice that if I hold this set of beliefs, the coercive nature of the Qur'anic ultimatum drops out of view. If disbelief is not an option for me, an ultimatum that demands "belief or else punishment" will seem unreal because given the urgency of the first disjunct, the second disjunct is an irrelevancy. Thus if I come to the choice of belief with a high degree of confidence in the fideist's conjunction, the choice to believe will seem to me a paradigmatically free act—not an instance of coercion, but an act of liberation.

By contrast, if I hold the fideist's conjunction with a relatively low degree of confidence, I will opt the same way—in the direction of belief—but with a greater sense of guilt, cognitive dissonance, alienation. and anxiety. For in this case, I come to the choice with the conflicted, alienated sense that while it seems that God exists and that belief in Him is good, the fact remains that I have doubts and incline toward disbelief, and cannot without loss of integrity disown my propensity to doubt and question His existence. In this case, it will not be obvious which option to take, and for that reason, the disjunctive formulation of the ultimatum will be more readily apparent. What will also be apparent is its coercive nature. If I believe but have doubts, and then face the possibility that disbelief will send me to Hell, it's an easy inference to the quasi-Pascalian conclusion (explicitly affirmed in the Qur'an 40:28–30) that I'd better keep believing lest I end up having my skin burned off for eternity.

This latter choice exacts a certain psychological cost. It eliminates (or diminishes) the immediate fear of damnation by replacing it with an equally immediate fear of *oneself*. Doubt and disbelief, after all, come from oneself, and if doubt is the enemy, so is its source. And so one lives with a self-imposed cloud above one's head, which finds expression as an endless series of pointless, arbitrary, and irresolvable doubts about one's moral character: *Do I disbelieve because I'm weak? Or is it because I'm immoral? Am I weak because I'm immoral? Or is it rather the reverse? Since it's one or the other, how* did I become so weak and immoral? What hidden flaw resides in me? What can I do to get rid of it? Will I be forgiven for it, or is my spiritual situation hopeless?

I doubt that there are entirely pure versions of either the "high confidence" or the "low confidence" believer. Most believers, I suspect, oscillate between the two extremes, as I did for years. The "high confidence" gambit inclines one to a sort of fanaticism. The "low confidence" gambit inclines one to self-doubt. The combination yields the sort of fanatical self-doubt exemplified by J. Alfred Prufrock's confession in T. S. Eliot's "Love Song of J. Alfred Prufrock":

> Should I, after tea and cakes and ices,
> Have the strength to force the moment to its crisis?
> But though I have wept and fasted, wept and prayed,
> Though I have seen my head (grown slightly bald) brought in upon
>   a platter,
> I am no prophet—and here's no great matter;
> I have seen the moment of my greatness flicker,
> And I have seen the eternal Footman hold my coat, and snicker,
> And in short, I was afraid.[13]

The fear disappears momentarily, as does the threat of the Footman, when one draws, in the moment of crisis, on the teachings of the Prophet. But only momentarily.

We are, I think, so used to thinking of the more dramatic instances of religious indoctrination that we miss the relatively self-confined drama of the sort of ultimatum I've just described. But though I've described the specifically Muslim version of the drama, and described it from my own experiences, it is one enacted in millions if not billions of lives every day. There are 1.25 billion Muslims in the world. The vast majority of them are coerced into religious belief in just the way I've described. Nor is the issue confined to Muslims. The details of my discussion have been Islamic, but *mutatis mutandis*, the same claims might be made of Jewish or Christian belief. The extraordinary fact, I think, is that they are so seldom made.

The Qur'anic Promise and the Wish for the Irrevocable

If the threat of damnation isn't enough to induce belief, the Qur'an offers the promise of paradise as a positive incentive.[14] The promise is typically described in economic terms, as "repayment" for one's faith and virtues,[15] but it offers up goods across the wide range of human experience—hedonistic, affective, aesthetic, and moral.

> [Prophet], give those who believe and do good the news that they will have Gardens graced with flowing streams. Whenever they are given sustenance from the fruits of these Gardens, they will say "We have been given this before," because they were [in their temporal lives], provided with something like it. They will have pure spouses and there they will stay. (Qur'an 2:25)

> Do not think of those who have been killed in God's way as dead. They are alive with their Lord, well provided for, happy with what God has given them of His favour; rejoicing that for those they have left behind who have yet to join them there is no fear, nor will they grieve; [rejoicing] in God's blessing and favour, and that God will not let the reward of the believers be lost. (3:169–171)

> God has promised the believers, both men and women, Gardens graced with flowing streams where they will remain; good, peaceful homes in Gardens of lasting bliss; and—greatest of all—God's good pleasure. That is the supreme triumph. (9:72).

> In whatever matter you may be engaged and whatever part of the Qur'an you are reciting, whatever work you are doing, We witness you when you are engaged in it. Not even the weight of a speck of dust in the earth or sky escapes your Lord, nor anything lesser or greater: it is all written in a clear record. But for those who are on God's side, there is no fear, nor shall they grieve. For those who believe and are conscious of God, for them there is good news in this life and in the Hereafter—there is no changing the promises of God—that is truly the supreme triumph. (10:61–64)

> [Believers] will have the reward of the [true] home: they will enter perpetual Gardens, along with their righteous ancestors, spouses and descendants; the angels will go in to them from every gate, "Peace be with you, because you have remained steadfast. What an excellent reward is this home of yours!" (13:22–23)

> [God's servants] will have familiar provisions—fruits—and will be honoured in gardens of delight; seated on couches, facing one another. A

> drink will be passed round among them from a flowing spring: white, delicious to those who taste it, causing no headiness or intoxication. With them will be spouses—modest of gaze and beautiful of eye. . . .
>
> They will turn to one another with questions: one will say "I had a close companion on earth who used to ask me, 'Do you really believe that after we die and become dust and bone, we shall be brought for judgment?'" Then he will say, "Shall we look for him?" He will look down and see him in the midst of the Fire, and say to him, "By God, you almost brought me to ruin! Had it not been for the grace of my Lord, I too would have been taken to Hell." Then he will say [to his blessed companions], "Are we never to die again after our earlier death? Shall we never suffer? This truly is the supreme triumph!" Everyone should strive to attain this. (37:40–68)

I previously described this promise as a "fraud." I think that actually understates the case. An act qualifies as fraud so long as it involves a trespassory taking, by stealth, of something of monetary value. A person who knowingly writes bad checks all over town is typically thought to be guilty of fraud, even if the checks are written for relatively small amounts. But ordinary fraud of that sort pales in comparison to the cosmic fraud we confront in the Qur'an. The most evil *Wall Street*–like tycoon promises innocent shareholders that they'll get rich quick, then cleans them out and leaves them high and dry. Even *he* doesn't promise a life of infinite felicity "perfectly proportioned" to virtue, where the virtue in question is performed by a finite being in a lifetime of finite duration.

The Qur'anic promise has two crucial consequences. The first is its subordination of alethic to nonalethic concerns: taken at face value, the Qur'anic promise asks us to regard considerations of truth as subordinate to considerations of desire. I take it as obvious that this is an inversion of the right attitude toward inquiry and cognition, and leave the matter there.

A subtler, complementary, but more invidious consequence is what I call the "false promise of the irrevocable." Suppose for argument's sake that there is no hereafter, but just a natural, temporal realm. On this assumption, the purely natural goods we seek, I would argue, have three features: They are *conditional* in the sense that they require appropriate action in the face of obstacles for their achievement; the failure to act appropriately entails the failure to achieve them. They are *limited* in the sense that every good has merely finite value and intensity, relative to our natural capacities of comprehension and pursuit. And they are *revocable* in the sense that once had, they can be lost. There may be differences in the degree to which natural goods are revocable, but at the limit, mortality puts an end to action, and with it, the pursuit of any natural good. When we speak of posthumous goods, on a purely naturalistic conception, we speak at best metaphorically.[16]

To illustrate: Almost all of us wish for life, safety, happiness, pleasure, tranquility, justice, beauty, and love. It is equally obvious, however, that in the natural world, not a single one of these goods comes with a guarantee of achievement, much less the promise of literal irrevocability. We die; we're injured; happiness, pleasure, and tranquility wane; justice is delayed or denied; beauty decays; love is lost. More painfully still, as Kant (among others) emphasizes, nothing in the natural world guarantees an invariant connection between virtue and reward, or between vice and punishment: virtue can in principle lead to injustice or misfortune, vice to success.[17] But on a naturalistic conception, conditionality, limitedness, and revocability are the best life has to offer us. We can like that or not and accept it or not, but dislike merely alienates us from the way the world is, and rejection merely puts us in the position of Don Quixote, tilting haplessly at windmills.

Things are quite different for the Muslim believer. Though the Qur'an expresses matters somewhat confusingly, its predominant attitude is that the world we live in is *teleologically subordinate* to the hereafter: this world is a "test" that determines our fate in the next, when we make our "return" to God. This claim has two crucial implications. The first is the idea that the next world is *superior* to this one: if X exists for the sake of Y, but Y exists for its own sake, then X has merely instrumental (hence inferior) value, while Y's value is intrinsic and ultimate.[18] A second and closely related implication is that the hereafter consists of unconditional, unlimited, and irrevocable versions of worldly goods. If we have faith in God—and only if we do—we enjoy *eternal* life, *guaranteed* felicity, *unconditional* justice.

This combination of commitments leads in the Qur'an to a consistent derogation of the present world in favor of the hereafter, and a derogation of this world precisely in virtue of the properties that distinguish natural goods from their supernatural counterparts. Conditionality, limitedness, and revocability thus become the fundamental axiological flaws of the natural world. And revocability is the deepest flaw. It is perhaps tolerable that natural goods must be achieved by action, and that our enjoyment of them is limited by our capacities. What seems less tolerable is that once had, we ever have to part with them. Hence the appeal of and wish for irrevocable goods—goods that can be had for an infinite duration without the risk of loss.

The result, I think, is that the Qur'anic promise—"Believe and you shall be rewarded"—exploits our desire for natural goods while subverting our understanding of their nature. What it trades on, specifically, is how difficult it is to be *wholeheartedly* committed to something impermanent and revocable, and how easy it can become to achieve wholeheartedness by flouting the facts in front of one. And so it holds out hope for a realm in which we can have those very goods precisely without the fear, grief, and risk-averse half-heartedness that they occasion here.

Mortality is the most obvious example. Life is a good, and in loving it, it's hard to resist the wish that it last forever. And yet on a purely naturalistic conception of the world, we know that it can't last forever: we have to face our own mortality as well as that of our loved ones. Confronting it brings the depressing realization that in the natural world, while life is revocable, death is not. It's not clear how precisely one is supposed to reconcile oneself to this fact, and the temptations to evade it—hedonism, nostalgia, risk-aversity—can sometimes seem overwhelming. The Qur'anic promise seems to offer a way out: paradise repeals the inevitability of death by conferring irrevocability on eternal life. Once one accepts this premise, the problem of mortality fades away, leaving nothing to face.

So it is with love and friendship: they too are goods, and like life, we want them to last forever. But like life, marriage and friendship come to an end, and in any case, unless one insists quixotically on the indissolubility of human relationships, we know that some marriages and some friendships are best brought to an end. But when? Some divorces are premature but some are too long in coming. One simply knows that in ending a relationship, one thereby ends the possibilities for happiness to which that relationship gave rise. And in ending it, one may even come to alter one's perception of the happiness one previously enjoyed. At any rate, sometimes the choice has to be made one way or another, and the rationalizations for not making it abound. Once again, the hereafter offers a way out: recall that in the Muslim paradise, we are offered "pure spouses" and virtuous companions, with just enough textual ambiguity as to allow us to fill in the gaps as regards their identity in the ways that imagination and desire require. We need never face genuine loss; paradise abolishes the need to face it.

Or consider justice. There is something stirring in the Kantian dictum that justice must be done though the heavens may fall: "The principle of punishment is a categorical imperative, and woe to him who crawls through the windings of eudaemonism in order to discover something that releases the criminal from punishment or even reduces its amount by the advantage it promises, in accordance with the Pharisaical saying, 'It is better for one man to die than for an entire people to perish.' For if justice goes, there is no longer any value in men's living on the earth . . . for justice ceases to be justice if it can be bought for any price whatsoever."[19] Such slogans are stirring, anyway, as long as one adopts a spectatorial conception of justice, as opposed to the perspective of anyone who's ever had to work to achieve it. On the latter conception, one gradually comes to the inevitable realization that rigorist justice is a chimera: justice *has* to be limited by considerations of time, price, and circumstance. We can abolish slavery; we can't design a world entirely free of its consequences. We can defeat the Axis; we can't give every Nazi war criminal the punishment he deserves. We can avoid imposing collateral damage in war; we can't abolish it. We can try to ameliorate the effects of poverty, but we can't abolish moral luck. We can fight "wars on crime," but we can never reduce its occurrence to zero. At what point, we may wonder, is justice so diluted by expediency that it loses its identity? It's hard to tell. One extreme leads to Machiavelli; the other to Inspector Javert (of Victor Hugo's *Les Miserables*). But the belief in a Divine Magistrate seems to offer a way out of this quandary, as well. And so, the believer infers, we can pursue justice even if the heavens fall. If we make a mess of the world in the name of justice, there is always the compensatory safety net of divine justice: in paradise, every crime will eventually be punished, every victim fully compensated, every good deed recognized, appreciated, and rewarded. (Recall the Qur'anic precept quoted above that the martyr for justice only *appears* to die but in fact enjoys supernatural life, an attitude taken to extremes by contemporary suicide bombers.)

It would, I suppose, be simple enough to choose between these conceptions of the good—the natural and the supernatural—if the choices were starkly simple. Either one believes in an afterlife or not. If one does, one subordinates this realm to that one and treats the goods of this realm as conditional, impermanent, revocable, and ultimately unworthy of the deepest concern. If one doesn't believe in an afterlife, one is obliged to affirm and reconcile oneself to the conditional, revocable nature of the good in this world.

But things are not that simple: it's possible to reject the supernatural and wish for the irrevocable all the same. In this respect, religious indoctrination has a sort of psychological half-life that radiates through one's psyche long after one rejects the doctrine in which one was indoctrinated. In the Muslim case, this is perhaps partly explainable by the Qur'an's ambiguous attitude toward this-worldly success, but at a deeper level, it is explained by one's self-indoctrinated complicity in the Qur'anic promise. The Qur'an's coercive ultimatum gets its power from one's credulity and fear. In that case, the remedy is simply to stop being so credulous and fearful. But the promise of the irrevocable gets its power from our attachment to the good, and there is no equivalent prescription that tells us to "stop desiring the good." And so one can find the wish for the irrevocable lingering in one's psyche, coloring one's view of life long after the conscious rejection of religious doctrine.

I'm reminded in this connection of some lines from Wallace Stevens's "Esthétique du Mal":

> The greatest poverty is not to live
> In a physical world, to feel that one's desire
> Is too difficult to tell from despair. Perhaps,
> After death, the non-physical people, in paradise,
> Itself non-physical, may, by chance, observe
> The green corn gleaming and experience
> The minor of what we feel. The adventurer
> In humanity has not conceived of a race
> Completely physical in a physical world.
> The green corn gleams and the metaphysicals
> Lie sprawling in majors of the August heat,
> The rotund emotions, paradise unknown.
>
> This is the thesis scrivened in delight,
> The reverberating psalm, the right chorale.[20]

The most lasting damage of religious indoctrination is the way in which one internalizes the alienation that arises from an otherworldly attitude, so that one experiences life in the natural world as the "minor" of what one felt while half-inhabiting the supernatural. The wish for the irrevocable, once stimulated, becomes an addiction that unfits one for a completely wholehearted existence in the natural world. To a person in the grips of this addiction, a life lived wholly in the natural world seems less "the thesis scrivened in delight" than one demanding reluctant resignation.

The Journey Back

There is a recurring motif in epic literature wherein the hero makes a journey to the afterworld, there to meet the ghosts and shades of eminent people, virtuous and vicious. Think, for instance, of the journeys to the underworld in the *Odyssey* and *Aeneid*, or the parallel journey to Hell in Dante's *Inferno*. The common theme here is that the mysteries of the afterworld illuminate life in our own. The hero journeys, converses with ghosts, and returns home with a newfound wisdom.

It's always seemed to me remarkable that there is no comparable literature describing the reverse journey, from the phantom existence of a life half-lived in the afterworld to one fully engaged with this one. The journey I have in mind is a sort of counter-indoctrination, but not one confined to doctrine as ordinarily understood. Counter-indoctrination begins, to be sure, with a reappraisal and often enough a rejection of the strictly doctrinal tenets in which one was indoctrinated—in my case, the existence of God, the veracity of Scripture, and the inevitability of the afterlife. But at a more fundamental level, it requires the rejection in oneself of what led one to take to indoctrination in the first place. It requires revisiting and reappraising not just one's adult beliefs, but the childhood traits of character that facilitated one's indoctrination—to revisit, that is, the childhood self-doubt that created the susceptibility to a coercive ultimatum, and the alienation from the world that created one's desire for the irrevocable. The lesson, I think, is that one achieves immunity from divine ultimatums by investing an inviolate certainty in the value of one's cognitive autonomy. And one achieves immunity from a desire for the irrevocable by coming to grips with one's existence as an organism—as a conditional and limited being.

I'm reminded, again, of a famous passage from the Wallace Stevens poem I quoted earlier, which, I suppose, at least approximates the literature I've envisioned here:

> ... How cold the vacancy
> When the phantoms are gone and the shaken realist
> First sees reality. The mortal no
> Has its emptiness and tragic expirations.
> The tragedy, however, may have begun,
> Again, in the imagination's new beginning,
> In the yes of the realist spoken because he must
> Say yes, spoken because under every no
> Lay a passion for yes that had never been broken.[21]

That is the way counter-indoctrination feels at first, when the half-life of self-indoctrination clogs one's psyche, and keeps one in the grips of the wish for the irrevocable. Gradually, though, the coldness yields to warmth and the vacancy to fullness when the "shaken realist" at last finds his footing in reality—to a self that lives for itself, in a world that exists on its own.[22]

NOTES

1. "In the name of God, the Lord of Mercy, the Giver of Mercy! Praise belongs to God, Lord of the Worlds, the Lord of Mercy, the Giver of Mercy, Master of the Day of Judgment. It is You we worship; it is You we ask for help. Guide us to the straight path: the path of those You have blessed, those who incur no anger and who have not gone astray." The Qur'an, sura 1, trans. M. A. S. Abdel Haleem, revised paperback edition (Oxford: Oxford University Press, 2005). All translations quoted in this chapter refer to this edition.

2. Cf. Bernard Lewis, "Religious Coexistence and Secularism," in *Islam and the West* (Oxford: Oxford University Press, 1993), 178: "Correct Islam is defined not so much by orthodoxy as orthopraxy. What matters is what a Muslim does, not what he believes."

3. Qur'an 2:177, 2:183, 107:5–6.

4. Qur'an 4:64–70, 4:115, 24:51–52, 33:36.

5. Salman Rushdie, *The Satanic Verses* (New York: Viking, 1989), 363–64.

6. This is perhaps the place to note that in recounting events from my life, I rely throughout this chapter on memories that might well be contested by other parties to the events described. With one exception, I am estranged from my blood relatives—the exception being my brother, six years my junior. Though my brother would likely concur with the general thrust of my account, he was too young to remember certain significant details of it. My grandmother and the "close Muslim friend from a proselytizing family" described in the text are now deceased.

7. There were perhaps some exceptions to the "no censorship" rule (e.g., sexually explicit movies, *Playboy*, the *Sports Illustrated* swimsuit issue, and so on), but they are irrelevant to the point I am making.

8. I borrow the term "psycho-epistemology" from Ayn Rand's "The Psycho-Epistemology of Art," in *The Romantic Manifesto*, revised paperback edition (New York: Signet, 1975), 18.

9. Cf. Alvin Plantinga, "Reason and Belief in God," in *Faith and Rationality: Reason and Belief in God*, ed. Alvin Plantinga and Nicholas Wolterstorff (Notre Dame: University of Notre Dame Press, 1983), 33. Plantinga defends a rather extreme form of the credulity I describe in the text.

10. This is a complex topic, and the relevant texts fall into the following three or four categories (depending on how one counts them). A first category of texts suggests (sometimes clearly, sometimes obliquely) that we are free to use our reason, and are thus responsible for what we believe (Qur'an 2:256, 3:86, 4:82, 4:137, 5:105, 6:11–13, 6:93, 6:104, 6:157, 6:164, 7:9, 7:36, 7:64, 7:147, 8:23, 8:55, 10:42–44, 10:100, 37:154–155, 50:45). A second and related category suggests that ought implies can: we can *only* be held responsible insofar as we are free (2:286, 7:42, 23:62). A third and divergent category suggests that God facilitates the belief of those who are antecedently committed to believing in Him, and vitiates the disbelief of those antecedently committed to disbelief (2:26, 3:7, 3:86, 5:41, 6:25, 6:88, 6:108, 7:27, 9:93, 10:25, 16:9, 16:106–109, 18:57, 19:7, 30:59, 35:7, 7:177, 17:45–46). A subcategory of this third category goes so far as to suggest that belief and disbelief are foreordained by God as such: believers are determined to believe, and disbelievers to disbelieve (2:6–7, 10:10, 10:96, 10:99–100, 28:56, 29:49, 36:10, 47:23).

A reconciliation (my own) of the preceding texts might run along the following lines: God gives us a basic irreducible choice to choose good or evil. Those who choose good are then (as a reward for that choice) entitled to divine guidance, and thereby come to believe in God, whereas those who choose evil are (as punishment for that choice) driven further into corruption, which in turn gives them a culpable propensity to deny God's existence. Since God creates the causal laws that govern us in this world (including those triggered by Satan), we could refer to the operation of, say, psychological laws concerning corruption of conscience elliptically as "divine action." In that (elliptical) sense, God could be said to "cause" the corruption and perversity of those who disbelieve.

Three points are in order, however. First, it is worth noting that this reconciliation is nowhere to be found in the text of the Qur'an. Evidently, then, God's message relies for its intelligibility on the exercise of human reason—a fact that raises the possibility of relying on reason while dispensing with God's otherwise unintelligible message to us. Second, the reconciliation just described solves the immediate problem while giving renewed power to the problem of evil: if God "causes" corruption even in this elliptical sense, it's fair to say that He is responsible for all of the evil in the universe in precisely the same sense, and it is hard to see how an omnibenevolent God can be *responsible* for evil. As the Qur'anic scholar Michael Cook points out, the Qur'an seems to make just this concession. See Michael Cook, *The Koran: A Very Short Introduction* (Oxford: Oxford University Press, 2000), 19–20, referring to Qur'an 113. Third, there are passages on this topic in the Qur'an that, all things considered, are in my view irremediably incoherent and thus beyond assimilation into a coherent interpretation of any kind, most notably including its account of the Fall and various related passages (e.g., 33:72).

11. This "test" is repeatedly described in the Qur'an as the very purpose of existence; see, for example, 7:168, 9:16, 20:131, 21:35, 21:111, 25:20, 29:2–3, 39:49, 45:22, and all of sura 44.

12. The coercive ultimatum I describe in the text is made so often in the Qur'an that citations ought to be superfluous, but the following is a (nonexhaustive) list of citations intended to forestall the inevitable apologetic objections: 2:81–82, 2:85, 2:121, 2:126, 3:19, 3:85–86, 3:105–7, 3:116–17, 3:131, 4:56, 5:10, 6:28–32, 6:123–25, 7:8–9, 7:36–37, 7:177–78, 8:55, 10:17, 10:45, 10:94–95, 11:18–24, 16:104–9, 22:19–21, 22:42–46, 22:56–57, 35:7, 36:59–64, 41:19–24, 44:40–50, all of verse 50, and so on.

13. T. S. Eliot, "The Love Song of J. Alfred Prufrock," in *Selected Poems* (New York: Harcourt, Brace, Jovanovich, 1964), 14.

14. A nonexhaustive list: Qur'an 2:25, 2:38, 2:82, 3:15, 3:136, 3:169–72, 3:198, 4:13, 4:40, 4:57, 4:74, 4:114, 4:122, 5:9, 6:132–35, 7:35, 9:72, 9:100, 10:25–26, 10:61–64, 13:22–26, 13:35, 15:45–50, 18:30–31, 19:59–62, 20:76, 21:47, 22:10–24, 25:76–77, 35:33–35, 36:54–58, all of sura 37, 38:40, 38:49–54, 39:73–75, 40:39–40, 42:22, 43:70–73, 45:22, 46:13–14, 47:15, 52:17–29, and all of sura 55.

15. I discuss this point in more detail in "Islam and Capitalism: A Non-Rodinsonian Approach," in *Business and Religion: A Clash of Civilizations?* ed. Nicholas Capaldi (Salem, Mass.: M and M Scrivener Press, 2005), 371–72.

16. This conception of value is based loosely on Ayn Rand's theory of value. See "The Objectivist Ethics," in *The Virtue of Selfishness: A New Concept of Egoism* (New York: Signet, 1964). For elaboration, see Allan Gotthelf, *On Ayn Rand* (Belmont, Calif.: Wadsworth Publishing, 2000), chaps. 8–11.

17 Immanuel Kant, *Critique of Practical Reason*, II.2.4–5 (Ak. 5:122–132), ed. Mary Gregor, introduction by Andrews Reath (New York: Cambridge University Press, 1997), 102–10.

18. Notable passages expressing this view include Qur'an 2:86, 2:96, 3:185, 6:32, 6:70, 6:130, 7:169, 8:67, 9:38, 10:24, 13:26, 16:41, 17:18, 29:64, and 40:39. Narrow theological differences aside, the Qur'anic view finds powerful philosophical expression in the work of St. Thomas Aquinas. Cf. *Summa Theologiae*, II.1, Q. 5, Article 3, *Treatise on Happiness*, trans. John Oesterle (Notre Dame: University of Notre Dame Press, 1983), 57; cf. Q. 2, Articles 7 and 8, Q. 3, Article 8, and Q. 4, Articles 7 and 8. Elsewhere, Aquinas writes that "it is necessary for true happiness that man have an assured belief that he will never lose the good which he has" (*Summa Theologiae*, II.1, Q. 5, Art. 4, Response).

19. Immanuel Kant, *The Metaphysics of Morals*, II.1.E (Ak. 331–332), trans. Mary Gregor (New York: Cambridge University Press, 1991), 140.

20. Wallace Stevens, "Esthétique du Mal," in *The Palm at the End of the Mind: Selected Poems and a Play*, ed. Holly Stevens (New York: Vintage Books, 1972), 262–63.

21. Stevens, "Esthetique du Mal," 257–58.

22. Thanks to Carrie-Ann Biondi, Peter Caws, Stefani Jones, and Ibn Warraq for invaluable feedback on previous drafts.

3

FROM FUNDAMENTALIST TO FREETHINKER
(IT ALL BEGAN WITH SANTA)

Raymond D. Bradley

> When I was a child, I spake as a child, I understood as a child, I thought as a child; but when I became a man, I put away childish things.
>
> —St. Paul, 1 Corinthians 13:11

In some ways I'm glad I was brought up as a Christian fundamentalist.

Not because fundamentalism gave me moral values that I cherish. On the contrary, many of the values I hold most dear were developed in opposition to those found in the Bible: a burning sense of justice, for example, arising out of abhorrence at the behavior of the Old Testament God; revulsion at the doctrine of hellfire preached by Jesus in the New Testament; and a strong sense of compassion for those who have suffered in this life and who, if Christian doctrine were true, would suffer even more in the next life for the simple sin of nonbelief.

Why then? Because the fundamentalist beliefs of my early years gave me something tough to chew on, something to cut my teeth on intellectually. Not for me the gummy mouthings of liberal preachers, dishonestly clothing the wolf of fundamentalism in the softer semantics of liberal theology. Their evasive, obfuscatory language could never satisfy my passion for truth. At least the fundamentalist sect in which I grew up knew what it stood for: that the Bible was the word of God, that mankind needed to be saved, that

---

This is a revised version of a talk I presented to the New Zealand Association of Rationalists and Humanists at their annual conference in August 2004 and published in three parts in their journal *The Open Society* (vols. 78, no. 4; 79, no. 1; and 79, no. 2). Links to some of my other articles in defence of atheism—including the two critiques of Flew—are available online at http://www.sfu.ca/philosophy/bradley/bradley.htm.

God had provided salvation through belief in the "Lord Jesus Christ," that we'd go to hell if we didn't believe, and so on.

What I discovered, as my critical powers matured, was that the fundamentalist beliefs of my family and forebears were almost totally without warrant in reason or experience. As I put it when I was about thirty-one years old, in my first public debate (with a Catholic priest in Australia), I eventually came to the conclusion that many of their beliefs—beliefs central to traditional Christianity—were both morally obnoxious and intellectually pernicious.

Strong words, those. So I'll say more to justify them in a while. For the present, it is enough to say that I doubt whether I would have come so readily to these conclusions had my starting point been that of an unchallenged, and unchallenging, churchgoer in a more liberal tradition.

Fundamentalist Roots

My starting point, I have said, was that of a Christian fundamentalist. To be more specific, it was that of an earnest young Baptist. I was born in Auckland, New Zealand: firstborn in a family of ardent Baptists, with a maternal grandfather—Guy D. Thornton—who was a much-revered Baptist minister and evangelist, and with a set of forebears on his side of the family that stretched back to such Christian notables as Robert and Mary Moffat, parents-in-law of the renowned David Livingstone.

One of my earliest memories is of an event that helped shape my childhood. It was Wednesday, June 13, 1934. I was three and a half years old. My parents had been summoned to the deathbed of my grandfather, and I of course went with them. For twenty years he had suffered grievously from a tropical disease, chronic bacillary dysentery. Contracted soon after he became the first chaplain of the Anzacs in Cairo in 1914, it was caused by one of those creations—the *Shigella* bacillus—that God, according to the book of Genesis, thought to be "very good." Now it was taking its final toll. My grandmother, however, explained it differently in her biography of her late husband: "A loving Father was not willing that His child should suffer more, nor was He *'willing that he should be so far from Him any longer.'*"

Before he departed, the good Reverend found time to pronounce a benediction over both his grandchildren—my younger cousin Sibyl and me—expressing the hope that if it were the will of God, we both might "tread the dark places of the earth to carry to those who sit in darkness the light that was lighting his own feet through the valley of the shadow." He concluded, in my case, with the words "I am casting my mantle over you." So it was that I felt destined to follow in my grandfather's footsteps.

And follow I did. In keeping with the Baptist belief in full immersion, I took the plunge, engaging wholeheartedly in scriptural and theological studies and church activities. My mind was filled with reflections on the foundations of my faith. And my teenage years were filled with church activities: Baptist Harriers (cross-country running) on Saturday afternoons and the Young People's Social on Saturday night; then, next day, Sunday School or Christian Endeavour at ten; morning service at eleven; Bible Class at two; evening service at seven; and the hours in between discussing theological problems on street corners with a handful of friends who also took their faith seriously.

Nor did my holidays afford a break. There were Bible Class camps at various "retreats" around Auckland. I competed in, and won, several sermonette contests. I even "won" several souls for Christ. There were annual Christian Crusader camps out on Ponui Island, during which Dr. Sam Martin preached about the sin of "self-abuse," a sin which we identified with masturbation while he (by innuendo) identified it with the sin against the Holy Ghost: the sin that will not be forgiven "neither in this world, nor in that which is to come" (Matthew 12:52). And there were the monthly meetings at the Bible Training Institute of the Young People's Missionary Fellowship, which I had helped to found. Even my days at Mt. Albert Grammar were infused by religion, especially when, at age fifteen, I became secretary of the Christian Crusaders, the junior version of the Evangelical Union.

My exposure to religious indoctrination was about as total as that of a Muslim child in a madrasa or a Jewish one in a yeshiva. Not as much rote-learning, perhaps. But the same suppression of critical examination; the same substitution of faith-based reasoning for evidence-based reasoning; the same elevation of unquestioning faith to a place of paramount virtue.

Yet being exposed to the disease of religion isn't the same as being infected. And even from my early childhood, I seemed fairly immune to it. Not that I was untouched. It took years for the scars to fade. My continuing aversion to all forms of faith-based reasoning, those in politics and economics as well as in religion, has its roots in personal experience of the harm I've seen it do to others as well as to myself.

Some children seem gifted from birth with artistic, musical, or mathematical abilities. I was not one of those. But I am fortunate enough to have the sort of mind that cannot curb the impulse to question and to have had the ability, from childhood, to detect ambiguities in words and fallacies in arguments. In short, I was an unpopular possessor of what is popularly called "a critical mind." That soon marked me out from my peers in the Baptist community. It eventually made me a heretic, repeatedly subjected to attempted religious reeducation at the hands of pastors and theologians. Parents looked askance and steered their offspring away from close association with me. Only two of my teenage friends stuck with me during that time. But neither of them—so they've said—had the moral courage to follow me into unabashed atheism until decades later. Societal pressures as much as intellectual timidity kept them in the closet of Christian conformity: for years, both preferred to think of themselves as agnostics. As for the rest of the friends of my youth, most of them became deacons, ministers, or missionaries—as did their own offspring in turn.

Does my own resistance to religious indoctrination prove it to be less dangerous than any other disease? Of course not. As with other plagues that have wrought havoc on humans, killing, crippling, or curtailing the development of most who are exposed, there have always been some whose immune systems sooner or later "kick in" and offer them some form of protection. That doesn't make any plague the less to be feared. So, too, with the plague of religion. I escaped the worst of its ravages. But most don't. A worldwide campaign to eradicate it—along with smallpox, polio, and other scourges—is as desirable as it is unlikely.

So how did I manage to break free from the Baptist belief system and emerge as a freethinker? Basically by asking questions and not being satisfied with evasive answers or spurious reasonings. That's a simple way of explaining it. But I can fairly say that from very early on I displayed many of the dispositions that later characterized my career as an academic philosopher. Among other things, I had a desire for conceptual clarity and a nose for the implications of beliefs, and for any inconsistencies between them.

Philosophical Predisposition

My atheism was, so to speak, homegrown, not a function of having been seduced away by other doubters. I knew little of the writings of agnostics or atheists until my fifties, some thirty-odd years after I'd staked out my own independent rejection of Christianity and all other forms of religion. I was seemingly born with an inability to accept beliefs on faith, an ineluctable determination—of the kind that David Hume extolled—to proportion the strength of my beliefs to the strength of the evidence for them.

The Demand for Evidence

For me, there was no escape from the demand for evidence. "Have faith," I was told. But faith in what? Why have faith in this rather than that unless there's stronger evidence for this rather than that? Why should I be a Baptist rather than a Catholic, a Christian rather than a Jew or a Muslim? These were questions that came to me in early childhood when I first became aware of the diversity of religious faiths and of sects within each. They couldn't be answered by invoking faith, since it was faith itself that I was questioning. They required an examination of the credentials of each of the rival faiths and of the beliefs of those who embraced no faith at all.

"But," some would object, "if you turn from theism to atheism, haven't you abandoned one 'ism' for another, one faith for another?" No. I don't believe there is a God for the same reasons I don't believe there are fairies: there's an absence of good evidence for the existence of such entities and an abundance of compelling evidence for their nonexistence. I am, as it were, an atheist—not a mere agnostic—about fairies as well as gods. Indeed, I'm an atheist about both for much the same reasons that Christians are atheists—not agnostics—about the whole panoply of heathen gods: Baal, Zeus, Isis, Osiris, and the more than two hundred other gods you'll find listed in a good book on comparative religion.

My Atheism Not an Intransigent Belief

My belief that no such supernatural entities exist, however, isn't an intransigent belief. If the heavens were to open tomorrow and remain open with God revealing himself to us daily by speaking publicly to all humans and exercising his much-vaunted powers and goodness by putting an immediate end to disease, warfare, injustice, and the whole realm of human and animal suffering, I'd consider revising my beliefs.

Woody Allen, I'm told, would be content if God would reveal himself by making a large deposit in Woody's bank account. I'd want a lot more evidence than that: a clear and unambiguous display of the supernatural powers that the theist's God is supposed to have—something like the instant transformation of earth into the heaven that he could have created in the first place. Maybe I'd then consider embracing theism once more.

But not before I'd got him to answer some pretty tough questions. Which theist God was he? The Judaic God, Yahweh, for whom Moses was chief prophet and Jesus an impostor? The Christian God who supposedly revealed himself two thousand years ago to a handful of people in a minor province of the Roman Empire? The Allah of Islam for whom Mohammed was paramount prophet? And if he declared himself the God of the Christians, I'd want to know his doctrinal affiliations. Had I gotten it right in supposing him to be the God of the Baptists? If so, why hadn't he made it unequivocally clear to rival Christian sects that we were indeed the true believers? Or was he, in fact, the God of one of these other sects?

I'd want to ask him: "Why did you wait so long to make your existence indisputable, to display your awesome powers, and to deal definitively with the problems of disease, disaster, and suffering to the solution of which compassionate mortals have dedicated their lives through the centuries?" I'd want to ask him: "Why did you create such a mess in the first place when you obviously could have placed us immediately in a heavenly world?" And most important of all, I'd want to ask him: "What are you going to do about all those people who never heard the name of your son, Jesus, or who—having heard—found no good reason to believe him to be your son? What are you going to do with apostates like me who, according to your son, are doomed to spend eternity suffering the tortures of the damned?"

I can't even conceive of any satisfactory answers. He might, perhaps, urge me to have faith in his wisdom, justice, and mercy. But these three qualities, together with faith itself, are precisely what I am calling in question.

"Have faith" is the last resort of those who have abandoned reason. To be sure, religionists often speak of faith as some sort of third way of knowing, recourse to which can lead one to truths beyond the reach of human experience and reason. But faith, I came to realize, is nothing more than resolute belief. And religious faith is usually intransigent belief: closed-minded belief, impervious to evidence of any kind. That sort of faith is a betrayal of intellectual and moral integrity. I wanted nothing to do with it.

My Pilgrim's Progress

In order to tell the story of how I became an atheist, I will depict my early years as ones in which I undertook a journey along a difficult and sometimes daunting path. And I will now revisit certain of its more salient vantage points, commenting on the incidents and episodes that occurred along the way, and pausing to reflect on the vistas that opened up as I journeyed onward. You may, if you wish, think of my journey as a kind of "Pilgrim's Progress," though one whose direction was contrary to that of John Bunyan's hero.

Childhood: A Period of Questioning

It all began with Santa. In hindsight, I see that it was questions about him that primed the pump of critical inquiry for me. Up until the age of six or seven, I believed in Santa just as fervently as I believed in Jesus and the nativity stories, in heaven as a place from which my grandfather—along with God—watched my every move, and in hell as a place where the bad people go. If anything, my belief in Santa was even more vivid, more compelling than these other beliefs. After all, I'd actually talked to him every Xmas when we went to the Farmers Trading Company on Hobson Street. And sometimes I see him again, half an hour later, in Milne and Choyce on Queen Street.

But soon I started asking questions. How many Santas were there? If—as my parents explained—the Hobson Street Santa and the Queen Street Santa were only "pretend" Santas, where was the real Santa? Was there, in fact, a real Santa as well as the pretend ones? If so, where did he live? How did he manage to visit all the children in the world on the very same night? How did he get down our chimney without being covered with soot or visit my bedroom without leaving visible footprints? It seemed to me that his ability to do all these extraordinary things made him something of a miracle worker, a bit like Moses and Jesus.

More worrying were some ethical questions. Why did Santa discriminate so blatantly by giving rich kids things like bicycles when my stocking contained trinkets like lead soldiers, a bag of lollies, and a few pieces of fruit? Why did he reward some of the nasty kids I knew more than good little boys like me? I was troubled even more when I discovered that some of the kids at school didn't believe in Santa any more. They said it was my parents who'd filled my stocking and nibbled at the cherry-topped cookie I'd left for Santa to eat.

When finally confronted with the whole package of my perplexities, my parents confessed that Santa stories were just pleasant make-believe. But that, too, troubled me. They had lied, I insisted. So how could I trust other stories they told me? And how could I trust my own beliefs to be true if in this instance they had proved to be false? How much of what I believed was myth? How much was based in reality? I resolved never again to believe just on the basis of someone else's say-so.

Many of my questions about Santa later found clear parallels in questions about religious matters.

Many Santas, Many Religions

My questions about how many Santas there were, and which, if any, was the real one, found any echo in problems about the diversity of religious sects and the question which, if any, was the true one.

This problem first thrust itself upon me when I was eight and wanted to play with the Kelly kids who lived just opposite. My mother objected vehemently. They were Roman Catholics, she explained, followers of what she described as "the whore of Rome." But, I objected, didn't they believe in Jesus? Weren't they Christians, too? Yes, she replied: they believed in Jesus; and yes they were Christians. But they weren't *true* Christians.

But if there were true religions and false religions, I reflected, how could I be sure that my one was the true one? If I'd been brought up as one of the Kelly kids, wouldn't I have been a Catholic too? Did I share the beliefs of my parents and grandparents only because I'd been brought up as a Baptist? Might not all the religions I'd heard of be fakes like the different Santas I'd seen in the shops? Was there in fact a true religion at all? Might not the Bible stories be just pleasant make-believe like stories about Santa?

Religious Experiences: Genuine or Spurious?

My childhood reflections on the rivalry between religions had other implications. We Baptists believed we had a special relationship with God. We spoke to him in prayer, and he spoke to us in return, sometimes providing vivid experiences of his presence in our lives. We believed we were doing God's will. Yet sincere believers of contrary faiths also believed they were doing God's will. They had religious experiences different from, and sometimes contrary to, ours. I was almost envious, for a time, of the Kelly kids' claim to see visions of the Virgin Mary. Why didn't God reveal himself to Protestants that way? Why were the miracles of Lourdes reserved for Catholics? Were they deluding themselves? Might I not have been deluding myself when, aged fourteen, I was immersed into the baptismal waters and felt the "indwelling of the Holy Spirit"? What with the church choir singing,

"Where he leads me I will follow" in tones of deepest solemnity, it was all very moving. But how significant?

Then I learned how, throughout history, competing armies—often fired up by religious conviction—would both claim to be fighting "in the name of God." And I heard, during World War II, that many German Christians believed God was fighting on their side, not ours. It seemed to me that only the most churlish believers could claim that their own religious experiences alone were genuine. Could it be that none were?

I came to question the status of religious experiences for other reasons as well. Evangelical crusades sometimes took place in the Auckland Town Hall, and I would be there in the midst of the massed choir arrayed behind the evangelist, the massive pipe organ reverberating through our bodies and stirring our emotions. Each night I saw the newly converted—often in paroxysms of guilt and grief—as they "gave themselves to Jesus" and were shepherded off into the wings for counseling. I could hardly doubt their sincerity. Or could I? What was I to think when some reappeared the next night, to be converted again, and sometimes still a third time? How much store could be placed in the intensity of such religious enthusiasm? I was first embarrassed. Then uneasy. Then skeptical of the evidential worth of subjective experiences like these, my own included.

Formative Reading

I spent most of my early years up to the age of twelve as a relatively solitary child, a joint consequence of my parent's religious exclusivism and frequent moves from one house to another. There weren't enough "suitable" children for me to play with. So I spent much of my spare time reading. And most of the books I read were religious ones.

One of the earliest was *Bible Stories for Children*. It retold, in simple terms, stories, many with illustrations, from both the Old and New Testaments: Adam and Eve, Noah and the great flood, Moses and the wicked Pharaoh, David and Goliath, Jonah in the belly of the whale, Mary and Joseph going down to Egypt, the three Wise Men, the Nativity, scenes from the life of Jesus, St. Paul's shipwreck. It sparked my desire to know more.

That's one reason why I turned to the Bible itself: the unvarnished and unexpurgated King James version. Another reason was that my parents had enrolled me in both the Auckland Sunday School Union and the Scripture Union, both organizations whose examinations on selected biblical passages

I sat successfully at frequent intervals, thereby accumulating quite a nice little library of novels by approved Christian authors.

One of my book prizes, *Ten Brave Boys*, left a special mark on me. It was filled with adventure. But some of the stories conspired with the sense of mission spawned by my grandfather's deathbed consecration to make me feel that I was indeed one of God's chosen, like some of the brave boys who had dedicated their lives to His service.

Another book that left its mark, one from my parents' library, was John Bunyan's *The Pilgrim's Progress*. I struggled with the difficult prose, and found its archaic worldview difficult to understand. But it encouraged me to think that, no matter what difficulties I might be encountering in understanding my faith, I—with help from on high—would win through in the end. I certainly did not envisage that my own intellectual pilgrimage would lead me away from the faith of my fathers rather than toward its reaffirmation.

My acquaintance with nonreligious literature was limited. But I took special pleasure from Arthur Mee's *Children's Encyclopaedia*, spending countless hours poring over its contents. I turned, also, to my own grandfather's writings and my grandmother's posthumous biography of his life. Guy Thornton wrote several books: *The Wowser* (a semi-autobiographical novel drawing upon his experiences among the loggers in the center of the North Island), *Out to Win* (a book on soul-winning), and the autobiographical *With the Anzacs in Cairo*. All three were effusions of the evangelical certitude that had characterized most of his adult life. It wasn't until I read my grandmother's biography of her late husband that I made a salutary discovery: at one point he had struggled with the notion that God could send people to hell, and had even gone so far as to avow atheism, albeit only briefly.

Unintended Consequences

Much of my reading had consequences that my parents surely did not intend.

From *Bible Stories for Children* I garnered the impression that these stories were akin to the stories of Hans Christian Andersen and various other fairy tales. The illustrations looked similar. There was an air of fantasy about them; and they differed, it seemed to me, only in so far as I was told that the Bible stories were true while the others were not.

My studies of the Bible itself sowed the seeds of a different disquiet. For I didn't confine myself to the sanitized selections that had been prescribed for examination. I would read on and on, often until late at night. And what I found was often deeply disturbing.

If God was a god of love, why did he punish Adam and Eve and all their descendants so severely? Why did he drown everyone except Noah and his family in apparent violation of his own commandment not to kill? Why did he "harden" pharaoh's heart every time pharaoh relented and wanted to let the children of Israel go? Hundreds of questions. I wanted answers but received none other than words to the effect that "God knows best."

The so-called problem of evil began to rear its head in various guises. Why did a perfectly good, all-powerful, and all-knowing God create a world full of so many natural disasters and suffering? Why did he knowingly create humans like Adam and Eve—or the Devil, for that matter—knowing in advance that they would sin? And—worse still—why was the Bible full of stories of his own evil deeds, ranging from repeated genocide to sending unbelievers to suffer eternally in hell fire? This last question, the problem of divine evil, troubled me even more than the problems of natural and moral evil.

Bunyan's *Pilgrim's Progress* posed another sort of problem. I found his personification of various abstract concepts in such figures as those of Mr. Obstinate, Mr. Pliable, and Mr. Legality troubling, even though I came to understand their role as literary devices in his allegory. I started to become suspicious of what philosophers call reification: treating an abstraction as if it were some real entity. This suspicion subsequently rendered much of Plato's philosophy foreign to my own way of thinking and came to fruition when, in my later years as an academic philosopher, I eventually got around to thinking carefully about abstract nouns such as "the mind," "intelligence," "consciousness," and the like, and came to the conclusion that they aren't names of substantial entities that we possess in addition to our physical bodies. Rather, they refer to properties of living organisms. My mind, intelligence, or consciousness can no more be detached from, or survive, the death of my body than can the smile of the Lewis Carroll's Cheshire Cat once his body has disappeared. To think otherwise is to indulge in the fallacy of reification and live in the fantasy land of Alice. So much for the soul and prospects of immortality.

Arthur Mee's *Children's Encyclopaedia* opened my eyes to a vast domain of information. Starting with religious subjects, I eventually branched out into other areas. It was then, I think, my passion for knowledge commenced. I was fascinated by the grand sweep of human history, by accounts of ancient civilizations, by the discoveries that then-modern science was making about the structure of the universe. Much of what I learned fell outside, and was clearly incompatible with, the worldview encompassed by the Bible and the belief that all had begun in about 4004 B.C.

Historical Questions Unanswered

I wanted to put the Bible stories into historical perspective. When exactly did Moses live? I knew something of the history of Egypt and the scores of pharaohs who'd ruled that ancient land. They were usually referred to by name. But the books of Genesis and Exodus simply talked about "Pharaoh." Which one, I asked. No one could tell me.

Again, I wanted to know more about the life and times of Jesus. When exactly did he live and die? And what else was going on at the time? No answers were forthcoming. Precise dates were given for countless other historical figures, such as Julius Caesar. But, strangely, not for the Son of God.

It gradually dawned on me that most biblical events were recounted in a curiously ahistorical way. Why? The question stuck with me and was reawakened years later, in my early teens, when I came across George Bernard Shaw's preface to his *Androcles and the Lion* and then Albert Schweitzer's *Quest for the Historical Jesus*. Only then did I realize that there was a serious issue here: one of which I'd had still earlier inklings when I'd thought of the tales in *Bible Stories for Children* as somehow akin to fairy stories, or—at the very least—to the ahistorical tales of King Arthur. I couldn't find dates for him either.

Until then, I had shared the standard assumption that Jesus had been born at the beginning of A.D. 1. For wasn't that the year which was supposed (by us in the West, anyway) to be the turning point of human history: the year in which God came down to earth? It took me years to discover just how questionable this presupposition is.

Theological Difficulties

At about the same time—when I was ten or eleven—I was starting to discern still deeper difficulties lurking within my Christian faith. One night, after being tucked into bed and saying my prayers, I asked my mother what heaven was really like. I simply wanted a concrete understanding of all the heaven-talk to which I was accustomed. Where was heaven located? Since Jesus had ascended to it, in which direction did he go? And how fast? What would its streets look like when we got there? What would we eat and do all day? She didn't even pretend to know. We would just have to wait until we got there.

Stymied on that one, I ventured to ask what God himself was like. I got the standard answer about the divine attributes. God could do anything, she began. God also knew everything. And . . .

God's Foreknowledge and Predestination

We didn't proceed further, to God's perfect goodness, because the concept of omniscience seized my attention. What exactly did his knowledge include? Did he know where my father had been all day? Did he know what I had been doing all day? "Yes, dear: God knows all that," she answered. At that point my mind kicked into gear. If God knew all that, did he also know what I would do tomorrow? "Yes dear, he knows all that." My head spun. If he knew what I was going to do tomorrow, and the day after, and the day after that . . . then surely I couldn't do anything tomorrow or at any other time, other than what he already knew I would do.

I had tried to flesh out, in concrete detail, exactly what it *means* to say that God knows everything. And the implications, when I thought about them, were profoundly disturbing. I checked on the Bible and found again passages such as Romans 8:29: "For whom he did foreknow, he also did predestinate. . . ." I had hit upon the theological problem of free will, God's foreknowledge, predestination—a problem which, in its more philosophical guise of free will versus determinism, I was eventually to address in my dissertation. At the time, however, the impact of this "discovery" about God's nature was visceral as well as intellectual. For weeks afterward I wandered about like a zombie, feeling like a mere puppet, God's plaything.

It was the problem of predestination that first prompted me—when eleven or twelve years old—to start reading the three-volume work that grandfather Thornton had bequeathed to me: A. H. Strong's *Systematic Theology* (published in 1907). One of the foundational works of fundamentalist Christianity, I consulted it frequently over the ensuing years. Yet it opened my mind to still more problems.

Christology

I read, for instance, that the prevailing Christology (theory about Christ's nature) among the early Christians, commencing in about A.D. 70 and continuing for a hundred years or so, was that of the Docetists. They claimed that Christ was a mere apparition, not a person of flesh and blood. It was Docetism—I subsequently learned—that prevailed prior to both the composition and circulation of the Gospel incarnation stories, and prior by several centuries to the orthodox doctrine promulgated at Chalcedon in 451. I wondered how the Docetists could have thought Jesus to be a ghostly apparition if he had indeed walked and talked among them or their fathers. And

I wondered why it took so long for the "correct" doctrine to prevail. Why couldn't God have made the "true" doctrine so indisputably clear at the outset that none of the heresies that tore the Church apart for several centuries could have arisen?

Inerrancy

I discovered, too, that there were several rival accounts of what it meant to say that the Bible was the "word of God," and read with increasing skepticism Strong's defense of the doctrine that in all matters to do with science, history, and morality, the Bible is inerrant. It didn't require much logical acumen to perceive the circularity of his argument that the Scriptures must be without error because they report that Jesus himself had accepted them as true.

As for Strong's attempts to explain away any apparent errors by providing face-saving interpretations, I wondered why God would leave so much room for contrary construals of his words. Didn't he mean what he had so clearly said? Or didn't he know how to say what he really meant? I could not help but wonder at the presumptuousness of those who put their own words into God's mouth, as if he couldn't speak for himself. For it seemed to me that here lay the source of most of the doctrinal rivalry that had bedeviled the history of Christianity.

Predestination and Free Will

As for the doctrine of predestination, I pored over Strong's unsuccessful attempt to reconcile it with the concept of free will, underlining over a hundred passages and writing twenty-odd comments in the margin of volume 1, chapter 3, "The Decrees of God." Twice, I was so outraged by his arguments that I simply wrote the expletive "Bosh!"

Worse still, when I turned to the Bible itself, I found not a trace of the idea that human beings—as opposed to God himself—possessed genuine free will. Rather, it was God himself who took responsibility for assigning each of us to one or the other of two camps: that of the elect who would, by virtue of his grace (and not of anything in ourselves) join him in heaven; and on the other hand, that of the reprobates who were foreordained to damnation in hell. And the Westminster Confession, which Strong himself (strangely) endorsed, put it clearly enough: "God did from all eternity, by the most just and holy counsel of his own will, freely and unchangeably ordain whatever comes to pass." No obfuscatory mincing of words there.

Teenage Years: Doubts, Dissent, and Final Freedom

Until near the end of my twelfth year most of my doubts churned within the confines of my own mind. Only occasionally did I voice them to one other person: my mother. Hers was a fairly simple and unsophisticated faith, certainly not versed in the theological doctrines that I was wrestling with. Sadly, in the close confines of our kitchen, and because of pressure from my persistence, our exchanges grew increasingly disputatious and confrontational.

The Search for Understanding

But then we moved house still again, and I found a wider arena for discussion. A handful of friends attending Bible Class with me at the Mt. Albert Baptist Church were also interested in my quest for understanding. Like me they thought that St. Augustine's motto "Faith in search of understanding" put the cart before the horse. For us, understanding was a prerequisite of faith. We wanted to understand, for instance, what sort of experience counted as being "born again." Had those of us who'd been born into the faith also been born "again"? If one had been born again, could one subsequently fall from grace and be damned? What of the comforting doctrine "Once saved, always saved"? What was the point of being a minister or missionary if everyone to whom you preach is already predestined to either salvation or damnation?

Our deliberations took place in Bible Class, on street corners, and in my closest friends' basement bedrooms. They were delicious days in which we experienced the exhilaration of thinking for ourselves outside the boundaries of orthodox dogma.

But the path of free inquiry seldom runs smooth. News of the difficult questions my closest friends and I were raising in Bible Class had consequences. My parents wanted higher authorities to put us in our place lest we contaminate others with heresy.

Combating Heresy

The church set up a monthly "Brains Trust." We'd submit questions, and the panel would reply. No opportunity for subsequent debate. A couple of us soon learned to preempt their puerile answers by couching our questions in more complex form. One that I remember submitting—in writing—went something like this:

My question is Q. You might want to answer A, or perhaps B, or perhaps even C. But if you answer A then you've got to deal with problems 1, 2, and 3. And if you answer B, then you're faced with problems 4 and 5. While if you answer C, then....

And so on. They rejected the last question I sent them. It was nearly four pages long. Our Brains Trust sessions soon came to an end.

Next I was referred to a couple of "experts" for counseling. My parents had long insisted that there were Christian believers aplenty who were much cleverer than I was. And I could not but agree. First, I spent an evening with the president of the Baptist Theological College, but he gave up before 9:00 P.M. Then came a day in the Titirangi home of the redoubtable Dr. E. M. Blaiklock, professor and head of classics at the University of Auckland, a friend of my father, "Uncle Ted" to me from childhood, and an occasional lay preacher at the church. As a youth of fifteen, I held him in awe, so prepared thoughtfully for the occasion.

Blaiklock on the Historicity of Jesus

Our daylong discussions ranged over a host of topics. One had to do with the historicity of Jesus. Blaiklock had recently delivered a sermon in which he had brought the full weight of his classical scholarship to bear on an attempt to prove that Jesus had in fact lived about two thousand years ago. Most of the congregation was incensed. Why belabor the obvious, the unquestionable presupposition of our faith? But I had been fascinated. And so I took up the question again.

By that time my own little quest for the historical Jesus had yielded a seeming inconsistency in the Gospels' accounts of the date of his birth. Matthew 2:1 said that he was born "in the days of Herod the king." And since Herod had died in 4 B.C., that meant that my old assumption of a birth at the beginning of A.D. 1 had to be wrong.

Worse was to come. For Luke 2:1–2 said that he was born "when Cyrenius [otherwise known as Quirinius] was governor of Syria." But that, so far as I could discover, was in A.D. 6. Blaiklock's proposed solution was to claim that Cyrenius must have been governor once before, during the period 6–4 B.C. That seemed good enough at the time, so we moved on to other matters.

Only decades later did I discover the truth. First, I discovered that Blaiklock's proposed reconciliation of the two Gospel accounts was spurious. Both he and I had failed to take account of Luke 2:1. For there we find that the governorship of Cyrenius during which Jesus was said to be born was concurrent with the period during which Augustus Caesar issued a decree "that all the world should be taxed." But that was during Cyrenius's second term, namely, during or after A.D. 6. The inconsistency with Matthew 2:1 is every bit as real as I had first thought it to be. So the Gospel accounts certainly can't be relied upon.

Second, I learned that independent historical evidence of Jesus' very existence, let alone his alleged date of birth, simply does not exist. In his book *Man or Myth* (1983), Blaiklock confessed, "Jesus is authenticated in no other way, outside the gospels, save by Josephus and a sentence in a Roman historian." But he didn't do justice to the fact that most New Testament scholars regard the passages in Josephus as interpolations originating in the fourth century. Many scholars think that they came from the hand of Bishop Eusebius. At all events, the passages were unknown to second-century Christian apologists, such as Origen, who had chided Josephus for not mentioning Jesus.

As for the Roman historian Tacitus, the "one sentence" Blaiklock refers to was written in about A.D. 109. It merely reports the belief by Christians of that time that the originator of their sect, someone they called "Christ," had been executed during the reign of Tiberius some eighty or so years earlier. Nothing conclusive in that.

Little wonder that when, in Appendix 2 of his book, the good professor gave a list of important dates of the period, he was able to be specific about many other figures, but not about Jesus. Seneca, he said, was born in 5 B.C. But 5 B.C. was only the "presumed" date of the nativity. And, betraying his uncertainty still further, he described A.D. 29 as the "presumed date of the crucifixion." He could confidently give dates of publication for many of the most important writings of the first century, but none for the Gospels.

So when, if at all, did the incarnation occur? The Gospels are full of inconsistencies, absurdities, factual error, and evangelizing propaganda. They are historically unreliable. And secular history of the time knows nothing of such a supposedly momentous event, or of others reported in the Gospels. The fact is that Blaiklock didn't know, and neither does anyone else know, when—or even if—God/the Holy Ghost/Jesus the Christ visited this insignificant planet of ours (all in order, supposedly, to save a few of the "elect" from his own unseemly vengeance).

Blaiklock on Evil, Free Will, and Responsibility

We spent most of the day, however, on the issues that troubled me most: the problems of moral and natural evil; the problem of hellfire and damnation;

the problem of particularity (why God would announce his plan for universal salvation to only a handful of people, at only one time and place); questions about the doctrine of salvation and why God would demand the sacrifice of his son in order to atone for the sins of a relative handful of his creatures; questions about how creatures created without flaw—Satan, Adam, and Eve—could fall from grace; why, according to the doctrine of original sin, God would impute sin to all descendants of Adam and Eve; and so on.

Questions about free will and responsibility predominated. Not only in connection with the doctrine of predestination, but in other contexts as well. It had become clear to me by then that although there was some sense in which I did in fact sometimes act "of my own free will" and was responsible for the actions I then performed, there was also some "deeper" sense in which I was neither free nor responsible. I couldn't see why the buck should stop with me. After all, I didn't choose who I was going to be, who would be my parents, or the nature of my soul (if I had one). How then could I be ultimately responsible for what I was, or therefore did? It was this deeper sense of both concepts that was threatened by predestination, of course, for—according to that doctrine—it was God who was ultimately responsible for my free acts and for my final fate.

My own ultimate responsibility for my free acts was also threatened, I thought, by other considerations having little to do with theological doctrine. World War II was raging, and it was all Hitler's fault. Or so we all believed. A curious question haunted me: "What if I had been Hitler?" Then, I thought, I would have done what Hitler had done; and it would all have been *my* fault. I wasn't asking merely, "What if I'd been *born* in the same circumstances as Hitler?" Rather, it was a question about identity, personal identity in particular: "What if I were identical with Hitler?" He didn't choose his identity—who he was—any more than did I. So was he really at fault for the acts that had flowed from the person he was?

I'm not too sure to this day how to answer the question, or even whether it makes logical sense. It is even more puzzling, perhaps, than the question posed decades later by the philosopher Thomas Nagel, who asked: "What is it like to be a bat?" But it did set me thinking about how lucky I was that I was in fact Raymond Bradley, not Hitler. Was it just luck of the draw, as it were? Translating my perplexity, and sense of good fortune, back into the theological context, I felt the force of the saying "There, but for the grace of God, go I." Was Hitler ultimately responsible? Was anyone? Other than God, of course. Blaiklock said it was all a mystery to which God would one day reveal the answer.

Hitler's name came up again in connection with the problem of moral evil. I wanted to know why God would permit his creatures, like Hitler, to commit so many morally evil deeds? Blaiklock's answer, in keeping with that of other Christian apologists, then and now, was that God has given us the gift of free will and couldn't take it away without transforming us into zombies.

But surely, I objected, there was a third alternative. God could allow Hitler, for example, to freely choose his policies but then, by means of a timely miracle, ensure that Hitler's intentions were frustrated. After all, we were encouraged to believe that God could perform miracles any time he chose. So why couldn't he strike Hitler down with a heart attack or ensure that there was a mechanical failure in the aircraft in which he was flying? Why couldn't he intervene in some such way every time anyone formed an evil intent? That wouldn't take away our free will. On the contrary, God would be intervening in much the same way as do good parents with their children. We'd soon learn not even to try to translate evil thought into evil action. And we would no more be zombies than are the millions of people around the world who are "struck down" by disease or mishap every year.

Blaiklock invoked the biblically spurious belief in free will, again, in order to answer my questions about natural evil: Why did God create a world rife with disease and disaster, fire, flood, famine, and the rest? Blame it on the Devil, was Blaiklock's answer. God's original creation, he claimed, was perfect, and God had very correctly surveyed it and said that it was "very good." It was the devil, Satan, who'd messed it up. God, I was supposed to believe, had given Satan, too, the gift of free will—a gift that he had abused by spoiling God's good work, at our cost.

But that wouldn't do, I objected. Since God was supposed to be all-powerful, he could easily at any time—and preferably sooner rather than later—deprive Satan of his awesome powers, rendering impotent Satan's evil intent. According to the Book of Revelation, God would eventually bind Satan in chains forever. So why didn't God do it now? Indeed, why hadn't he done it in the first place, the moment Satan began his evil career? Again, all was mystery.

Blaiklock did his best. But it wasn't good enough. Calling it all a deep mystery simply heightened my desire to penetrate mystery's inner workings. And when I did, I came across indefensible and contradictory doctrines at its very heart. I had to use reason to do get at the truth. Faith tried to lock the door on mystery and then hide the key.

At the end of a day that tested my intellectual stamina beyond anything I'd experienced before, he had a simple confession: "Ray. I can't answer your questions. All I can do is ask you to go to the Bible Training Institute Bookroom and buy the following books . . . Read and pray." He wrote out a substantial check. I purchased the books, among them C. S. Lewis's *The Problem of Pain* and *The Screwtape Letters*. I read. I prayed. But the heavens were closed.

About twenty years later (in 1965 or 1966, as I remember it), Professor Blaiklock and I crossed swords again, but on a more even footing. By then I had been appointed as Professor and Head of Philosophy at the University of Auckland and was asked to engage my "Uncle Ted" in a series of ten lunch-hour debates. Our final session went on for over two hours before an audience of a thousand or so. He began patronizingly by telling how he'd known me since my early childhood and went on to predict that I'd someday return to the faith of my fathers, if only on my deathbed. His rhetoric was unmatchable: he was, after all, university orator. But my arguments were unanswered. In many ways we simply talked passed each other.

The previous year, I'd had a similar series of ten debates with Professor Val Chapman of the Botany Department, at the end of which I was told that the president of the Student Christian Movement had lost his faith and didn't get it back again until they'd worked on him for three weeks. That's why the one of the campus chaplains had recruited Professor Blaiklock in the hope that he would prove a more worthy opponent. Which he did.

Other Milestones on the Way to Apostasy

But back to my teenage years. It is worth mentioning a few other milestones in my attempts to pursue truth wherever it might be found.

The year before my Titirangi talks with Blaiklock, our Fourth Form English and History teacher, Maurice Hutchings, decided we should learn the art of debating. The topic chosen was "Creation Versus Evolution." I volunteered, along with a Seventh Day Adventist classmate, to take up the cudgels on behalf of Creation. I began researching all the anti-evolutionist literature that was heaped on me once my mission was known.

The Evolution Debate

Some three weeks later, the debate occurred. That night I had to report on its outcome to my parents. They detected my reluctance to elaborate on the simple statement that we had won by a vote or two. Only under pressure did I confess that, in spite of winning, I could no longer believe that for which I had argued.

In my view the anti-evolutionist literature I'd read was full of spurious arguments against crude caricatures of what evolutionists actually said. And I'd thought the opposition's arguments for evolutionary theory were pretty convincing. Besides, I pointed out, there was a difference between believing in creation (that the universe owed its existence to a creator-god) and believing in creation*ism* (that the world was created in the way depicted in Genesis complete with species that reproduced only "according to their kind"). My parents were outraged. I was, they said, "possessed by the Devil." No assurances to the contrary had any calming effect. I finished up spending most of a frosty night shivering in a concrete shelter among the sheep in the crater of Mt. Albert. But I never did recant.

Christian Crusaders

Then a year later, in 1945, the very same teacher, Maurice Hutchings, spotted me wearing my Christian Crusader badge. He asked me if I knew much of the history of the crusades and suggested I might want to find out more. I did the research. And I threw away my badge.

Buddhism

The following year, when I was in the Sixth Form, I won an essay competition and selected *The Life of the Buddha* as my prize. The ethics of Siddhartha Gautama Buddha, I discovered, had anticipated most of the much-vaunted Sermon on the Mount, by more than five centuries. And Siddhartha himself came across as rather more wise and virtuous than Jesus. I couldn't buy into his doctrine of *samsara*, the wheel of reincarnation. But the idea of *karma*, the fruits of one's actions (in this world at least), made sense. And his notion of *nirvana*, a state of nothingness where there are neither sensations nor ideas, and in which all personal identity is lost, seemed both more plausible and more pleasant than the Christian prospect of an eternity in heaven, for a few, or in hell, for most.

I did flirt with Madame Blavatsky's Theosophy—one of Buddhism's nineteenth-century spin-offs—for a month or so, but rapidly came to the conclusion that it was mainly mumbo-jumbo.

By the time I was seventeen, attending Auckland Teachers College by day while commencing a part-time degree at the university by night, I'd pretty much given up on Christianity and all other forms of revealed religion.

Deism

Yet I thought for a while that some form of deism might be defensible, deism being the belief in some sort of Supreme Being who created the world and then left it to its own devices. I tried out the standard philosophical arguments—the Cosmological Argument, the Teleological Argument, and the Ontological Argument—in the senior sermonette contest at a Bible Class camp in Orewa. I tied for first place with one of the students from the Baptist Theological College but was criticized for being "less evangelical" than my rival. Actually, I was surprised at having been ranked so high, for the arguments I'd propounded had seemed to me unsound despite my best attempts to give them a positive spin. That was the last time I really thought I might find a rational basis for belief in any sort of god. Nevertheless, I did preserve—for a while—the liberal Christian idea that the Jesus-myth was worth preserving for the moral values it enshrined. But then the doctrine of hellfire got to me again, and I came to the same conclusion as Mark Twain. As he had put it, "The palm for malignity must be granted to Jesus, the inventor of hell."

As for agnosticism, that seemed to me a refuge for the timid and spineless, for those who couldn't see, or wouldn't face up to, the implications of the fact that they were atheists, not agnostics, about Santa Claus. So, by the age of eighteen, I was an atheist about all gods and other creatures of imagination, myth, and superstition. First, a closet atheist; then, a bit later, a publicly unabashed one. No longer in fear of the Devil, I saw no need to cower before the unfashionable word "atheist."

Postscript

Given my story so far, it might be supposed that my struggles to free myself from the bondage of Baptist beliefs occurred in an atmosphere of sweetness and light. How about the darker side that we normally associate with the term "fundamentalism"? Condemnation of films, dancing, immodest clothing, lipstick, alcohol, and the like? Prohibitions against work—even homework—on the Lord's Day? Blasphemy charges? Book burnings? Beating those who dared to differ?

Sad to say, I experienced all these at the hands of those who most sincerely sought to save my soul from perdition: my parents. The book burnings occurred when my biology teacher, Peter Ohms, lent me a textbook outlining evolutionary theory and a novel depicting St. Paul as a misogynist who occasionally sought relief in the warm flesh of a woman of the night. Both books disappeared mysteriously from my shelves. It was only when questioned that my parents revealed the fate of both. They'd thrown them into a bonfire along with "other garbage." My teacher was magnanimous. But that didn't erase my shame and outrage.

The beatings, in particular, left their mark on me—not least in a broken nose inflicted after the evolution debate, before I'd fled to the mountaintop. They had begun, when I was ten or eleven, with the kitchen confrontations with my mother over issues to do with God's foreknowledge. They continued, with increasing severity, as my apostasy became more evident and fears for my soul grew more intense. And they ended only when our closest neighbour, Balfour Joseph, intervened and threatened to call the police were they to occur again. These ugly, but all-too-common, manifestations of fundamentalism were not the cause of my loss of faith. They were its effects. But I shan't dwell on them.

Suffice it to say that, once embarked on the path of a freethinker, I never turned back. Up until the 1980s my public opposition to the fundamentalist beliefs of my childhood took the form, mainly, of debates with those who wished to challenge my disbelief: first, that debate with the Catholic priest in Australia; then those debates with Professors Chapman and Blaiklock in Auckland; and during the 1980s and early 1990s, various debates with representatives of the Campus Crusade for Christ (including philosopher-evangelists Michael Horner and the redoubtable William L. Craig) in Vancouver, B.C. But then I started writing a series of papers for publication in print or, later, on the Internet.

Among the most recent of these are two critiques of philosopher Antony Flew: "An Open Letter to Professor Antony Flew," and "Antony in Wonderland." Flew had long been regarded as one of the icons of twentieth-century atheism. But recently he's become an apostate in his own way. Having been seduced by the spurious "intelligent design" movement, he's now reverted to belief in God—albeit a deist one rather than the theist one of his childhood.

Blaiklock had predicted a similar fate for me. But he was wrong. No deathbed conversion awaits me. I'd bet my life on that. For with every passing day, my conviction strengthens that religious belief—especially of the fundamentalist, "faith-based," kind—is the most dangerous phenomenon of our times. The world desperately needs a savior: a new age of reason and enlightenment.

4

GROWING UP TO QUESTION CATHOLICISM: EMOTIONAL SUFFERING, THE *EUTHYPHRO*, AND THE LIFE OF THE MIND

Damien Alexander Dupont

Introduction

There are those who believe the issue of the morality of indoctrination is no more a problem for religious indoctrination than it is for indoctrination in general education. I agree there is some truth to the idea that indoctrination of *some* kind must play a role in education of *any* kind. But I claim that anyone cognizant of the history of ideas would acknowledge that the tension between those dedicated to the advancement of knowledge above all and those dedicated to the preservation of morality above all has often been tremendous, to put it mildly. And those who might truly be said to hold both goals equally dear have been few and far between. As such, my purpose here is guided by my view that the possible moral concerns regarding indoctrination become more acute when handled by organizations and institutions that by their very nature are supposed to be fundamentally and particularly concerned with morality.

I will proceed by first relating what is a very personal account of my religious indoctrination and how it affected my intellectual and social development, as well as my development as an autonomous individual. I believe my memoir will leave little doubt that in my case, and likely in the case of almost any devout Roman Catholic youth, the education received is indeed *indoctrination*, and is so in the most pejorative sense of the term.

I understand "indoctrination" most generally as a method or methods for instilling the fundamental aims and beliefs of a group in an individual, with the intention of the indoctrinators that these aims and beliefs should be critically accepted and adhered to by the individual as an adult, according to the individual's considered judgment. I understand indoctrination in the pejorative sense to be the *intentional* molding of a person into one who will wholly accept and make every attempt to strictly adhere to the aims and beliefs in question, according to the standards of those who instill them. More specifically, "pejorative indoctrination" is (1) using of methods of indoctrination on individuals who could not ask for the aims and beliefs to be so acquired at the time the process would begin *and* who in the future would reject the use of those methods and their intended results for their child selves, and (2) using such methods on adults who have not asked for such treatment and who would not seek it unless they had, by their considered judgment, already come to basic acceptance of the aims and beliefs to be instilled.[1]

During and after the relating of my story, I will offer some reflection and finally some critical analysis of what happened to me, and why. I will conclude by arguing that since children cannot choose to be indoctrinated, and many adults would rather have not been indoctrinated as children, and since successful religious indoctrination is very harmful to certain types of people,[2] successful religious indoctrination of children is often immoral. Since the point of any indoctrination is to be successful, and Roman Catholic religious indoctrination aims to create subservient disciples, such indoctrination should not be inflicted on children. Attempting to shape a person so drastically, especially one who if he or she could choose would not want such dispositions or beliefs, is immoral.

My Story

My Hometown

Most residents of Greenville, South Carolina, think of it as a great place to raise a family. I was born and raised there and came to believe there are many reasons to think that belief unfounded. For my purposes here, I will focus on the massive influence of the fundamentalist and evangelical climate in the city. While beautifully situated geographically, the self-styled "buckle of the Bible belt" exhibits an ugly strain of religiosity. At the center of it, and incredibly influential in Greenville's local politics, are Bob Jones University and its alumni. They fervently pursue political manifestations of their worldview, and they, like so many other religious groups, want nothing more than to spread their beliefs. Worse still, their reputation for bigotry is, in my opinion, almost completely deserved. It was my personal experience that one of the groups they have particular contempt for is Roman Catholics.

Growing up devoutly Catholic in a city that is incredibly conservative, xenophobic, overwhelmingly Protestant, intensely Southern Baptist, and influenced by anti-Catholic sentiments in many community leaders was, to say the least, a challenge. Unfortunately, the Catholic community of my youth did not escape related flaws and bred them in me. Perhaps because of the overwhelming feeling of being looked at as a curiosity barely to be tolerated, the Catholic community of my youth was insulated and felt very tightly knit. I soaked that feeling in, making my Catholicism essential to my identity. In some ways, it just *was* me.

My Childhood

Upon reflection I now see that a main component of my indoctrination, a pillar of my faith, was something of a syllogism, though of course I did not know that at the time. First, I was taught and believed fervently that the Catholic Church was the one true church. Second, I knew that since my father had divorced his first wife, my parents' marriage was not sanctioned by the church. Therefore, since my parents' marriage *didn't exist*, I was born out of wedlock, which is to say that I was illegitimate. I was baptized, but at a very young age I came to believe what seemed obvious: that since my parents were continuing to "live in sin," I should not have been baptized. To my knowledge this is the correct interpretation of doctrine, and if it is not, it certainly is the de facto interpretation in numerous parishes around the world.

This fostered shame and along with it, a feeling of great indebtedness to the church. I was the lucky recipient of an undeserved gift, and the best possible one at that. I had always felt "provisional," as if at any moment my tenuous membership in the church could be revoked by some misstep on my part. I felt inadequate and marginal in the eyes of the church, and so in the eyes of God. As such, that I was welcome at all was something comforting yet terrifying. And I dutifully worked to keep from wasting my good fortune. It is hard to relate how strong the feeling of barely skating by in the eyes of God, or the strength of the attachment one feels to his faith, is for a boy growing up as a devout member of a religious minority in a largely intolerant city.

Though I was given all the sacraments and had religion classes every year of my life from primary school through high school, nothing was ever done to address this humiliating and deeply painful concern. Some might lay the blame on me or my parents, but I think the reasonable conclusion is that my indoctrinators should have looked for signs in my behavior. Children often don't have the self-possession or self-awareness to know why they have the feelings they have, much less what to do about them. We would not blame a child who was terrified of losing its parents' love and acceptance for never asking of them certain things—we would wonder at the parents. And when it comes to religious upbringing and community, the church is your mother, and God is your father.

My conviction that it was *right* for me to be considered a bastard repeatedly reinforced feelings of inadequacy, indebtedness, and obligation that led me to embrace the church and do everything I could to earn and hopefully keep its love and acceptance. This meant becoming an altar boy as early as was allowed and remaining one until I broke from the church more than ten years later. I also became a lector, and eventually a Eucharistic minister. It raised many eyebrows that a young boy was allowed to read Scripture in front of the whole congregation, and little else could have made me happier.

My psychological dependence on the church led to an attitude of uncritical acceptance of its authority in general, and over me in particular.[3] It also produced a feeling of being completely deserving of any punishment or "trial" that God might choose to give me. As I grew, this expanded into antisocial behavior in that when I got to public school I felt compelled to much moralizing and hectoring of acquaintances for their "misbehavior," a practice that often alienated me from boys and girls who should have been my friends. And I was silently horrified by many others. My "saintly" attitude and social awkwardness led to a lot of loneliness and hurt feelings, which led me deeper into the arms of the church; I was fairly safe until, because there was no parochial high school, it was time to matriculate at Greenville Senior High School. Then I invested tremendous amounts of time and effort in my parish's youth group.

A Devout Teen

Considering all the temptations and urges a teenager has, when I look back I am quite impressed (and more than a little disturbed) at how devout I was. As most people are aware, much of socializing in high school revolves around "adult" behavior such as drinking and sexual exploration, but my faith made me believe both were wrong for someone my age; and so I avoided not only high school parties but any association at all with the girls who went to them, as I saw them as immoral and so a negative influence. Of course eventually I compromised in that I just couldn't resist at least trying to make friends with several of those girls I judged better behaved than average. (It is more than a coincidence that most would have judged them among the prettiest, too.) Unfortunately, they mostly found me just too nice and boring to take seriously.

It is no surprise, then, how I took to both my parish's youth organization and the related Confraternity of Christian Doctrine. Very quickly these two groups accounted for nearly all my social life and, to my mind, were the only possible places to meet good girls who would talk to me. Unfortunately for me, most of them found me nearly as shy and awkward as the girls at school did. Still, if I hadn't played JV baseball and made friends with a handful of my teammates, the youth organization and the confraternity would have accounted for all of my socialization outside my family. I was deeply involved in the workings of both. I was elected class representative, then vice president, and finally president. In this capacity I was appointed as youth representative on the parish council. And because of that position, I was appointed one of a handful of youth delegates representing the Upstate region at the historic 1995 Synod of Charleston. In addition, I was an avid participant in the parish's youth basketball program from fourth grade through twelfth grade. In short, I took every avenue I could to enmesh myself in the church. From the standpoint of religious indoctrination I was a total success, a shining example of what well-structured indoctrination can do, especially when the student has a disposition toward dependence and trust as I did.

It might be asked if I was really a success, considering my unhappy and unhealthy psychological state and my (overall) poor socialization. Consider the mission statement, the "philosophy," of my parochial school (italics are mine):

> The *primary mission* of St. Mary's School is to *invite* our students to *follow* the Lord Jesus Christ as *obedient disciples* in faith, hope, and love, and *every activity* in the school is *subordinated* to this *apostolic purpose*. In our curriculum, academic excellence, athletic challenge, artistic expression, and character formation are *integrated* in the *effort to serve* the *evangelical mission* of St. Mary's Church and School.
>
> *In addition to transmitting the Gospel* to our students, we seek to instill in them all of the human virtues celebrated in classical wisdom and Catholic tradition. By teaching our children to love righteousness in all its forms, we *prepare them to serve* Christ and His Church by respecting the human dignity of each person, and through regular participation in the Most Holy Eucharist and systematic catechesis, our students are *introduced to the Christian life* in all its richness.

> Our program is not restricted only to extraordinary students, but it is *intended only for children of families with deep commitment to the Gospel* of Jesus Christ and *genuine respect* for the classical forms and disciplines of *Christian* education. The faculty and staff of St. Mary's School are dedicated to the *integral formation* of our pupils, and we work with our parents as a single community of many families to *serve each child* and *motivate every student*.[4]

Both the devotion to God and the church that molded and motivated me, and the behavior that evinced it, were *exactly* the results my religious "education" wanted to achieve. Of course a fundamental reason this is pejorative indoctrination is that you can't really *invite* students to follow Jesus as obedient disciples.

So I was given an "invitation" that I really could not accept, to be shaped into a humble servant, a disciple of Jesus, and thereby be a part of the next generation of evangelical Catholics. It turned out I could not turn it down either. Now compare this statement of the mission of my public high school: "Our mission is to foster excellence by empowering students to become critical thinkers, productive citizens, and lifelong learners."[5] Or even this much more ambiguous statement of the mission: "The mission of Greenville Senior High School Academy of Academic Excellence is to continue our tradition of providing a stimulating environment of unity with spirit conducive to learning and a meaningful, challenging curriculum that prepares our diverse student body to be responsible, contributing members of a global society."[6]

The first is practically heretical compared to the mission of my parochial school, and the second is not much better. Unfortunately, they were unable to override the indoctrination I had already received.

Still, I would have been relatively lucky if the extent of the damage done by my religious indoctrination had been only to make me the moralizing, lonely, and socially backward boy that I was, incapable of any criticism of the church. The reality, however, was much worse. Due in large part to my indoctrination and my psychological state, so helpful to the indoctrination process, I became the easy prey of the Pastor of my parish, who molested me from the time I was in second grade until about my sophomore year in high school. Sadly, my self-imposed high frequency of being an altar boy, along with his quite frequent appearances at confraternity classes and youth events, gave him many opportunities to seek me (and I imagine many others) out.[7]

When I was very young, say third to fifth grade, I just didn't "get it." But sometime around my arrival in middle school I began to realize what was happening was not supposed to happen. I remembered teachers saying that adults weren't supposed to do certain things, and that we were supposed to tell someone if they did. Sadly, I was simply *incapable* of following that advice. As I did start to understand and become more and more uncomfortable when it would happen, my guilty conscience and my sense of indebtedness short-circuited any response. My family was much less well off than those of most of the kids at school, and I knew very well my parents couldn't really afford the tuition; I knew we were getting education at a discount rate. And consistent with my general feeling toward the church, I felt incredibly grateful for the opportunity. Moreover, I was constantly reminded that public school was horrible, with bullies and criminals everywhere, and offered little chance to go to college. The prospect of leaving my school seemed like a nightmare, and my sisters needed to be at the school too, so I could never do anything that would call negative attention to my family's great benefactor.

I suppose the best way I can put it is that I felt like this episode in my life was a trial, a test of responsibility. And I was never sure that I'd be believed even by my parents, or how they would take it if they did believe me, considering how strong I perceived their devotion to be. But the most troubling thing of all, a very influential fact in my understanding of what was happening to me, is that it would often happen in front of at least half a dozen adults. I was absolutely shocked that the lector and a deacon or two would be less than ten feet away, the cantors would be warming up their voices just as nearby, and the priest would simply walk right up to me, and often enough to the other altar boys there. I always admired the guts of those who came running when he walked over, but was terrified for them at the same time—what a risk they were taking! To my mind at the time the public nature of his behavior was a sort of legitimatization of his actions and that, along with the aforementioned pressures, kept me almost completely silent for a very long time.

Even when he was removed from the parish after allegations of misconduct stemming from previous parish assignments, I kept my mouth shut. The very few people I have told about what I was subjected to all have asked me why I never came forward and have often encouraged me to do so. For a very long time my view was that whatever ability the church had to mitigate the influence of the evangelical, conservative forces that, I felt, demonized my religion would very likely be compromised by such accusations.

And I felt certain that the cohesiveness of the Catholic community would unravel. In addition, I saw no benefit after he was put out of commission, and I personally could not ever spend any money I might have been awarded by a "victory" in court.

At this point I've decided that perhaps this outlet is the best, as it may help to educate those who are directly interested in questions about religious indoctrination and education in general by pointing out the very real dangers in many ways specific to religious indoctrination: I believe pedophile priests are much more capable, and have much more opportunity to satisfy their gross desires than most pedophiles just because their prey are religiously indoctrinated. With the gravitas and authority that their position carries in the mind of an indoctrinated person, especially an indoctrinated *child* such as I was, it is a wonder they are ever caught at all.

Catholic in College

Throughout all this my devotion was strong. And it remained very strong through my freshman year at Vanderbilt. Within a week of being on campus I had made the acquaintance of the Catholic mission on campus, and I immediately signed on as a lector and Eucharistic minister. I also became known among my friends in the Hispanic student organization as quite religious; I was the guy who always insisted on praying before meals and who called to remind people to come to church.

I also made some acquaintances that were quite anti-Catholic and got into very many heated arguments with them. I'm sure this behavior alienated many people otherwise sympathetic to me. But I saw myself as a defender of the Faith and could not let any slight go uncontested. Looking back I don't know how my hallmates ever put up with me, but I do see why I did not get invited to many outings.

But a fascinating thing happened in my own dorm room. I was assigned to room with a very devout Methodist from rural Texas. Eye-opening does not begin to describe the experience. Though he too wore his religious convictions on his sleeve, I couldn't help but notice differences in our demeanors. I perceived him to be the stereotypical all-American "aw-shucks" type. He was a big strong kid from a farm in Texas who loved Christian rock and would never have considered drinking alcohol or having premarital sex. He was simply a sweet person who prayed on his knees at the foot of his bed twice a day and completely trusted God would work things out for him. On my best days I was a combination of our two religious modes. On my worst days I was both highly critical of him and yet ashamed of myself in comparison to him for my perceived failures.

I remember very well one night toward the end of my freshman year, at a point where I had become what I thought was a fairly regular drinker. My roommate had a habit of waking up and looking at me, shaking his head sadly, when I came in after a night of drinking. But that night I was quite self-conscious and in no mood for dirty looks, so we had a confrontation about it. I finally explained to him that though it was terrific of him to be so pure, and though he was a good example to everyone, some people are simply unable to exercise that much control, to deny themselves repeatedly all manner of pleasures. And that I wasn't even sure anymore that that was really a good idea. He was shocked, apologized profusely for hurting my feelings, and thanked me for the tremendous compliment.

When I realized what I'd said about myself, I too was shocked. Not long after this confrontation I decided my biological urges had gotten the better of me and that I ought to abstain from drinking for a while. So I began a practice of one month on, one month off, to prove to myself both that I did love God and that I really was a good Catholic. I would prove that I could have something of a normal social life while still being devout.

With this decision I had survived the first serious tension between my wants and my faith. But as I became more social, I realized very quickly that I was an incredibly naïve person relative to the other students I knew, and that it was much more obvious to most people than it was to me. This new problem worried me to no end; what was it about me I, often wondered, that marked me out so much? How did girls seem to know to avoid me, why did fraternities seem so uninterested, how come I had to ask around so much to hear about parties? Why was I never "one of the guys"? I was at a loss. I decided I must not be very physically attractive, and I focused that feeling on my mild cerebral palsy. Surely what kept me back, I reasoned, was that people simply discounted me immediately when they saw me walk up to them with my distinctive gait. It never once occurred to me that my attitude and demeanor, inspired by my religiosity, could be the problem.

This realization led me to what I now recognize as a bout of depression: over the course of the next year my grades were horrible, I was even lonelier than ever, and I was having trouble finding my usual solace in the church. And I didn't know exactly why. By the end of my sophomore year, during which I had been on academic probation, I lost my generous financial aid package and was left unable to pay tuition. Over the next two years I had to work two and sometimes three jobs to save money and was only able to afford one semester of school.

Philosophical Awakening and the Loss of Faith

One thing happened that bleak sophomore year that would eventually prove to be my "salvation." My Introduction to Philosophy course was unlike anything I'd ever experienced. I recall feeling excited at the prospect of reading about Socrates, a character who I knew little of but whom I was fascinated with since his portrayal in the puerile comedy *Bill and Ted's Excellent Adventure*. But I had no idea what I was in for. One of the readings was Plato's *Euthyphro*, and studying it changed my life.

Simply put, that dialogue showed me that questioning religious authority was a real possibility, something that, strange as it might sound, had never fully occurred to me up to that point. I was simply dumbfounded, yet completely invigorated. I'd had doubts here and there—during the time leading up to my confirmation, I had wondered why children who died unbaptized would not automatically end up in heaven—but never did I think that the church had really gotten something wrong, or that I'd made some kind of mistake in being so devout. The only mistakes were my own and in spite of the church's help and counsel.

The *Euthyphro* convinced me, like so many others, that fundamentalism, dogmatism, and naked appeals to authority in general are intellectually unacceptable. And that human excellence consists not simply in devotion to God, but in understanding proper devotion. So I had a new syllogism operating: First, God gave humans intellect that separates us from the animals. Second, God wants humans to be good and holds us responsible for our successes and failures. Therefore, God must want us to use our minds to be good. Plato had taught me that blind obedience to authority, even spiritual authority, was certainly undignified and probably immoral. My immediate thought was that I'd have to accept that my failings were due to my laziness. I was making the church do all the work rather than using my head. I thought if only I'd studied my religion more and really understood the truth therein, I would be much happier and more successful.

As I mentioned, however, my academic awakening was put on hold because of my financial circumstances. Though I wasn't going to be taking another philosophy class for a little while, I did become very studious about the history of the church and of Christianity in general. I read Gnostic scriptures and other apocryphal writings, and books and essays such as *The*

Imitation of Christ. However, in the one semester that I was able to go to school during the two-year period that I spent largely away, I was introduced to David Hume's *Dialogues on Natural Religion* and Bertrand Russell's *Why I Am Not a Christian*. I was very anxious at the time, realizing that the "old me," the dogmatic and intellectually lazy me, would probably have declined to read the former and would never have considered reading the latter even if had known it existed, given that I eschewed such blasphemous subject matter. As it was, Plato's argument had gotten to me the only possible way something so potent could have, totally under the radar. But these two I read consciously, realizing that what was in them would be at least challenging.

I had a decent idea what these two books would be about, but I was not ready for how persuasive they would be. Because of them I looked at myself, at my life to that point, at revealed religion, and at divine command theory in hot-faced and stunned confusion. I was blindsided and devastated upon realizing just how much damage the beginnings of critical thinking sparked by Plato and set ablaze by Hume and Russell had done to *me*. The combined weight on my mind of these three texts *completely broke me down*. Once the image of the church and of the divine that my identity and my whole worldview were predicated upon was shattered, I was left with no compass or bearing. That was when fear *really* set in.

I vividly recall a week's worth of nights I spent reading and rereading these books and my notes in bed, then thinking over my childhood lessons. During these marathon sessions I tormented myself, punching pillows and viciously yelling at myself for being a failure. Most of those nights I broke down into tears as struggled to find a way back to where I had been, to what I used to believe so fervently. I had indeed been well indoctrinated—I required no outside coercion to stay in the church, I was doing it to myself. Still, I knew I was facing a very serious, intensely frightening dilemma; several times I asked myself point blank whether I should stay an active Catholic when in my heart of hearts I didn't believe in it any more or whether I should leave the church and go to hell when I died. What a question! I was sobbing like I hadn't since I was a little boy when I finally came to the agonizing decision that I simply would have to go to hell. God made me the way I was and in my best effort to please him, I had come to the conclusion that the belief structure and the organization I had thought perfectly well grounded, and that had aided my desire to please him, was useless. Not long after some more intense soul searching I decided further that if God really would send me to hell for being intellectually honest, I could not respect him. And that I would rather be punished unjustly than be rewarded by a being I did not respect. Not long after this self-implosion, this tearing down, I concluded *that no one should have to face such a crisis* and soon became unable to even set foot in a church, a fact that remained true for five years, until filial obligation and tragic circumstance led me to my father's funeral.

Though today I am more of an agnostic than an atheist, the real residuum from my theistic years is the thought that the beliefs and feelings I was given by my indoctrination *severely negatively impacted* my intellectual autonomy and my personal growth. They damaged my socialization, especially in my dealings with women, homosexuals, and non-Christians, until late in college, and they generally stifled the possibility of the very things I thought my beliefs would eventually guarantee—my personal happiness and success. I think it is quite telling that if you look in any of my mother's photo albums you won't find a picture of me relaxed and smiling after about the second grade until when I graduated from college.

Though I thought I was fulfilled by the spiritual sustenance I had been raised on, I was plainly now quite empty inside, starving mentally and emotionally. Below I'll analyze my religious indoctrination and explain how and why this came to pass. I conclude that the mental anguish I experienced is practically inevitable for anyone pejoratively indoctrinated as I was. Once something triggers the development of critical analysis of belief, and the process of asserting oneself as an individual begins, the sustenance provided by religious indoctrination no longer nourishes.

The Human Cost of Escaping Religious Indoctrination

Before turning to my philosophical analysis, I want to give some indication of the cost to me and my family of my choice to leave the church. I will say at once that no one ever explicitly coerced, or tried to explicitly coerce me to stay—my prior indoctrination was enough to take care of that. But there was a lot of what I will call "passive coercion." When I returned home after the one semester I was in school between 1998 and 2000, I refused to go to church any more. My father was furious, and my mother was distraught. They had no idea what had happened to me. Even after I made it clear I did not want to go to church, I still got a knock on my door every Sunday, just to "double check." My parents feared that my going to school far away had been an awful choice and didn't want me to go back again. I got occasional worried calls from friends wondering why I wasn't at church even though I was in town. I quit being an altar boy more than a few times only to have my name constantly reappear on the schedule. This hit me harder than you might think; not showing up to a scheduled mass increases the workload and responsibility of the others you are scheduled to serve with, and many of us had grown up together. And in one rather chilling episode one afternoon at a local mall, I was reminded by a former youth minister and basketball coach that I couldn't actually quit being Catholic, I would just be a bad Catholic for the rest of my life. Once my parents decided I was just going through a phase, I managed to get through those tough, awkward times with relatively little injury—relative to the injury I would feel when my father was diagnosed with pancreatic cancer.

In January 2001, when I heard my dad had gotten sick and that it was gravely serious, I knew religion was going to be a very big issue. It very quickly brought up old, never healed wounds in my relationship with my parents. Both they and my sisters started asking very tough questions about God, faith, and mortality, questions that I found incredibly challenging to answer the way I wanted to. My family was given a tremendous break when my father courageously fought off that cancer. And immediately my mother became convinced that it had been a miracle; the families' prayers had worked. Since I didn't pray, this left me looking, in my parents' eyes at least, rather bad.

Still, they were very happy and willing to forgive my doubt. Unfortunately, however, my father's cancer returned in 2003 and claimed his life. My mother and my sisters repeatedly insisted on knowing where I thought dad was now that he was dead. I refused to answer several times until finally they all sat me down and confronted me together. My mother was particularly crushed when I explained I thought that when you die, that is the end. She hugged me, crying. I could see she was trying to understand what had happened to her boy. Since then my poor, brave mother has lost her mother and her father as well. I, as well as she, have been very pained by the religious divide between us. Though she has now stopped going to church as often as before, she still looks for spiritual and emotional solace, and several times she's come to me. I cannot tell you the pain a son feels when he realizes he cannot give his mother solace and be true to himself, when he realizes he will have to betray himself and lie to her to give her any comfort. Though we love each other very much, religious indoctrination has made it nearly impossible for me to relate and commiserate with my mother about the losses we've experienced. And I can only sit back and wish things weren't this way.

Philosophical Analysis

Below I offer a philosophical discussion of my religious indoctrination with the intention of explaining what can be generalized from it. The way I understand indoctrination in general allows for the possibility that for some individuals indoctrination is acceptable. And it is also logically possible that it might even be of some benefit to an individual, if judged valuable by that (capable) individual. As such, I will not argue that religious indoctrination is necessarily abusive of every recipient. But I will argue that specifically in the cases of certain types of children, children such as I was (and likely for any child), being religiously indoctrinated is in fact (and likely necessarily) immoral in ways not attributable to other forms of more benign indoctrination, because it fosters psychological dependence and intellectual laziness, all of which is deeply harmful to the development of an autonomous self. I think that my case demonstrates that religious indoctrination is a sort of malnutrition, a purposefully limited supply of critical evaluation and an inadequate elucidation of alternative or competing sources for education and understanding. Further, I think my experience makes a strong case that the pain and suffering I went through was nearly inevitable when a person like me is religiously indoctrinated as a child.

Metaphysics and Theology

I'll begin with some troublesome metaphysical or theological points about religious indoctrination. The Roman Catholic Church, like all other Western religions, is based on (at least) three fundamental claims: (1) There is only one God; (2) God requires us to worship and obey him; and (3) there is (at least) one person, the founder of the religion (Jesus), who has the definitive answer to how to properly show God that we do worship and obey him, as well as to any other questions about the ultimate nature of reality. Furthermore, according to the church, the way to salvation is through acceptance of God's son, the founder, as your savior. Except in exceedingly rare cases, this is considered the *only way* to get to heaven. This is effectively what the founder said, and until recently it was pretty clearly the church's position. Whether or not this is current dogma, I can vouch that this is still what is understood by most of the Catholic faithful; and in practice belief in this is tacitly encouraged and allowed to flourish.

WHO GOD IS TO A RELIGIOUSLY INDOCTRINATED PERSON

It is important, too, to keep a clear picture of *who* it is that is the key to salvation. God in the Old Testament exhibits jealousy, vengefulness, spite, and murderousness. He also seemed quite keen on keeping humanity generally ignorant in as much as he severely punished them for gaining the knowledge of right and wrong. In the New Testament God is comparably merciful, forgiving, and loving, but at the same time, Jesus isn't so much intent on being the "Prince of Peace," claiming that he comes to tear families apart. True enough, most learned religious people would rather not think of God this way, but the bad qualities are all there in the same texts that showcase the more likable ones. No doubt this is not a coincidence. And clearly the philosophy of my primary school was consistent with the desires of God as understood by the Roman Catholic Church.

The obvious goal of indoctrination into this religion is the creation of *real* Catholics. Real Catholics, those truly committed to the life of Christ, are supposed to be first and foremost humble, obedient, worshipful servants of God. Anything that would get in the way of that is to be rejected. Only in quite enlightened quarters is literal understanding of the sacred texts frowned upon, and even then inconsistently, sporadically, and not at all severely. Real Catholics ought to follow the Bible and the teachings of the pertinent leaders. Real Catholics believe—fervently—that Jesus (and his church) is *the Way, the Truth,* and *the Light.* In these intellectually freer times we forget who the God of religion, the God of the average devout, indoctrinated person, is to them and for them.

Based on my experiences and what I take as fundamentally true about church dogma, I now think that appeasing such an emotional, intellectual, and physical *bully* as God makes the indoctrinated scared, starved, and ineffectual on the inside and hostile paladins on the outside. To *make* a person this way when a child is unconscionable.

I bring all this up because though it is common knowledge, it is easily forgotten and easily swept under the rug in philosophical debates such as these. But with these facts fresh in our minds we can more fully consider the actual issues surrounding religious indoctrination rather than simply engaging in academic debates about the theoretical issues.

BOUGHT ON STOLEN MINDS

One issue in particular strikes me as largely and mistakenly ignored, namely the factors involved in the decision to put children into, for example, parochial schools for the purpose of religious indoctrination. Clearly these schools exist, first and foremost (if not exclusively), to provide religious indoctrination. But of course children are not capable of choosing (in any relevant way) whether they want to be engaged in religious indoctrination. They are at the mercy of their parents, and this is highly problematic because parents have to make this decision under very suspect circumstances.

I contend that, at least in the case of the devout family, the situation the parents are in presents something of a dilemma. Consciously or not, they must consider that either (a) they put their children in the hands of those who intend, above all else, to religiously indoctrinate them, or (b) they do not do this. If they select (a), then if the child meets an untimely end, it will be accepted by God. If they select (b), then if the child meets an untimely end, it will end up in purgatory, and perhaps hell. And that will be the parents' fault. Put simply, devout parents considering submitting their children to religious indoctrination have to decide whether or not they want themselves and their child to be punished by God in the event of their child's untimely end. In the case of a devout family with poorly educated parents, which I imagine is the most common case, the situation is particularly bad, since such parents usually have fewer "resources" to draw on to see other possibilities. And they are likely quite disinclined to raise the child without religion. In the very best case of a well-off, well-educated, open-minded yet devout family the parents may wonder whether it is wiser to let their child grow up with a free mind so that it may later to choose to accept salvation, or whether to do what they can now to ensure acceptance of the Faith, and so salvation. Given the spiritual, psychological, and emotional strain, and the social pressure involved in such a decision, it would be quite contentious to say that the decision to involve their children in religious indoctrination was freely made. Why then, are parents "asked" to make it?

When done efficiently, religious indoctrination is supposed to be fundamentally formative and permanent. So the question can be asked another way: why would God want souls harvested out of fear, naïveté, and stress?[8] While this is a worthwhile question, it would take me too far afield to answer it here.

Practical or "Matter-of-Fact" Criticisms

If the choice to have one's child religiously indoctrinated is so fraught with difficulties, what can be said for those who are happy to oblige the church by deciding to do so? Is it immoral to religiously indoctrinate a child? The short answer is yes, it is immoral. But things are a bit more complicated than that. As I noted, it does seem that plain indoctrination is generally allowable. And in the case of an educated consenting adult, one could convincingly argue that religious indoctrination could be beneficial to some. But as a matter of fact, religious indoctrination is very often abusive. In this section I will argue that, extrapolating from my personal experience, we can sketch out the position that there is a type of child that will seriously suffer from religious indoctrination, and that when this indoctrination is done well and produces its intended consequences, this type of child, a child with an emotional, intellectual, and psychological makeup like mine, *will* have been abused. And there are plenty of such children. Most simply put, this argument is based on a claim I take to be obvious, that it is shameful to hold hostage a mind capable of more than blind obedience. To religiously indoctrinate such a mind is quite immoral even if "noble lies" are generally acceptable or even sometimes beneficial, as it serves to hide open-minded critical thinking from one who would benefit from it.

Religious indoctrination in my case was immoral. My parents should not have subjected me to it, but given their circumstances the real responsibility for my suffering lies with those who took advantage of my parents' trust and obedience.[9] The Roman Catholic Church, by their proxy, my parish school, took the responsibility for religiously indoctrinating me. And cases like mine in particular, but also cases of religious indoctrination in general, press upon us to ask what religious organizations like the church care about the most in religious indoctrination. I believe it clear from what has been said thus far that for the church the goal of indoctrination is creating and maintaining subservient, reverent Catholics. The facts of my experience strongly support this, and from the view of my indoctrinators, my religious indoctrination was normally performed. In addition to these facts, I will continue to argue that it is intellectually compelling to think that religious indoctrinators would want to produce subservient and reverent Catholics with the expectation that the then (well) indoctrinated would want to remain this way.

Given this background, it is easier to see that my case demonstrates a fundamental problem. Religious organizations like the Roman Catholic Church are not usually thought to be consequentialist (concerned with results, independently of methods). The church represents itself as being deontological (following divine commands) and is usually so seen. But I think this is a misrepresentation.

Now consider whether or not the propagation of the flock, the training of subservient, reverent Catholics, is merely *a* goal of a parochial school or whether it is the fundamental purpose of it. Again, the facts are in our favor;

my parochial school says it has the fundamental purpose of creating such people. As the educational arm of the parish and so the local educational arm of the Roman Catholic Church, the parochial school is fundamentally designed and operated to create devout Catholics. I add that this goal will be pursued at the cost of personal autonomy, overall emotional health, and a free intellect if necessary. In fact, there are good theological reasons, discussed above, to suggest that it is *necessary* in very many cases.

Thus, it seems that one of three things is true; either (1) Roman Catholic indoctrinators have an honest (though highly suspect and ethically questionable) belief that if you are not religiously indoctrinated, you will suffer and likely be damned by God; or (2) they believe more practically that if they get you young, human psychology being what it is, and the methods and content of indoctrination being what they are, the chances are good that they can keep you in the church, whereas is if they wait until you are older, they'll likely not get you to submit to religious indoctrination and so they will lose you; or (3) both (1) and (2) together. To decide, we must ask what a religious indoctrinator deems more desirable: obedient, humble servants of God, or autonomous, free-thinking individuals with their own beliefs and practices.[10] The facts would seem to make the answers clear: from the point of view of religious indoctrinators the goal has to be to indoctrinate as many people as possible, at a very young age, and make them emotionally, spiritually, and intellectually dependent on the Roman Catholic Church.

That this is so can also be evidenced somewhat from the point of view of the initiate. What is the point of getting religiously indoctrinated? Since I am focusing on children, I won't discuss what the point might be for an adult. The first thing I note is that I have no recollection of a time when I didn't have "God" in my vocabulary. My parents were pretty devout, so this is not a surprise. When it was time to officially begin my religious indoctrination, I was wide open to the content. But as I was rather curious, I did develop an avid interest in it in addition to the pure internalization that is a large part of indoctrination of a child. I wanted to know what God was really like. I wanted to feel his love, and I wanted to be sure to do just what he wanted. I imagined the reward—happiness and eventually salvation— and it motivated me immensely. I remember my second-grade teacher, Sister Carmelita, gave me a small reproduction of a painting of Jesus for my birthday that year. I brought it home and tacked it to the wall above my bed, and I would sit in my bed and talk to Jesus all the time, about all sorts of things. Eventually as I got older, this desire to understand God and his creation grew. I'll call this the desire to understand ultimate reality. My belief is that many religiously indoctrinated adults are motivated to stay that way in no small measure by the desire to be a part of the ultimate reality of Roman Catholicism. It helps give one hope and peace of mind, and makes one feel at home in the immensely large and often cruel world. Being well indoctrinated, then, might seem quite desirable to a child, and remaining so would seem quite appealing to an invested adult.

The actual goal of religious indoctrination is both derivable *from the point of being religious* and identifiable from things like the "mission statements" or "philosophies" of religious schools, and the practices of these schools and of related youth ministries. They show that mental and behavioral control are paramount objectives, even though this may be so for "noble" intentions. More specifically, though, the control is quite good at fostering intellectual laziness, openness to suggestion, and generally a noncritical stance toward the church. This is of course quite important when an individual's experiences begin seriously challenging assumptions learned at church. Poor indoctrination can be overwhelmed by serious stress just as good indoctrination can be overwhelmed by serious attention to internal criticisms and the will and ability to follow them through.

And the facts must again be brought up. It is clear in both dogma and in practice that the Roman Catholic Church has a very low opinion of the idea that almost any Catholic who is not clergy might pursue knowledge that would go against the church's teachings and interests. While we can skip recounting the volumes of historical cases that evince this, I must remind you not to be overly impressed by the fact that the church is no longer as vigilant or ruthless as it once was in prosecuting those who do pursue such knowledge. Indeed, it is not clear *at all* that the church would not be very vindictive and punitive if it were able to be. Further, the recent history of largely Catholic liberal societies like Quebec makes it plain that the church is more than happy to exercise as much control over a population's lifestyle as the population will allow. Further still, the more "liberal" stances taken after Vatican II are experiencing serious backlash, even reversal, from more traditional Catholics. And in my experience the church at local levels quite actively discourages serious questioning of the Faith. But this should be no surprise when the psychological realities of religious indoctrination are considered.

Psychological Criticisms

I can attest from my own experience that religious indoctrination is harmful. My indoctrination created various issues I've had to deal with, which is bad enough, but what seems just as bad or worse is that these issues were hidden from me during the time I was indoctrinated. But as I have tried to argue, I was not an anomaly. In fact I think, in addition to what I have already said, that the harm is also rooted in the reason *why* a person wants to be indoctrinated. We agreed that the point of religious indoctrination is to create devout, humble servants of God. And by the standards of the Roman Catholic Church I exemplified this very well: the message was deeply inculcated, and at the time it made me feel as if I was doing something right, something I needed to keep after vigilantly. I felt that, flawed as I was, I was developing properly. I think it likely the reader will agree that hindsight has shown this to be false.

I felt like I was doing something right, I was convinced I was fulfilled, in no small measure because it is *desirable* to have certain psychological needs filled, and the Roman Catholic Church attempts to do this completely. Thinking your religion is right, thinking that you have found the key to ultimate reality and so to salvation is an amazing feeling; it becomes something of a prized possession and, as I tried to stress in my memoir, is a large part of one's identity. And the church promises this to its devout members, those who have been properly religiously indoctrinated.

Now, it is right to distinguish between those religious folk who "check their brain in" completely and those who do so only on certain days. But any indoctrinated Roman Catholic takes on a lot of beliefs purely on faith and submits himself to some quite strange practices because of the authority of tradition. And living in a community that doesn't share these beliefs and practices makes you quite aware of these facts. So it is that there is a lot of psychological benefit to membership in the Roman Catholic Church.

By the same token, it is quite disappointing to be told that other ways of looking at the world are equally valid. And such a belief, contradictory to the teachings (or at least the apparent intentions) of the founder(s) as they are, creates psychological tension in the one indoctrinated. So at best accepting the idea breeds pity and sometimes contempt for the nonindoctrinated, while denying it creates serious cognitive dissonance as well as subverting the possibility of the benefits that might have been garnered by taking other points of view seriously.

The End of the Road

I've argued that religious indoctrination, by and large, is abusive of children, especially certain types of children, because in practice, and quite often by necessity, it limits their general development as autonomous individuals by manipulating their emotional needs, informational deficiencies, and so on, for the church's benefit. *That is its nature.* And so it is immoral. One final note: one of the strengths of the way I've argued for this is that I can admit that though this *might* apply as a matter of fact to other forms of indoctrination, say liberalism or a "scientific" metaphysics, this does not make it acceptable. These other indoctrinations aren't supposed to work that way, in fact liberalism and science only meet their goals when they do not work that way. But religious indoctrination in its purest, most consistent form *aims to work that way,* and so is abusive of children in a way not attributable to other types of indoctrination.

NOTES

1. Relatedly, I understand *education* as being about creating a person capable, generally or in a specific field, of deciding who would count as someone knowledgeable on the subject, and being able to explain why they have so judged in reasons that a disinterested party would find intellectually appreciable. Basically, I am paraphrasing Plato's account of one who knows from, for example, the *Phaedo* and *Meno*.

2. What I have in mind by certain types of people is the types of people who as adults prefer to answer questions about matters like ethics or metaphysics in a philosophic or scientific manner rather than a religious one. I realize this is incredibly hard to predict—this is part of the problem of religious indoctrination—but one reasonable method might be to think of gifted students, and students with a psychological makeup predisposing them to dependence and trust, among others, as being likely candidates, though I take it as obvious that many very gifted people are theists and even religious, and that some overly trusting individuals prefer to keep their neuroses. Still, it seems some such test would be in order if it could be found out: while it may be that some adults would feel they were denied a very important gift, such a belief would be completely question begging.

3. I argue below it is rather obvious that the dependence was created specifically to breed uncritical acceptance of the church's authority.

4. St. Mary's Catholic School, http://stmarysgvl.org/theschool/st-marys-catholic-school-philosophy (accessed June 30, 2006).

5. Greenville Senior High Academy of Academic Excellence, http://greenvillehigh.greenville.k12.sc.us (accessed June 30, 2006).

6. Greenville Senior High Academy of Academic Excellence, http://greenvillehigh.greenville.k12.sc.us/academics/op.htm (accessed June 30, 2006).

7. He has since been convicted of at least one count of committing a lewd act on a minor, removed from active service, and is required by court order to stay away from children. But I do not know if I am the first person from his time at my parish to bring up his abuses there. See Lyn Riddle and Deb Richardson-Moore, "Former Greenville Priest Suspended After Abuse Allegation Surfaces," *GreenvilleOnline.com,* the *Greenville News,* May 29, 2002, http://www.thegreenvillenews.com/news/2002/05/29/2002052924012.htm (accessed June 15, 2006).

8. Relatedly, why are children confirmed at the beginning of puberty, when they are so vulnerable to social pressure, rather than at the end of puberty or later?

9. It's worth pointing out here that being my primary educator, the RCC also had access to my standardized test scores and knew me to be a bright boy who would have likely taken very well to what I defined in note 1 as "education."

10. One might be tempted to respond that what they want is *both*. But here again the facts belie this: it is really only the clergy that gets any serious theological, hermeneutic, or philosophical instruction regarding the dogma and doctrine of the church. Further, as we'll see, having such followers is rather disruptive for the more intellectually docile majority of Roman Catholics.

PART 2

RECONFIGURING THE MORALITY
OF INDOCTRINATION

5

BITING INTO THE HERMENEUTICAL APPLE:
BIBLICAL LITERALISM AND THE LURE OF UNCERTAINTY

Amalia Jiva

If I consider the issue of morality in terms of the intentions behind a certain act, I would be required to impose agency for my indoctrination as a Baptist fundamentalist on a particular actor. And if I were to attempt to place this burden on someone's shoulders, whose shoulders would they be? The old-fashioned pastor's at my hometown Baptist church in Arad, Romania? My grandparents', who converted to the Baptist faith after fleeing from the Stalin famine? My mother's, who hoped church would be a parenting aid for raising two children by herself after a painful divorce? My friends', who buoyantly raised their hands to accept Christ as their Lord and Savior with me in the crowded church balcony after a particularly charismatic sermon? My own, since I willingly and eagerly chose to confess my sins in front of four hundred church members and be baptized by immersion at fourteen? Didn't we all participate in this process of indoctrination?

Or should I blame the institutional efficacy of the Romanian Baptist Union, whose members risked arrest and detention at times to assure that the church could express itself freely? Should I turn against Jerry Falwell and my Liberty University friends, some of whom went to jail sincerely protesting as Students Angry Against Abortion? The RA's in the women's dorm, who, though tedious in their earnestness, prayed with me and for me when my father died? Is indoctrination the fault of the Southern Baptist Convention whose folds once included the humanitarian president Jimmy Carter? Is it the responsibility of history, of Luther and the Reformation movement that first led to the splinter soon to grow into the Protestant denominations? Should I quarrel with John Smith and the Anabaptists for their successful proselytizing, which inspired German Baptists to bring the Baptist faith to Romania? Where would the chain of questions stop?

I will never know if any of the individuals who participated in the mysterious process that blends interpretation practices with social dynamics did so self-consciously. Just as no one individual is responsible for, or can personally effect, significant changes in a given language, though each individual participates in and therefore leaves her imprint however feebly on language, as a Baptist I, along with most others I knew, functioned within the institution and spoke its language; we cannot be severed from that context and the doctrinal flow and ebb of action and reaction to it in order to be tried for our allegiance. For if anyone was responsible, I would be the first.

But there is another way of perceiving the morality of an action, and that is in terms of its consequences. And the consequences of the type of indoctrination I received and participated in are significant because they affect the very core of autonomous self-realization. Indoctrination limits not only the ability to choose, but the very awareness of choice; it imposes a perspective that follows the individual in his or her most private thoughts and intimate moments; it is insidious and invasive, all the more so because it purports not to exist.

It was with some difficulty that I traveled back in time to retrieve, as truthfully as I could, my state of mind while a Baptist in Romania and at Liberty. Fearing my memory alone might be unreliable and revisionist, I spoke with friends who knew me then, listened to family stories, and pored over correspondence from that time. And it surprised me above all to find almost no traces of conflict and doubt, no signs of dissatisfaction. It appears I was a very happy Baptist.

In communist Romania, I was part of a thriving community of Baptists, where I had a tight-knit circle of friends and where church was my life. I had no thoughts of being at an ideological periphery, and I never examined my views to see if they held up against other perspectives, because no other perspectives were available to me. Communism ensured that religious conversations would not pepper everyday discourse; and when they happened, they happened usually because they were initiated by attempts to proselytize, which put those involved at risk. And because the regime needed isolation from the outside world in order to maintain the happy-worker farce it was promoting, there was no free press, no uncensored TV programs, no controversial books, and very little information about the rest of the world that might challenge its tenets. If communism, either through its propaganda or through isolation, was ultimately not successful in actually convincing many individuals of its own worth, the dearth of information provided a perfect backdrop for the success of the Baptist movement there.

It was against this backdrop that I flowered into a dedicated Baptist. I had certainty about my place in the world and about the afterlife. I knew that when I died, I would go to heaven praising God among the angels and meeting biblical prophets and dead loved ones. I knew that I would be assumed into the sky when Jesus came, and that the unbelievers would find my toothbrush in the sink, water running, and clothes on the floor once I'd disappeared. I proselytized during the "patriotic labor" tomato-picking weeks that began the school year, I sang carols with the church youths on Christmas Eve, hoping to convert the Orthodox and the unbelievers, and I sat down during the prom dance to signal my difference. I did this honestly, and wholeheartedly, assured every Sunday in my church filled with "repentants," as we were called by the "outsiders," that this was the straight but narrow way. I memorized Bible verses and went on mission trips to remote villages, and knew without a doubt that I was going to heaven and everyone else was going to hell. This certainty I shared with each person in my home and in my church, and though the "world" thought us strange, I felt safe and comforted in this social cocoon.

And if I was so isolated that I never learned the customs of my schoolmates and the Orthodox majority with their saints and icons, their prayers for the dead, and their empty rituals, I knew enough from the pulpit not to feel any sense of loss. They, I was told, were performing a meaningless formality, wearing a mere mask of religion, not thinking through their beliefs and not practicing their Christian life day in and day out as I was. Much freer were we for being baptized as teenagers, or adults who willingly declared our passion for Christ in front of the entire congregation after weeks of catechism, than those who simply did good deeds, lit candles, and hoped, ever unsure, for salvation. How else, I was taught, to distinguish a Baptist from an Orthodox if not by our regular church attendance, our incessant reading of the Scripture, our surreptitious proselytizing, our certainty of heaven, and our lack of jewelry?

I went to church three times a week, and it was there rather than in high school that I experienced all the teenage angst, while gossiping with girlfriends, flirting with boys, breaking in and out of cliques, and proving my popularity when selected to play Potiphar's wife seducing Joseph at a New Year's skit. High school had none of the social functions it has in the United States, at least not for me, because I made very few friends among my classmates. That I wasn't allowed to dance or wear makeup, that I wasn't encouraged to see movies and date, only buttressed my feeling of otherness and superiority. It didn't bother me that every now and then boys on the street would yell "repentant" after me as I sauntered on to church in my Sunday attire. I didn't want the things I couldn't have because they were worldly and wrong. I thought it perfectly justified to show off my saintliness to my friends and rebuke the girl who wore mascara in church. So when my homeroom teacher called my mom in to admonish her for not letting me attend the school dance, I was proud. I wouldn't have gone anyway. I was chosen for a different path, one of dedication to God, one of renouncing the world. When, at twenty, I said good-bye to my church friends and Romania, it was with a big raffle party where I bequeathed my prized possessions, a wooden flute, a black bow-tie, and a Moody Blues record, to the lucky few; we sang church hymns, prayed together, and ate homemade pizza squares sporting Bible verses as fortunes.

It was only much later I came to learn of the price certainty demanded. I had the occasion to reflect anew on the church's role in the dissolution of my parents' marriage when a deacon from my home church in Romania on vacation abroad visited our Florida home. Over coffee and cookies, he updated my mom with news from home, and eventually the subject of my mom's divorce presented itself among the memories. Our guest had been on the committee my mom appeared before when she sought her reintegration in the community. He reminisced about the church's strict position on divorce and explained how the attitudes had since changed in light of new interpretative insight into the biblical stand on the matter, after much study and prayer.

As my mom remembers, when she first considered separation, the church had seen only five divorces among its members in the past thirty years. With trepidation, my mom sought counsel from a church elder at the end of a Sunday morning service. He asked her inside, where they sat on an empty pew, and he read to her from Matthew 19:6: "Therefore what God has joined together, let man not separate."[11] He then prayed for her and sent her home. After another year of failed reconciliation attempts she again sought help, only to be read the same verse and exhorted to be strong in the Lord and stay together for the sake of her children. Precisely for that reason, she separated soon after and filed for divorce. And while no one noticed, she denied herself communion for two years, feeling guilty in the eyes of the church, though sure about the wisdom of her decision for herself and for my brother and me.

When she later wanted to feel absolved, active in her faith, and to participate fully in the community, she took it up with the church committee. They invited her to their weekly meeting, where she was questioned about details from her marital life by twenty Bible-carrying men. After much debate, they agreed to consider her a healthy member of the community once again and to allow her communion, on one condition: that at thirty-five she was to stay single for the remainder of her life or remarry my father. As long as my father was alive, these were her only options. My mom complied.

I wonder what might have been if the church's revelation, that they understand both divorce and remarriage are possible within the doctrine under the right circumstances, had come two decades earlier. I cannot know whether my mom, who continues to believe that divorce is sinful but that remarrying after divorce is even more sinful, might have lived more fully and prized personal happiness more, but I do know that within the confines of the Baptist fundamentalist ideology, she denied herself the very possibility. And she is certainly not alone. Before departing, the deacon added that the committee members were not planning to share their new understanding on marriage, divorce, and remarriage with parishioners for fear of encouraging this behavior.

The very same doctrinal principles that affected my family's life so profoundly also ensured my own isolation from ideas, from my culture, and ultimately from myself. As an adolescent, my rebellion, though I would not have termed it so at the time, took the form of going to the theater and the opera, listening enraptured to Franz Liszt's rhapsodies, and cutting school to watch art documentaries at the public library. I consorted in these trespasses with my Orthodox high school friend, since most of my church friends found no solace in art and literature. I did seek them out, though timidly, not knowing how to reconcile the joy and personal enrichment I found there with the Baptist tenets. Relying entirely on the Scripture for meaning and personal knowledge removes the incentive as well as the desire to foster aesthetic experience.

When I needed some distance from my own thoughts on how I had been personally affected by my upbringing in the Baptist church, I decided to speak with my long-time Orthodox friend, who I hoped might have a fresh perspective. I asked her how she remembers me and our interactions from our adolescent years. Without prompting, she pronounced on both the benefits and the costs of my Baptist affiliation: "You were a normal adolescent, with the same hopes and desires as I had. But you denied yourself many of these. What you had was certainty. What you did not have was the ability to establish for yourself what your system of values was going to be. You were not free."

She added, frankly, that I had strong prejudices, the bias against Orthodoxy being the main one. I was not surprised. Skepticism against the Orthodox

Church was part of the very fabric of what it meant to be born-again for me. A telling joke I often heard speaks to this: an Orthodox dies and goes to heaven. As Saint Peter leads him to his final place of rest, the Orthodox notices that as they are passing a small, unadorned room, full of men in jackets and women with their heads covered by scarves, the church father starts walking on tiptoes and speaks softly, almost in a whisper. When the Orthodox, puzzled, finally asks why, Saint Peter answers: "Shhh. . . . This is the mansion of the Baptists. I don't want them to see you. They think they're the only ones here."

To emphasize the denomination's ahistorical stance and underline its rootedness in unmediated Scripture, the Romanian Baptist doctrine states that "the Bible is the only authority in matters of religion; it is sufficient for our teaching."[12] The following sentence is directly addressed to the Orthodox: "Therefore, there is no need for the support of tradition." Answering to other Orthodox tenets, the statement on salvation makes clear that "the means of salvation is the Lord Jesus who was crucified in our place. There are no other means (cross, holy mysteries, saints)."[13] Similar distinctions are made in the pivotal article on baptism, a rite that must be performed through immersion, not sprinkling, and administered to adults, not children as it would be for the Orthodox.

There are many historical reasons for the present distance between the Baptists and the Orthodox, most of them related to the favored position the Orthodox Church had, at least officially, during the communist regime. Yet this separation created rifts between individuals and removed their cultural connection. I never went to Orthodox services, never understood Romanian holiday traditions, never participated in the wondrous midnight Easter liturgy, and did not connect with those who did. A visit to the Web site of a Romanian American organization, where I had hoped to learn more about the resources available to students in the Romanian diaspora, reminded me of my alienation from this cultural heritage, in which a majority of Romanians base their identity. The site greeted visitors with an image of an Orthodox icon superimposed upon a Romanian flag and the map of the country. I did not feel I belonged, and even as I write these lines, I am not sure how to recover this piece of what might have been my history.

When I left for Liberty University, however, I had no concerns about faith or identity. I had been in the States for a year by then, and departing Romania for the United States a year after the 1989 revolution was our first trip abroad. As I was trying to make sense of the American dream bicycling to work in the Florida heat to earn my minimum wage at the cash register of a hardware store, my transition was made easier by letters from home about my friends' spiritual quests: like me, they were trying to decipher whom God wanted them to date, where God wanted them to work, whether God would return this year or the next.

Needless to say, Liberty seemed the ticket to a new and much more promising life. Friends from the Romanian American churches I attended raved about their experiences there, and my mother, who was as uncertain of how to navigate the American educational system as I was, and of few means, felt relieved knowing I would be studying in a school with values she herself held. I left for Liberty on the Greyhound bus and was thrilled to discover my very first vending machine at a bus stop: I had heard rumors of their existence from a Radio Free Europe program in Romania, on the forbidden shortwave radio smuggled from Russia. I joined the other Romanians there, was granted a generous scholarship, and felt welcomed, rescued, and blessed.

In one of my first letters home, beaming with enthusiasm, I described to my family the prayers before math class and the Christian concert I had just attended: "Can you believe it, mom? It is excellent!" Elatedly, I wrote about my freshman seminar where each class session the instructor asked for personal requests and led the whole group in prayer; about how groups such as the Sound of Liberty delighted us in convocations; about how an altar call after a musical interlude led to dozens of conversions; about how everyone was friendly, if a little more exuberant than I was used to. I closed my letter asking everyone not to worry about anything because "God brought me here and He will take care of me. This is what I believe!"

Liberty is a relatively small school, and I found it easy to bridge the differences between my cultural background and those of the other students. Assisted by our shared beliefs, I soon managed to make friends with an assortment of students from among the black-clad alternative crowd, the Bible-in-a-lace-jacket southern belles, the preppie J-crew elite, and the stylish international students. We all wanted Liberty to grow, we all joined hands during the Jericho walks around the school praying for fiscal stability, and many shared their excitement for the Christian mission of Liberty, together with their tolerance for the strict rules that governed student behavior. We were united by our love for Christ and by our common dress code: until 4:00 P.M., during school days, girls had to wear skirts, and boys shirts and ties.

I may not have mentioned this in my letters home, but along with spiritual growth, I was also very busy negotiating the cultural shift. If in Romania I needed to carefully switch between my school persona and my church one, here church and school were one. I tried to adapt as soon as I could—

dyed my hair, changed my wardrobe, and started dating a bass player in a Christian rock band. The famed Liberty rules, no kissing, no handholding on campus, no drinking, no smoking, no coed dorms, no going off campus without permission, no R-rated movies, seemed terribly familiar and only made for a most exciting and adventurous life spent bending and breaking them. What might have been my first Liberty kiss was interrupted by a flashlight in the car window with security leaning in to ensure propriety.

Soon, however, I began to learn of the unrest behind the uniformity. While I was safe from the outside in Romania, behind the double curtain of communism and fundamentalism, the hill city of Lynchburg, Virginia, could not remain as secluded. By my junior year, we began attending a Presbyterian church on off-campus weekends and learned about different approaches to Christianity. Some started criticizing the shaky scientific method of Christian Apologetics classes and the quasi-literary approach of the Bible as Literature class. I began to listen more closely to the sermons during convocation and wondered why, in the midst of the festive, if mandatory, weekly gatherings, thousands of Christian college students were subjected to incessant messages against homosexuality and abortion.

I sometimes skipped church entirely to debate the merits of the various Protestant denominations over coffee at the Drowsy Poet. No longer swayed by the Liberty rules, we snuck into the dollar theater to R-rated movies, risking suspension. My most egregious misdemeanors amounted to no more than hiding in the closet during room check to avoid yet another sermon against the ills of liberalism, smuggling wine coolers past the security guard, and celebrating a friend's graduation with a bottle of wine paid for with a check on which was written prominently "Liberty University." By the time I graduated, I was intrigued and conflicted but still unable to coherently voice my doubts as I did not have the necessary conceptual tools.

Liberty's doctrinal foundation was almost identical to that of the Baptist message I grew up with. Its main line was the insistence on the Bible's ultimate veracity and unmediated transparency, making dialogue across denominational lines impossible. And Liberty's educational principles were closely tied with its beliefs. If many of the professors were rigorous in their area and also took an interest in students' lives, they could not provide multiple perspectives on the subject of religion. They could not because many held views consistent with Liberty's, and those who did not could not have made that public. Professors, as I understood it, had to make clear their beliefs when hired, attend Jerry Falwell's Thomas Road Baptist Church, and maintain proper doctrinal perspectives in all their classes. Religion, in fact, was not a subject of study when I was there. There were classes on ethics, theology, the New Testament, and the Old Testament; and all these topics were presented in a manner conforming to the Baptist fundamentalist doctrine. There was no opportunity or instruction on how to conduct a metaconversation on the very idea of constructing a system of religious beliefs, because this would have allowed for the notion of pluralism, and pluralism was directly incompatible with the isolationist aims of Liberty ideology.

It was not until I began graduate studies that classes on philosophical hermeneutics and religion in light of various approaches to language, as well as conversations with other graduate students with similarly conservative backgrounds, started to compensate for my educational lacunae. Hoping to gain the vocabulary to speak of my own indoctrination, I focused my master's qualifying paper on the role of fundamentalist discourse in establishing and maintaining group identity.

Examining Southern Baptist statements of faith, I saw the increased attempts to convert doctrines to truth claims. Dropping the phrase "we believe" from the 1925 article on the Bible turned the doctrinal statement into an assertion: "The Holy Bible was written by men divinely inspired."[4] In a similar revision, the words "the record of" were removed from "The Holy Bible ... is the record of God's revelation."[5] And perhaps most surprising, the role of Christ as hermeneutical guide was reconsidered, causing Jimmy Carter, for one, to sever ties with the Southern Baptist Convention. The 1963 version of the article on the Bible states, "The criterion by which the Bible is to be interpreted is Jesus Christ." The 2000 version revised this statement as follows: "All Scripture is a testimony to Christ, who is Himself the focus of divine revelation."[6]

The direct emphasis on homosexuality and abortion, issues of great political import in recent years, found its way into doctrinal statements as well. In the 2000 version of the statement of faith, the article on Christians and the social order adds to the list of sins Christians should oppose "all forms of sexual immorality, including adultery, homosexuality, and pornography." About abortion, the article also mentions that "we should speak on behalf of the unborn and contend for the sanctity of all human life from conception to natural death."[7] What I had witnessed during my Liberty years had finally become official doctrine.

As I made sense of the issue at the time, and based on my own experience, the process of indoctrination succeeds by assuring church members of their very freedom of thought. This is why the platform of the self-evident truth of Scripture is crucial to the propagation of Baptist fundamentalist doctrine. This doctrinal cornerstone is so foundational that it is never truly questioned by someone born into the denomination. It functions as a primitive, basic truth on which all other assertions are based but which itself remains unchallenged.

Surely there are myriads of proofs offered by the church regarding the veracity of Scripture, but they are not for believers. They are weapons to be used if needed in defending this core tenet against outside attacks, rhetorical ammunition of archeological, historical, logical, or scientific provenance. Was it possible for Jonah to have survived for three days in the belly of the whale? Did the plagues really exist? Could Jesus have been a mere man? Is the Shroud of Turin the real veil wrapped around him in the tomb? Can rocks really speak? There are answers at the ready for each of these questions and scores of others like them. But the believers themselves have assimilated this notion and have based their entire self-definition on it, and truly engaging in meaningful dialogue that might chip away at this certainty is often too costly to consider or simply outside the noetic possibilities of most.

Once the truth of Scripture is taken as a given, the question of how it is to be read arises. And the Baptist fundamentalist answer is well known: literally. The perils of this method are many, as my grandfather's reading of certain verses can attest. He considers wearing a suit jacket in church an absolute necessity, even on the hottest day, and protests loudly if someone else dares to remove his. He quotes Matthew 22:12 for justification: "'Friend,' he asked, 'how did you get in here without wedding clothes?' The man was speechless."[8] In Romanian the word for "clothes" is the same as the one for "jacket." He doesn't finish the verse to realize it refers to a wedding robe meant to distinguish the invited guests from wedding crashers or that it comes from a parable about the kingdom of God. He is upset when my mother goes to church without a scarf, as the Bible says, in 1 Corinthians 11:6 that "if a woman does not cover her head, she should have her hair cut off; and if it is a disgrace for a woman to have her hair cut or shaved off, she should cover her head."[9] He is not troubled by the conflict that arises when my mother points out that he himself does not wear his hair long and sport a beard as might have been the fashion in Jesus' time, or when she posits that cutting one's hair off is perhaps not the sign of dubious moral worth that it once was. He does not recognize that he has simply found it convenient to use Bible verses to sanction agreed-upon conventions. For him the Bible has become a repository of individual verses to be employed, often out of context, as support for the norms Baptists follow at a particular moment in history. My grandfather chooses to wear a jacket because jackets have always been worn in church in his experience. He has internalized the Baptist code and is finding biblical evidence for it.

The presentation of Baptist doctrines as flowing effortlessly from a literal reading of Scripture is what gives them their endurance and their hold on the lives of churchgoers. It seemingly empowers everyday readers to examine and see for themselves that what is expressed at the pulpit is biblically grounded. And Baptist statements of faith underline the importance of the priesthood of believers, which entails direct, unmediated access to both God and the Bible. While the readers, confident of their intellectual independence, peruse the Scriptures on their own or in groups, they are slow to realize that in fact, what they are finding in the Bible is always and only what has been already framed for them as the Baptist perspective.

But fundamentalist Baptists, as shown by the Southern Baptist Convention's Baptist Faith and Message, are careful of any accusation of creedalism. Their statements of faith must declare limits on the power and reach of doctrines in order to keep the Bible and its truth and its inerrancy at the fore. Otherwise, the system will not work. Doctrines are described as "a consensus of opinion" meant to serve the purpose of "instruction and guidance" of believers but they are not considered "complete statements of our faith, having any quality or finality or infallibility."[10] They do not have "authority over the conscience" as the only "authority for faith and practice among Baptists is the Scripture of the Old and New Testaments."[11] Yet if doctrines are assigned their proper place in the official statements, when individual doctrines are presented, they are always shown to be "statements of religious conviction drawn from the Scripture."[12] Since "the sole authority for faith and practice . . . is the Scripture,"[13] doctrines are in fact reinforced by their origin, making it logically impossible to disagree with them but agree with the truth of the Scripture, from which they are derived.

The system is thus closed, resting on the all-encompassing assertion of the truth of the Bible. The first hermeneutical principle I was given, at the catechism course preceding my baptism, was "Scripture interprets itself," a principle that makes sure one never ventures outside the hermeneutical confines of Baptist answers. Within it, doctrines function as gatekeepers to define the group mostly in terms of what it is against. The "outside" context then, whether as broad as naturalism, modernism, and postmodernism, or as specific as Orthodoxy, sexual orientation, and abortion rights will determine the content of certain doctrines. Grounded in the overarching claim of biblical inerrancy, doctrines will function in part to react against the societal norms that will help the group gain definition. In other words, doctrines will nimbly change according to the issues worth opposing, while rejecting the very reality of change.

I am certain there are many other ways to describe the process of indoctrination or the method of building a fundamentalist system. There are also many religious and social systems that fit some of the characteristics here described. Most religious systems consider their claims truthful, often defining truth through the prism of their most grounding claims. And in order to gain coherence, they must define clearly their ideological contour. But not all religious and social systems require that their foundational statements be unchallenged and rely on opposition and isolation for their architectural soundness. They do not all "rebel against a world of many competing signals and build figurative walls around themselves," as Martin Marty explains, and they are not all defined by their impetus to "re+act." It is the domain of fundamentalism to "gather into enclaves," deny that "they are selective" in their approach to the Bible, and stand "sure that their God is calling them to be militant in defending their own faith and keeping all others at a distance." Not all systems remove the very possibility of genuine interaction with other systems through their very self-determination. In my experience, the certainty and comfort offered by a construct such as fundamentalism are incalculable. But so are the consequences.

After years of clarity and assurance about present, past, and future, the notion that the ground created by the doctrine of inerrancy might be giving way felt disorienting and alarming. The possibility of giving up the safety of my previous world was anything but freeing. I felt overwhelmed with guilt for questioning the principles that had framed my worldview and had governed every aspect of my private and social life. As I researched my thesis, questions about the consequences of what I was finding came to the fore: What will replace the moral absolutes found in the Scriptures? What is the cost of doubting the reality of afterlife? Will all of my sources of stability be overcome by relativism?

Eventually I began to see confusion as salutary. It was a sign that I had accomplished the most difficult task, namely becoming aware of my intellectual confinement. Seduced by the insights of philosophical hermeneutics, I hoped to continue my progress by studying issues of interpretation in my doctoral program. I had denied myself the beauty of literature; and the Bible, read only through the prism of literalism, had long been opaque and barren. I hoped to learn how to release its riches and become a reader who participates in the creation of meaning while respecting the otherness of the text. I also wanted to explore how language, confined as it is in time and space, can hope to express the divine.

More than Schleiermacher's quest for the author, his reflections on translation surprised me with prescient intuitions of the embodied nature of language and the necessary connection between all speakers linked by their being human. Saussure's attempts at a linguistic system left room for his admission, which I shared, that no scientific model can do justice to the puzzle of language in use by a particular speaker at a particular time. Ricoeur helped me appreciate the multilayered nature of meaning in spoken discourse, the elusive nature of writing despite its apparent stability, the world-creating power of metaphor, and most important, the ever fruitful connection between language and experience. Gadamer's fusion of horizons revealed the text in all its interpretative vulnerability and displayed all participants in the hermeneutical play together with their necessary historicity.

The enigma posed by language of the divine found more answers in Michael Sells's study of the unsayable. Iser's phenomenology of reading spoke of engaging the text in apophatic terms. Farid al-Din Attar's *Conference of the Birds* showed me the importance of community, of sentences in a text, and of souls in their spiritual quest. The Qur'an's oral emphasis pointed to the power of the text as breathed into life by its speakers and breathing life into its speakers. I saw language distrusted in Dante's ascent through Purgatorio, turned against itself by St. Teresa of Avila's metaphors, melding into experience in Dionysius' "Divine Names," and denied its expository role by John of the Cross's night. I realized the inherent tension in Christianity's fear of reification and gratitude for revelation. Most important, I came to see that my task was no longer to understand how to speak of the divine, for that was impossible. We do not speak of the divine when we speak of the divine. We speak of ourselves and our limitations. We recognize our effort is in vain, and still we go on speaking. My hope now is to find out why.

In no small measure because of my journey, I am no longer in the thrall of literalism, but I am still burdened by its discontents. I could, if necessary, speak coherently of the hermeneutical poverty of fundamentalism. I could discuss the contradictions of offering interpretations while denying the very act. I could point out the ethical implications of holding a text as rich as the Bible prisoner and of denying a reader her authentic communion with it. I could explain to a fundamentalist the human history of how the Bible came to be the Bible he or she knows, and describe the efforts made to create cohesion between the Old and the New Testament.

But I am not sure that is my prerogative, and I am not convinced that it would be fruitful. I have learned that one has to find his or her own way out of a system of indoctrination, though I would help if asked. I also wouldn't presume that the path I followed is suitable for all. I am grateful for my own chance, but I cannot promise that the dismantling of someone else's assurance would have the same results. With guides too many to mention, I have come to treasure uncertainty and the discovery it allows. I am a theist without a Christology; I long for the community of a church but cannot subject myself to a new doctrinal system; I cherish my Baptist past, and also revolt against its ills; I understand materialism, but prefer the fiction of the dualism of body and soul.

What I could reveal is that leaving the enclosure of fundamentalism has not delivered me into the abyss. I have discovered new insights, found new means of expression, taken inspiration from new sources, and I have been restored to myself anew. I ate from the apple and saw that it "was good for food and pleasing to the eye, and also desirable for gaining wisdom" (Genesis 3:6).[14] What now of God? I am uncertain. That is the wisdom I gained: of not knowing and of not saying.

NOTES

1. *The Bible, New International Version* (Colorado Springs: International Bible Society, 1984). http://www.biblegateway.com/ (accessed July 17, 2006).

2. Romanian Baptist Church, "Marturisirea de Credinta a Cultului Crestin Baptist" (The Romanian Baptist Confession of Faith). http://www.baptisti.ro/ (accessed July 17, 2006).

3. Ibid.

4. Southern Baptist Convention, "Comparison of 1925, 1963 and 2000 Baptist Faith and Message." http://www.sbc.net/bfm/bfmcomparison.asp (accessed July 17, 2006).

5. Ibid.

6. Ibid.

7. Ibid.

8. *The Bible, New International Version.*

9. Ibid.

10. Southern Baptist Convention, "Comparison of 1925, 1963 and 2000 Baptist Faith and Message."

11. Ibid.

12. Ibid.

13. Ibid.

14. *The Bible, New International Version.*

6

AUTONOMY AND INDOCTRINATION IN EVANGELICAL CHRISTIANITY

Tasia Persson

Evangelical Christianity is a form of Protestantism that holds that the only way to attain eternal salvation is to accept the divinity and humanity of Jesus Christ, believe in the atonement sacrifice of his crucifixion, and maintain hope in the eternal physical and spiritual life that His resurrection signals. More than any other Christian position, it privileges the Bible, especially the Gospels, as literal truth and the final authority on reality. I was raised in this tradition: my father was a member of the pastoral staff of a conservative evangelical church that my family attended regularly on Sundays. My siblings and I were very involved in the evangelical community, helping to run the church camp every summer and attending evangelical schools and midweekly youth meetings at church. It was not until I gained philosophical training in graduate school that I began to think more critically about my evangelical beliefs. Even then, I continued to retain these beliefs, despite nagging doubts about them. Recently, I began changing my mind, though, throwing off those beliefs which struck me as unethical or simply false. As I went through this change, I asked myself why it had taken me so long to seriously question and reject them—especially since they appear patently objectionable or false to me now—and I realized that my inability to seriously question and reject these beliefs had to do with the effects that the process of indoctrination into the evangelical faith has had on my life. The following is my attempt to analyze the experience of indoctrination in order to both gain insight into my own experience and explain the wider ethical concerns it raises.

I would like to thank Greg Novack for his helpful, extensive comments on this chapter.

I will begin with an insider's perspective on indoctrination into evangelical Christianity, conveying what committed adherents believe concerning the moral value of their beliefs, and accordingly, the importance of their children's acceptance of these beliefs. I will go on to discuss some trends in evangelical thought and rhetoric that make it more likely that parents will indoctrinate their children. Indeed, my primary concern here is that the temptation to use indoctrination is always present for the majority of moderate evangelicals, who are influenced by the more extreme camp, the members of which tend to be prominently featured in the evangelical community and vociferous in their insistence on indoctrination. Next, I will point out some common methods used by evangelicals to indoctrinate their children and will show that such methods violate children's right to autonomy, putting them at risk of moral corruption in the form of dirty-hands conflicts and moral drift. As such, I will argue that the use of these methods is morally impermissible, despite attempts to justify their use. Finally, I will discuss how evangelicals might avoid the harms of indoctrination without compromising the importance they place on passing on their faith to their children.

I understand the term "indoctrination" to indicate a greater level of coercion than some of its denotations, such as "to teach" or "to imbue," would suggest. I understand the term in the present context to signify instead "to brainwash," historically used in cases like the "instruction" of POWs or "persuading" people to convert to communism. Although most evangelical indoctrination does not qualify as brainwashing in the most commonly understood sense of the term (i.e., the use of torture, drugs, or special psychological-stress techniques in order to alter attitudes and beliefs), this does not imply that certain methods used to bring initiates into the faith are not coercive or that they must be less effective than common brainwashing methods. On the contrary, those who are brought up and maintain close emotional ties with the people who indoctrinated them may have a harder time escaping the effects of the indoctrination than those who undergo common brainwashing techniques at the hands of strangers or political opponents.

Further provisos are in order before I lay out my argument. I will assume a parent-child relationship when I discuss indoctrination, although I am aware that this is not the only relationship in which indoctrination can occur. Since indoctrination affects children throughout the course of their lives and some of the effects that I will discuss manifest at different ages depending on maturity level, I will use the term "initiate(s)" as a catchall to signify indoctrinated children at various ages. I will sometimes use the term "adherent" instead of parent, especially when I want to emphasize the parents' commitment to their faith as opposed to their investment in parenting. When I speak of biblical values or biblical truth, I will mean by this the *evangelical* understanding and interpretation of the Bible, since strict Roman Catholics, for example, interpret and understand the Bible differently. Also, I acknowledge that not all of the methods used to introduce children of adherents to Christianity are objectionable, and not all evangelical adherents use coercive techniques to bring initiates into the faith. I have known several people in my community of faith who were willing to discuss and debate the validity of the Bible and doctrine with me in open-minded, intelligent, and non-threatening ways in order to assuage my doubts and concerns. Furthermore, most members of my evangelical community have acknowledged the importance of freedom of choice in matters of faith, even those who also advocated the coercive methods of indoctrination that I will discuss later. Since evangelical doctrine requires that a "free choice" must be made for God in order to attain eternal salvation, evangelicals at least pay lip service to the importance of the freedom to choose for or against God, even if this freedom is not always properly understood, valued, or practiced.[1] While objectionable methods may be used to a greater extent by parents who are controlling quite independently of their faith (or alternatively, solely as a function of the strictness of their adherence to the faith as it is commonly understood and practiced), more moderate evangelicals may in fact find that applying methods of indoctrination to their children is distasteful, or even morally repugnant, as I will discuss shortly.

Moral Value of Indoctrination for Evangelicals

Adherents of evangelical Christianity believe that the general body of evangelical beliefs, which includes a defined range of accepted interpretations of biblical scripture and widely held beliefs extrapolated from these interpretations, gives them a corner on moral truth that outsiders lack. As David F. Wells, professor of historical and systematic theology at a prominent evangelical seminary describes it, "Character . . . is . . . not simply the cultivation of natural virtue but the intensely conscious sense of living morally before God. Without this sense, built into character, our moral conduct disintegrates."[2] For evangelicals, the truth about God to which Wells refers is accurately captured by central biblical beliefs regarding God's perfect character and the demands that this perfection places upon humans. "Truth about

God and about what is morally right are always implied in each other, and these are made of no account by those who are fallen" because "suppressing inconvenient or unwanted knowledge [about moral truth] is the tell-tale sign of a nature that is fallen."[3] To be negligent in insisting that one's children adhere to these beliefs is to shirk the most sacred responsibility that God gives to parents and to put one's children in danger of people who stifle moral truth, accept false beliefs, and commit immoral actions, in other words, people "who are fallen."

Relativism is the favorite whipping boy of prominent evangelicals: it is the moral void into which youth will fall if they do not cling to biblical belief as the key to moral clarity. As Josh McDowell, an influential evangelical writer and speaker, argues, young people must learn biblical truth and values in order to be able to tell objective right from wrong; simply put, attesting to these beliefs is to gain knowledge of objective moral truth.[4] In his public television program *On Faith and Reason*, Bill Moyers characterizes this belief more generally by saying that since Christians see God as the ultimate lawgiver, any set of moral beliefs that do not depend on his character do not have a firm footing and therefore fall down a slippery slope into relativism or nihilism.[5]

It is important to realize that evangelicals are not simply claiming that Judeo-Christian ethics are better reflections of objective moral truth than the other ethical systems. There is a deeply metaphysical claim operative here as well: born-again Christians are understood to receive the Spirit of God within them when they convert. In the absence of a sinful lifestyle and in the presence of regular church attendance and reading of the Scripture, the committed adherent has spiritually gained insight into absolute truth, including objective moral truth. So an adherent has firsthand access to moral knowledge that others who do not convert to Christianity—and therefore who do not receive the Holy Spirit—either lack or only gain secondhand access to by way of association with Christians. However, this secondhand knowledge does not do the nonbeliever much moral good, because one needs the Holy Spirit in order to have the power to act on what is right, rather than indulging in sinful wrongs. Children who are not exposed to evangelical beliefs or fail to accept them, will not receive the inner guide that would give them direct access to objective truth and the ability to act on that truth.

While it is true that evangelical parents believe that passing on their beliefs to their children is the supreme indicator of being a good parent, it would be a mistake to believe that all evangelical parents find indoctrination morally unproblematic. Certainly, a distinction must be drawn between the evangelical parent who undergoes a strict course of indoctrination from the time of childhood and the evangelical parent who either had religiously permissive parents herself or who came to the faith as an adult and therefore escaped the indoctrination process. While there will always be variation, in my experience the strictly indoctrinated parent is on the whole more likely to indoctrinate her child with less moral awareness of the harms incurred as a result of the process and when moral concern about indoctrination is raised by others, with little or no tolerance or uptake of those concerns. The more permissive parent, however, is more likely to view methods of indoctrination with concern or doubt.

Even so, perhaps under the weight of influential evangelicals' claims in favor of indoctrination and the evangelical community's acceptance of those claims, parents who are reluctant to indoctrinate may be able to get past their concern by rationalizing that however bad the indoctrination process might be for their children, the alternative—the failure of their children to accept their beliefs—is worse. As might be expected, the negligence or failure in passing on beliefs to children also reflects poorly on evangelical parents, which gives them additional motivation to ensure that children accept their faith. James Dobson, founder of the influential evangelical organization Focus on the Family, conveys how crucial it is for evangelicals to convey their beliefs to their children: "What is at stake here is nothing less than the faith of our children. Our ultimate object in living must be the spiritual welfare of our sons and daughters. If we lost it there, we have lost everything."[6] Evangelicals who are willing to indoctrinate their children gain a feeling of comforting assurance, because evangelical belief gives parents a strong expectation that children will not stray from their early training later on in life. In discussing the long-term efficacy of evangelical indoctrination, Dobson claims, "Leaders of the Catholic Church are widely quoted as saying, 'Give us a child until he is seven years old and we'll have him for life'; their affirmation is usually correct, because permanent attitudes can be instilled in these seven vulnerable years."[7]

As well as the assurance of their children's spiritual well-being, there is also the claim of "free choice" to ease hesitant parents into indoctrinating children. In my introduction, I nodded at a sort of double-talk about autonomy in evangelical circles: they talk about a "free choice" for salvation, even when in practice no such choice is given. Apparently, "free choice" is often understood to refer to the absence of recognized methods of brainwashing, such as the use of mind-altering drugs and torture, rather than to the avoidance of threatening and manipulative tactics. Unfortunately, the term "free choice" itself carries the patina of autonomy, so it can be used in many ways. It can be used to emphasize that adults accept these beliefs as a result of independently considered thought (and some adults do), but it can also function to deemphasize children's lack of freedom of choice when coercive and manipulative methods are used to bring them into the faith. Therefore, evangelical parents who indoctrinate their children may succeed in believing that a "free choice" is operative in the child's attitude toward the faith, and the initiate herself may understand her salvation experience (*qua* assent to the propositions of evangelical belief) as a freely made commitment, even though she has been subjected to threats and manipulation that prevent her from truly having a choice in the matter.

Trends and Beliefs That Encourage Indoctrination

Evangelicals believe that failure to pass on their beliefs to their children leaves children vulnerable to influences that will ultimately lead to moral confusion that will in turn cause them to engage in immoral conduct, finally propelling them away from the truth of Christianity. Children's estrangement from biblical truth is dangerous, because it risks damning them to the eternal punishment reserved for nonbelievers. Certain beliefs that are already contained in Christian doctrine cause evangelicals to fear for their children's welfare—for example, the belief that those who do not accept certain basic Christian beliefs will be condemned to eternal punishment in hell. However, there are also some more recent disturbing trends in contemporary evangelical Christianity that tend to heighten fears grounded in doctrine. For example, evangelical sermons and publications tend to employ war rhetoric when discussing secular influences on evangelicals. Dobson talks about the "great civil war of values," a "bitter conflict" and "struggle for the hearts and minds of the people" on the part of the biblical traditionalists against "secular humanists."[8] Another writer insists that "planners of the other side" are plotting the downfall of America in the same way that America's Communist enemy plotted their revolution: by corrupting the young, controlling the media, and encouraging civil disobedience.[9] Yet another evangelical leader writes, "Daily, perhaps hourly, we seem to be losing the war for America's heart and mind."[10] War rhetoric is most often employed in the context of the specific fear that secular humanists are at the helm of the media machine and are in league with Satan.[11] Evangelicals believe that one of the humanists' key tactics is to use the liberal media to influence children against being convinced of the truths of Christianity. Dobson describes media influences as brainwashing adolescents, conditioning them until the "freedom of youth is traded for slavery and domination."[12]

The prevailing belief among evangelical writers who are concerned about media influences seems to be that a permissive attitude toward these influences would be devastating for children. Dobson uses extreme examples of harm to encourage parents to shield their children from these influences: youngsters who watch, read, or hear sexually explicit media messages fall easily into sexual promiscuity, which, he emphasizes, can lead to sexually transmitted diseases. He also maintains that there is a "slippery slope" directly from pornographic media to Ted Bundy's heinous actions.[13] The effect of extreme examples and the polarizing rhetoric of war is to impress on the reader that accepting any of the tenets of liberalism, secular humanism, and the like is to defect to the enemy: there is no middle ground on which those who accept moderate beliefs can still be said to "belong" as evangelicals. It is also clear that if one does not shield one's child from these bad influences, that child could easily defect to the enemy. Dobson and other prominent evangelical leaders often employ this war rhetoric—which highlights constant attack from the enemy, conveys great urgency, and in my experience, tends to be successful in inspiring anger and fear in evangelicals—for the purpose of encouraging vigilance about ensuring children's (continued) acceptance of the faith and, as a result, their moral and spiritual well-being. He warns, "Warfare has always been exhausting, dangerous, and expensive. But how can we remain uninvolved when the welfare of our children and subsequent generations is on the line?"[14] These concerns among evangelical commentators are not relegated to the upper echelons of evangelical thinkers: as I was growing up, they were well known in our community of faith, and they continue to hold an apparently unchallenged place. At a small church service I recently attended, the pastor commented in his sermon that media influences lead to loose morals, with no apparent effort expended to support or justify this statement.[15]

With secular threats to children's well-being constantly looming, it is no wonder that Dobson responds to a concern that a child should be able to "decide for himself" and not have religion "forced down his throat" in the following way: "When parents say that they are going to withhold indoctrination from their small child, allowing him to 'decide for himself,' they are almost guaranteeing that he will 'decide' in the negative. . . . If the early exposure has been properly conducted, he will have an inner mainstay to steady him. That early indoctrination, then, is the key to the spiritual attitudes he will carry into adulthood."[16]

Given the alleged serious risks of eternal damnation and immorality posed by secular influences, coupled with the belief that allowing children to decide for themselves will inevitably result in their rejection of the faith, parents are highly motivated to use tactics that they believe will ensure children's acceptance of their beliefs. With the constant threat of the evil influence of the liberal media and the fires of hell waiting to take their children, it is not surprising that evangelical parents are willing to embrace methods of indoctrination in order to ensure their children's futures.

Methods of Indoctrination

Several methods are commonly used to indoctrinate initiates. First, initiates are inundated with preferred beliefs while being prevented from gaining exposure to incompatible beliefs. The biblical injunction to "train up a child in the way that he should go" leads many evangelical parents to regularly read Bible stories to their children. They are sent to Christian youth groups, youth camps, and schools (or are home-schooled). Many among my evangelical acquaintance never set foot in a secular educational institution; they went from elementary school through college (and sometimes, graduate school) at evangelically affiliated institutions. At the same time, most of us were prevented from exposure to competing beliefs and ideas by having our relationships and entertainment monitored for agreement with evangelical beliefs. Like most evangelical children, much of my schooling took place at private religious institutions for the express purposes of placing limitations on the curriculum I was taught (i.e., no evolution or "safe sex" lectures) and encouraging me to associate primarily (or ideally, solely) with those who shared my religious beliefs. Every evangelical church that I attended from the time I could remember taught that one permissibly may have non-Christian acquaintances, but intimate relationships with them were strictly forbidden. Any association with them was to be undertaken for the primary purpose of "persuading them of the Truth" of evangelicalism. The suspicion that one was forming too close a bond with a non-Christian for the wrong purposes (for example, romantic attachment or close friendship) inevitably led stalwart churchgoers to quote the following verse from 2 Corinthians, "Do not be yoked together with unbelievers. For what do righteousness and wickedness have in common? Or what fellowship can light have with darkness?"[17]

As may be expected from the influence of Dobson and other prominent evangelicals concerned about secular influences over evangelical parents, we were not allowed access to media that depicted situations or expressed values that were considered "worldly" or "sinful," that is, contrary to evangelical doctrine and values.

A second indoctrination method is for adherents to treat initiates' misgivings as mere obstacles to faith rather than as valid reasons for concern. When my friends and I began to ask probing and critical questions about the tenets of our faith, our misgivings were met with formulated answers. (I have tried asking the same questions of adherents in different evangelical churches throughout the country, and I almost invariably received some version of basically the same answer to my questions.) However, if an initiate pushes her concerns and doubts past the formulated answers and arguments (or less often, the creative, on-the-spot pseudo-philosophical argumentation), the response is some variation on the theme to trust God with the "seeming" inconsistencies. Trusting God generally signifies replacing critical assessment of beliefs with "biblical discernment," which means making biblical truth the primary or sole authority in deciding whether or not to accept a belief or engage in an action.[18] The epistemic rationale for believing that biblical discernment should be trusted over and against one's own judgment is that reliance on this type of discernment will not lead one into error, whereas one's own understanding and conscience can lead one into false beliefs and bad choices. Though widely accepted, this rationale may yet prove unsatisfactory for the initiate. If she makes it known that she continues to believe that her doubts have merit, she will most likely be met with one or all of the responses I have experienced. These responses range from concern ("We'll pray that you develop more faith"), to indignation ("You've been spending too much time with those no-good Liberals"), to outright anger and fear ("Don't go spreading your doubts around and poisoning other peoples' faith!").

Finally, the person who insists that her doubts and concerns are well founded is threatened with punishment. Dobson warns that there will be "hell to pay" and the "wages of sin is death" for those who do not embrace Christian beliefs and morality.[19] Often, this method boils down to threatening the initiate that God will punish her if she continues to treat her doubts seriously. Evangelicals worry when people give credence to their doubts and concerns about evangelical doctrine, since they believe that the doubters are not "really saved." They therefore face the punishment of a miserable, immoral life, and after that, eternal damnation. The concern about giving credence to doubt here is telling: doubt is the signal that the process of indoctrination has failed in this person.

The bombardment by threats of eternal punishment and becoming a bad person, coupled with the mind-numbing formulated answers to pacify my concerns, succeeded in causing me to cease asking critical questions about the faith in my childhood. After struggling with the terror of hell for years, I was finally able to renew my inquiry regarding my doubts and concerns. I attribute this renewal to the effect of prolonged training in a system of liberal education, in which I was not only encouraged, but expected to think critically and make considered judgments about beliefs that I had always taken for granted. Developing these capacities and attaining a greater measure of confidence in the conclusions to which they brought me helped me to overcome the threats and manipulations involved in the indoctrination process.

Autonomy

Basic to my moral analysis of indoctrination will be Thomas Hill's discussion of autonomy in *Autonomy and Self-respect*. He discusses the notion of autonomy as a right, as opposed to competing notions of it as a psychological capacity or freedom from irrational desires.[20] For Hill, such a right is "a moral right against individuals ... (a) to make one's own decisions about matters deeply affecting one's life, (b) without certain sorts of interferences by others, (c) provided certain conditions obtain."[21] The choices he mentions in (a) are limited by "principles of justice, noninjury, contract, and responsibility to others" and do not include the freedom to control the lives of others.[22] The kinds of interferences that Hill has in mind in (b) are physical coercion, threats, and manipulation. On this definition, autonomy is not merely moral permission to make one's own decisions, but a prohibition on another's use of these kinds of interferences to prevent one from making important life decisions. Hill contends, "Respecting individuals' autonomy means granting them at least the opportunity to make their crucial life-affecting choices in a rational manner."[23] While a minimal capacity for rational choice is required, Hill is careful to point out that the requirement of respecting autonomy should not merely be extended to those who are likely to make rational decisions. It also applies to those who may make irrational and foolish decisions. So, to have the opportunity to make important choices in a rational manner simply refers to being granted the chance to deliberate among a set of options that is not limited by the perception-distorting effects of manipulation or fear experienced as a result of threats.

When applied to one who has not yet developed the ability to judge truth and falsity and right and wrong for herself, the methods of bringing initiates into the evangelical faith I have discussed—inundating with preferred beliefs while preventing exposure to other beliefs and ideas, treating misgivings as mere obstacles to faith rather than valid reasons for concern, and threatening those who are reluctant to believe with both earthly and eternal punishment—are forms of manipulation and coercion that make it very difficult or even impossible for the initiate to develop and maintain the ability to make rational choices about whether or not she will embrace evangelical beliefs. Indeed, the intended effect of these methods is to prevent or shake her reliance on her own critical assessment and moral judgment in favor of reliance on evangelical doctrine. As a result, the initiate may never learn to develop, rely on, or regain critical assessment skills that could alert her to reasons for justified concern and doubt. In particular, she will be unable to seriously consider whether or not the extent to which evangelical belief narrows her choices and affects her well-being is acceptable. Since these methods prevent the initiate from having the opportunity to make important choices about religious belief in a rationally deliberative manner, use of these methods of indoctrination violate the initiate's right to autonomy.

It is important to realize here, however, that the right to autonomy is defeasible, as Hill points out. One may permissibly override it to prevent a major disaster. Evangelicals might argue that eternal punishment and immorality are indeed major disasters, and so the indoctrination of their children is justified because it is for their own protection. There are also other rights that can trump the right to autonomy. For example, one might claim that the parents' right to pursue their own notion of the good includes bringing up children who accept their religious beliefs and is at least as important as the initiate's right to autonomy. I now consider whether these contentions nullify my claim that indoctrination violates the initiate's autonomy.

Preventing Disaster

Immorality

As I pointed out earlier, evangelicals claim that biblical belief is the indispensable key to moral clarity and right behavior. Two concerns with the evangelical claim to direct access to objective moral knowledge immediately present themselves: (1) committed evangelicals accuse other committed evangelicals of incorrect belief and wrong conduct, and (2) some evangelical belief and practice is discordant with basic ethical principles.

Implicitly, evangelicals acknowledge that biblical belief does not clearly reflect objective moral truth. For example, evangelical leaders criticized other evangelical leaders who signed a document along with Catholic leaders that constituted an agreement not to proselytize between the two faiths. Those who asserted that evangelical doctrine requires proselytizing non-Protestant Christians were labeled "sheep-stealers," whereas those who argued that evangelical doctrine is inclusive of non-Protestant Christians were accused of refusing to recognize the scope and importance of missionary work.[24] Another evangelical charges that "the worst enemies of Bible believing Christians now seems [sic] to be other Bible believing Christians," as a result of the phenomenon of some evangelical Christians insisting that evangelicals with differing beliefs are not truly members of the faith.[25] He comments that those who condemn others in this way are in reality "being used by Satan to further divide the body of Christ."[26] A more recent example can be found in Ronald J. Sider's book *The Scandal of the Evangelical Conscience*. He argues that the emphasis of widespread evangelical beliefs and messages on the idea of forgiveness of believers' sins has led to believers exhibiting an inordinate amount of immoral behavior, treating salvation as nothing more than a "one-way ticket to heaven," while living "like hell."[27] He insists, "Notions of cheap grace are at the core of today's scandalous evangelical disobedience."[28] He is concerned that among pastors and other leaders of the faith, "too many evangelicals in too many ways give the impression that the really important gospel is forgiveness of sins."[29]

The evangelical explanation of these disputes is that some of these "committed" adherents are in fact being led astray by sin. It might be plausible to believe that a few evangelicals are purported to be committed to the faith but are in fact living in sin, and therefore get wrong ideas and cause these controversies with those who really are committed. However, when there are two fairly large camps of recognized evangelical leaders that differ in their beliefs of what is right and wrong, my experience with the faith is that it is highly implausible that all of the evangelicals in one camp are living in sin and yet have all managed to keep it hidden from their Christian community and retain their leadership positions. For if church members submit the children of adherents to the scrutiny and monitoring that I have described, that scrutiny goes double for adherents' leaders. What is more plausible, and more consistent with my experience of these sorts of disputes in the church, is that they are in fact the product of sincere ideological disagreements among people who are careful to live out their beliefs and are heavily invested in their Christianity and the welfare of the church. If I am correct that these disputes are not evidence of the hidden sin of one camp of evangelicals and that they are instead merely ideological disputes, then the claim that avowing biblical belief successfully prevents confusion regarding the requirements of objective morality is simply untrue.

Not only does adherence to the evangelical faith fail to provide the moral clarity that it is claimed to, but also it seems that *prima facie* some evangelical beliefs are actually contrary to objective moral principles. The following is an example of how widespread evangelical belief and practice diverge from a basic ethical standard of fairness. There exists among evangelicals a strong belief that men are the "spiritual leaders" in a marriage: they are charged by God to be disciplined in maintaining their Christian beliefs and consistent in acting on them. As stated in the Southern Baptist Convention, "Therefore, be it RESOLVED, That we . . . reaffirm God's order of authority for his church and the Christian home: (1) Christ the head of every man; (2) man the head of every woman; (3) children in subjection to their parents—in the Lord."[30] One evangelical writer explains "headship" as a position that has both spiritual and practical implications: "The headship of the husband is not one of domination, but it is still headship in the sense of providing directions, offering guidelines . . . in his role as Christ's representative."[31] That the husband acts as Christ's representative to the wife indicates a spiritual hierarchy (not just a practical method for resolving disputes between husband and wife, as evangelicals are fond of claiming). As a consequence of this headship position, husbands are understood as the primary decision-makers in the marriage (although not the sole decision-makers, as evangelicals rush to point out in the face of feminist objections). Since evangelicals believe that God has ordained this role uniquely for husbands, wives are expected to be submissive to this leadership. However, my experiences with evangelical wives have convinced me that women have characteristics that make them just as capable in spiritual leadership roles as their husbands. To deny Christian women the status that should come with their matching abilities is to undervalue them and, as I have noticed on several occasions, ultimately leads them to undervalue themselves.

At the same time, Christian beliefs also require that those who "give themselves away" sexually outside marriage or in marriage with non-Christians are rebelling against God's law, because they have engaged in physical intimacy outside Christian marriage or have committed to those who are not fit to be the spiritual leaders in their marriages. While in this rebellious state, a woman will be seen to have even less spiritual aptitude and standing than the wives who entered into Christian marriage. As Michael R. Cosby explains, "Loose sexual behavior is totally unacceptable for Christians . . . true spirituality will be reflected practically in standards of ethical purity far above those of the surrounding culture."[32] As for women with non-Christian partners, while dating a non-Christian is questionable behavior for evangelicals, as many evangelicals have told me time and time again, marrying such a person would be totally unacceptable and would cast doubt upon one's commitment to the faith. The irony of this nexus of beliefs is that while evangelicals support the idea that women can only be appropriately valued in a marriage entered into under God, in reality Christian women in intimate relationships are devalued by other Christians whether or not they enter into religious marriages. In fact, it seems that the best chance that an evangelical Christian woman has of being appropriately valued by her community is to avoid intimate relationships altogether.[33] To box Christian women into this very limited position is unfair, because while Christian men remain limited by the prohibitions on marriage to non-Christian partners and sex outside marriage, they can be appropriately valued (or more accurately, comparatively overvalued) by their Christian community and enjoy intimacy in Christian marriage at the same time.

In response to the charge of immoral practices, I have heard evangelicals argue that we are simply mistaken about the nature of the moral value in question, in this case fairness. God determines what morality really requires, and therefore our considered judgment of what constitutes fairness is simply wrong. However, if one wants to take this route, one must bite the bullet: one must admit that human conscience is inconsistent with God's moral standards. This claim is often justified by pointing to the sinful nature of humanity, and it makes the Bible the final authority on truth. The problem with this notion is that I have shown that evangelicals differ in their interpretations regarding what the Bible says about certain moral issues. If there is no other court of appeal, such as one's conscience, considered moral judgments, and reason, then it is not clear how such disputes could ever be resolved.

Perhaps a final objection to my argument might be that while the evangelical faith may not guarantee moral rectitude, it may give the adherent a better shot at attaining it than those who embrace incompatible beliefs, such as atheism, Judaism, or Islam. I do not know whether this claim is true or not (and the scope of this piece does not allow me to explore it sufficiently), but whatever the case, it is not the claim that evangelicals are making about morality. Instead, they set up a false dichotomy between evangelical beliefs and relativism when arguing about objective morality. For example, by identifying secular ethics at the university level with relativism, McDowell sets up a straw man that anyone with a coherent claim to objective truth may knock down. He does not acknowledge other claims to objective moral truth, such as a secular moral system that predicates its claim to objective truth on our responsibility to each other as fellow moral beings. In other words, far from making a nuanced claim about an improved prospect of living a moral life as a result of adherence to evangelical belief, evangelicals tend to fail altogether to acknowledge the possibility that the appeal to God's moral authority is not the only viable option for grounding a coherent system of objective ethics.

These examples make it clear, I hope, that accepting evangelical beliefs does not give the assurance of moral clarity and rectitude promised by evangelicals. Even if one remains unconvinced that some of the tenets of contemporary evangelical Christianity are themselves false or unethical, as in the case of fairness to women, simply acknowledging that evangelical belief is vulnerable to infection by beliefs and attitudes that support immoral behavior is sufficient to support my contention that indoctrination does not guarantee the correctness of adherents' beliefs or the moral rectitude of their behavior. The violation of the right to autonomy that indoctrination poses, then, cannot be justified by the claim that acceptance of evangelical belief and practice provides insurance against holding incorrect beliefs and practicing immorality.

Eternal Punishment

Evangelicals also believe that adherence to certain basic tenets guarantees them salvation from eternal punishment. It is important to realize at this point that the notion of freedom of choice in matters of salvation and damnation cannot merely be a figure of speech for evangelicals, because evangelicals recognize the validity of freely chosen beliefs. Indeed, the very purpose of eternal punishment is to separate those who have freely chosen to reject God from those who have freely chosen to embrace evangelical beliefs. Without freedom of choice, the initiate's salvation would be a function of merely being at the right place at the right time: in other words, she would be lucky rather than meritorious. Even those evangelicals who adhere to the doctrine of predestination do not believe that people can skate into Heaven purely on the basis of luck—in order to be saved, the individual must still make a choice in the absence of knowledge concerning whether God preordained her for salvation or not. Also, in such a case the initiate's acceptance of the faith would not be a product of her recognition of the overwhelming truth of the evangelical message, as evangelicals claim, but instead her inability to ward off coercion. Finally, since evangelicals predicate merit on the freedom to choose, God would not be justified in assigning some people to hell and others to heaven if each of those people were not afforded freedom of choice to accept or reject him. He would instead be a capricious torturer who sends people to hell for no good reason (i.e., luck), or at least no good reason that humans can recognize. That God is just is one belief that evangelicals are very concerned to be able to defend in terms of recognized principles of human justice.

Since freedom of choice is a requirement for an authentic conversion experience, indoctrination fails to achieve its intended result, and from an evangelical standpoint, throws the initiate's claim to salvation from eternal punishment into doubt. Strictly speaking, the initiate who accepts the message as a result of threats has not freely chosen the doctrine, since a decision made as a result of manipulation or coercion is not compatible with the notion of autonomous choice. Evangelicals who inadequately understand the notion of freedom of choice recognize only three alternatives: a "free choice" to accept God (i.e., the initiate claims to have accepted biblical beliefs), a "free choice" to reject God (i.e., failure to accept biblical beliefs), or no choice at all as a result of common brainwashing techniques.[34] With the exception of those who understand what the notion of freedom of choice truly requires in order to be consistent with the other beliefs I mentioned (and a few do recognize this), evangelicals do not tend to recognize that the threats and manipulation that they employ in indoctrination are the sorts of practices that can undermine the authenticity of the initiate's salvation experience. This lack of recognition does not change the fact that the authentic conversion of those who are indoctrinated is untenable on the evangelical model of salvation. For the doctrine requires actual, as opposed to merely claimed, freedom of choice in order to achieve an authentic salvation experience. However, threats and manipulation deprive the initiate of the freedom to choose whether she will accept or reject God, and therefore use of these methods does not guarantee an authentic salvation experience.

I have shown that use of coercion and manipulation does not afford the initiate an authentic salvation experience, and therefore does not successfully prevent the danger of hell in a way that is consistent with evangelical doctrine. As such, the violation of the initiate's right to autonomy posed by indoctrination also cannot be justified by the claim that it must be used to save the child from the major disaster of eternal punishment.

Justified Paternalism

One might object that a child does not necessarily possess a right to autonomy because, depending upon her age, she may not meet the criteria for the "minimal rational capacity" that Hill requires. In that case, preventing children from accepting dangerous beliefs and practices, and even threatening them with punishment if they do constitutes justified paternalism and is just what parents are supposed to do for children who cannot choose for themselves, so long as it is reasonably in the child's best interest. Additionally, several theorists have recognized that parents have a further right to pursue their own notion of the good life. For example, Amy Gutmann argues that parents' notion of the good life may include the right to discipline, educate, and socialize their children in ways that are consistent with deeply held beliefs and values.[35] Since children do not generally have a right to full-fledged autonomy (excepting the rare instance of the extremely self-aware, precocious child), it might be argued that the parental right is the only operative right in the circumstances.

The child *qua* minor may not have a right to full-fledged autonomy until she reaches a certain age, but she has the right to the autonomy that comes with the minimal capacity for rationality, and the parent's right to pursue her own notion of the good does not trump the initiate's right to autonomy once she reaches this minimum threshold. This is because negative duties (e.g., to not harm others) are more stringent than positive duties (e.g., to cultivate one's moral personality). If the parent's pursuit of the good ends up damaging or destroying the child's ability to make important life decisions in a rational manner when she does reach this minimum threshold, then the parent has violated the initiate's right to autonomy. As I have pointed out, the right to autonomy requires that others may not deprive the agent of the opportunity to make deeply important, life-affecting choices with rational deliberation, but this is just what indoctrination does.

Indoctrination's Effect on Autonomy

If evangelical children are forbidden to associate with nonevangelicals except to proselytize them, they will not learn how to engage in sincere dialogue about differences in beliefs and negotiate these differences in close relationships. Furthermore, from a very young age it causes initiates to view those who do not agree with their core religious beliefs as bearers of agenda, rather than as persons with beliefs and perspectives that should be seriously considered and respected. Restricting children from exposure to all ideas and situations that are incompatible with preferred beliefs and all occasions where they may receive unvarnished exposure to such ideas and situations insulates them too heavily from the rest of the world. It does not afford them the opportunity to form and express their own ideas about these ideas and beliefs; ironically, it keeps them from developing the critical thinking skills that would help them pick out what might be wrong with certain secular ideas. However, it also keeps them from deciding what—and this is what the committed evangelical is afraid of—might be right about these ideas and situations. For example, children in my church were not allowed to watch, read, or listen to material that depicted sex outside marriage in an appealing manner. However, one of the problems that evangelical parents face is that their children eventually learn the truth that sex can be very appealing, independent of marital status. Parents who avoid or deny evangelically unpopular truths do nothing to help children to understand and manage these truths when they manifest in adult life, such as how to deal with the allure and intensity of sexual attraction outside marriage.

"Moral Drift"

More alarming than the effect that a lack of self-determination would have on the initiate's quality of life, however, is the possibility that she ultimately will be unable to identify and reject unethical or even evil principles and practices, especially those that are already embedded in, or may in future become part of the religious belief to which she has deferred. In other words, the major danger to those who are indoctrinated is the undermining or corruption of their moral character—a phenomenon that psychologists John Sabini and Maury Silver call "moral drift." As applied to the initiate's circumstances, this phenomenon would result from the initiate's failure to reproach evangelical behavior that she finds morally concerning on grounds that are independent of evangelical belief, such as secular ethical principles or the stirrings of her conscience. Sabini and Silver maintain that this failure makes the agent more likely to be unable to resist evil in the future, because it prevents her from clearly establishing the immorality of the deed in her own mind.[36] As they describe it: "In making a moral reproach an individual's subjective, personal, inarticulate, and vague moral impressions become externalized for himself and others, and thus become part of the social process. . . . If the making of a reproach clarifies and concretizes moral precepts, the failure to do so allows them to remain unclear both for others and for oneself."[37]

Sabini and Silver point out several reasons why an onlooker may not criticize behavior that disturbs her. First, she may not have standing to condemn the wrong done, and second, distinctions between morally legitimate and illegitimate ways of acting may be obscured by the circumstances in which the act took place. Both of these reasons explain why an initiate would fail to make moral reproach. For the initiate whose primary community defers to the authority of biblical belief is not likely to view her as having the standing to make such a reproach. This results from the fact that her community of evangelical adherents equates moral legitimacy with evangelical doctrine, and her position within this community can muddle her attempts at determining whether the beliefs and practices that she finds morally concerning are indeed morally legitimate. If indoctrination is successful, the initiate will see her only legitimate appeal as stemming from the set of beliefs that already contains the supposed justification for the wrong behavior, leaving her with no recourse for reproaching morally disturbing facets of evangelical belief.

"Dirty Hands"

Unfortunately, the risk to the initiate's moral integrity does not end even when she is able to escape the indoctrination effects that prevent her from relying on her own considered judgment. As I have pointed out, the doubletalk about "free choice" not only eases reluctant parents into the indoctrination process, but also obscures the reality that the initiate never truly chose the faith but instead was forced into it. For those who buy into this doubletalk and into evangelical beliefs about the permanency of indoctrination's effect on an initiate, genuine reconsideration of evangelical beliefs is not recognized as an option. In fact, no legitimate reason is recognized among her community for her to depart from these teachings. An initiate's later disagreement signals to adherents that she has fallen away from the faith as a result of capitulation to evil and sin, rather than as a result of her newfound ability to express her sincere doubts and concerns about the faith. If adherents acknowledged that the initiate had been forced to accept their beliefs, there would not be a trust relationship between them and her; if, on the other hand, adherents did not expect permanent acceptance at all, then the initiate's change of mind would be relatively unproblematic for them. However, as indoctrination now stands, the adherent experiences the initiate's change of mind as a betrayal, and the initiate will at least be aware of this perception, even in the rare cases in which she herself does not also experience her change of mind as a betrayal of her community.

As a result of the trust placed in her by her community, the initiate who later decides for herself that evangelical beliefs are invalid but still maintains ties in her community of faith faces a difficult choice between several morally unpalatable options, including (1) betraying the trust placed in her as a fellow member of the faith by abandoning her former religious beliefs and announcing her change in belief to community members, (2) lying to her community by claiming either implicitly or explicitly that there has been no change in her beliefs in order to avoid (1), or (3) suppressing reasonable doubts and concerns about evangelical beliefs in order to avoid (1) and (2). This conflict might be understood in terms of Michael Stocker's "dirty hands" problem, in that all the alternatives involve no less than "a violation and a betrayal of a person, value or principle," and no matter what the initiate does, in some sense she does what she should not.[38] For she must make the painful choice between self-respect and loyalty to her community. This is not to say that there can be no morally right choice in this situation, only that there are morally objectionable factors about each of the alternatives presented to the initiate. The morally right choice will be the one that represents the lesser evil in the situation, but the initiate cannot escape the conflict without acting on an alternative with morally objectionable feature(s)—something that in all likelihood she will regret.[39] This catch-22 prevents her from fully repudiating what is wrong about the alternative she finally chooses, since full repudiation would constitute a complete refusal to act on the morally objectionable feature(s) present in each of the alternatives. Her moral integrity is thereby jeopardized: her desire to act in the morally best way in the situation requires her to act in a manner that is in some sense wrong.

I have argued that the use of threats and manipulation in evangelical indoctrination violates the initiate's autonomy, which places her at risk for suffering moral corruption as a result of "moral drift" and "dirty hands" problems. As such, the use of widely accepted methods of evangelical indoctrination is morally impermissible.

Conclusion: A Response to the Problem of Indoctrination

At this point, the concern might arise that there is nowhere for evangelical parents who do not want to compromise the importance of their faith to go from here: how can they be good evangelical parents by ensuring their children's faith and yet at the same time respect their children's autonomy? As an initial attempt to answer these questions, let me say that being a morally good parent and being a good evangelical parent need not be in tension. Evangelical parents need not buy into the idea that making sure that their children accept their beliefs is a mark of good parenting. If the choice for God really is intended to be a free one, then evangelical parents would do well to ensure that their children are given the chance to make autonomous choices by allowing them to develop the capacity for rational decision-making. Methods that foster a child's confidence in critical thinking skills and allow her to express doubt and concern without fear of threat could be used to teach children about evangelical Christianity while at the same time giving them leeway to develop and rely on their own judgment. When trying to determine morally appropriate methods for instructing children in the evangelical faith, perhaps the most important factors to consider are whether the methods in question will foreseeably compromise the child's ability for critical assessment and moral self-determination.

The final problem is the problem of hell: must evangelical parents avoid mention of this part of the doctrine in order to avoid indoctrinating their children? I do not think so. It may permissibly be raised as a tenet of the doctrine once a child learns to think critically, so long as it is not presented in such a way that it could become the primary motivator for her to accept evangelical beliefs. (For example, it might instead be introduced as a potentially viable theological option to be evaluated for its consistency with ethical principles, notions of God's character, and other standards that the child has already considered and accepted.) While Pascal's wager is undoubtedly a good motivator, it is an ethically and theologically unacceptable approach for motivating children to accept and adhere to the faith. Evangelicals who want to respond to objective moral requirements and who understand God as a Being who values human autonomy, especially in making decisions to accept or reject his gift of salvation, would do better to focus their energies on creating and using teaching methods that do not manipulate and coerce their children.

NOTES

1. Even Pat Robertson, a televangelist and ex-politician who tends to have an aggressively coercive agenda, acknowledges (at least in theory) the importance of this freedom in claiming, "[God] is not going to force anyone to accept him. It has to be a free choice" (http://www.positiveatheism.org/hist/quotes/revpat.htm).
2. David F. Wells, *Losing Our Virtue* (Grand Rapids, Mich.: William B. Eerdmans Publishing, 1998), 16.
3. Ibid., 161.
4. Paraphrased from Josh McDowell and Bob Hostetler, *Right from Wrong* (Dallas: Word Publishing, 1994).
5. Bill Moyers, *On Faith and Reason*, PBS, June 23, 2006.
6. James Dobson, *Children at Risk* (Dallas: Word Publishing, 1990), 55.
7. James Dobson, *Dare to Discipline* (Wheaton, Ill.: Tyndale House Publishers, 1970), 157.
8. Dobson, *Children at Risk*, 20.
9. Thomas Wang, "Must History Repeat Itself?" in *America, Return to God*, ed. Thomas J. Wang (Sunnyvale, Calif.: Great Commission Center International, 2006), 126.
10. Erwin W. Lutzer, "We Must Seek God," in Wang, *America, Return to God*, 106.
11. This worldview may seem ridiculously paranoid, especially when one considers that (a) what the media airs is generally profit-driven by its audience base (and evangelicals are conspicuous among these groups), and (b) the consequence of the Bush administration's conservative evangelical stance was that evangelical interests received widespread and generally positive coverage. However, far from being a marginal belief by a few extremists, this concern continues to be a widely accepted evangelical mainstay.
12. Dobson, *Children at Risk*, 5.
13. Ibid., 8.
14. Ibid., 41.
15. Ray Kollbocker, "It's All Relative: Finding Time, Pt. 2" (sermon, Parkview Community Church, Glen Ellyn, Ill., May 28, 2006).
16. Dobson, *Dare to Discipline*, 156-7.
17. Second Corinthians 6:14 (New International Version).
18. Bob Smithouser, "Mind Over Media," Focus on the Family, http://www.family.org/fofmag/pf/a0026144.cfm (accessed June 2, 2006). The author's article is just one of many on Dobson's "Focus on the Family" website featuring discussions of the evils of the secular media.
19. James Dobson, *When God Doesn't Make Sense* (Wheaton, Ill.: Tyndale House Publishers, 1993), 184.
20. While autonomy may in fact also be consistent with these notions, I will focus on autonomy as a right for the purposes of this argument.
21. Thomas E. Hill Jr., *Autonomy and Self-Respect* (New York: Cambridge University Press, 1991), 32.
22. Ibid., 48.
23. Ibid.
24. Christian Century, "Evangelical-Catholic Statement Criticized," http://www.findarticles.com/p/articles/mi_m1058/is_n17_v111/ai_15405264/print (accessed June 2, 2006).
25. Don Koenig, "We Have Met the Enemy and They Are Us Evangelical Christians," The Prophetic Years, http://www.thepropheticyears.com/comments.com/ (accessed June 2, 2006).
26. Ibid.
27. Ronald Sider, *The Scandal of the Evangelical Conscience: Why Are Christians Living Just Like the Rest of the World?* (Grand Rapids, Mich.: Baker Books, 2005), 58.
28. Ibid., 59.
29. Ibid., 58.
30. Southern Baptist Convention, "Resolution on the Place of Women in Christian Service," http://www.sbc.net/resolutions/am Resolution.asp?ID=1090 (accessed June 2, 2006).
31. Donald G. Bloesch, *Is the Bible Sexist?* (Westchester, Ill.: Crossway Books, 1982), 88-89.

32. Michael R. Cosby, *Sex in the Bible* (Englewood Cliffs, N.J.: Prentice-Hall, 1984), 116.

33. Christian history suggests the true nature of this value: "Women could shed their femaleness by becoming nuns, and by becoming virgins they became, in the words of one of the fathers of the Church, 'honorary males.'" Karen Armstrong, interview for *Christianity: The Second Thousand Years* (A&E Television, 2000).

34. However, even this last claim is somewhat dubious for most evangelicals, since they view ancient Christians who repudiated their Christianity under Roman torture as traitors to the faith. On the other hand, it appears that a healthy respect for the effect of mind-altering drugs is sufficient to convince most evangelicals that any admission of unbelief under this kind of influence would not impugn the adherent.

35. Amy Gutmann, "Children, Paternalism, and Education: A Liberal Argument," *Philosophy and Public Affairs* 9 (Summer 1980): 338–58. Gutmann acknowledges that the parents' right to pursue their notion of the good life is constrained by children's right to the "necessary precondition[s] for the development of capacities to choose a conception of the good life" (350).

36. John Sabini and Maury Silver, *Moralities of Everyday Life* (New York: Oxford University Press, 1982), 49.

37. Ibid.

38. "Dirty Hands and Ordinary Life," *Plural and Conflicting Values* (New York: Oxford University Press, 1992), 18. While Stocker claims that a planner with an immoral design is generally the cause of the existence of the dirty-hands conflict, he leaves open the possibility of dirty hands without such a planner. I believe that at the least an immoral design is necessary, whether it is the result of the foreseeable and morally culpable actions of an institution, community, or person. To the extent that it is foreseeable that indoctrination will cause parents and adherents confusion with respect to the moral value of autonomy and place thoughtful believers in moral catch-22's, encouraging indoctrination is an immoral plan.

It is also worth noting that the dirty-hands problem is not limited to initiates. The risk of moral corruption cuts both ways, also affecting thoughtful adherents who are considering whether or not it is right to indoctrinate their children. Pointing out to parents the ethical problems that Christian indoctrination poses is unlikely to produce the full-fledged remorse and change of behavior that one might expect from those who realize that they have jeopardized their children's autonomy. Evangelical parents face the difficult choice between ensuring their child's spiritual well-being and violating the child's right to autonomy.

39. Bernard Williams believes that choosing to fulfill one's obligation to the detriment of another in a moral conflict leaves a "remainder"—unfulfilled obligation(s) that often cause the agent to feel guilt. For discussion of moral remainder, see "Ethical Consistency," in his *Problems of the Self* (New York: Cambridge University Press, 1973), 166–86.

7

INDOCTRINATION, AUTONOMY, AND AUTHENTICITY

Glen Pettigrove

The Wesleyan Church traces its roots back to John Wesley and the Oxford "methodists" of the 1720s and 1730s. But as a distinct denomination it was born a century later, when a number of churches in the United States opposed to slavery and desirous of church reform seceded from the Methodist Episcopal Church to form the Wesleyan Methodist Connection. Its early identity was shaped by a concern for social justice and personal holiness. But over time, the latter came to overshadow the former, and holiness came to be defined in increasingly legalistic terms. By the mid-twentieth century, the church was a fundamentalist institution whose membership was restricted to those who did not defile themselves by drinking, dancing, smoking, or playing card games. This was the church of my grandparents and great-grandparents on both sides of the family. My mother graduated from the oldest Wesleyan college, and my father from the largest. Two years after earning his bachelor's degree, my father left his job as a school teacher to become a Wesleyan pastor. I was born not long after he entered the ministry, and spent all of my childhood in Wesleyan parsonages, at Wesleyan campgrounds, and in Wesleyan church buildings. I am, you might say, a child of the Wesleyan Church.

I am also the product of a Baptist private education. Starting with kindergarten, my parents sent me to a Baptist school in a small town in rural Michigan. The school was begun by a congregation affiliated with the General Association of Regular Baptist Churches. To the list of "Thou shalt not's," the Regular Baptists added, among other things, going to the movies and listening to secular music.

Because both the Wesleyans and the Regular Baptists were on the far right end of the Christian theological spectrum, each viewed the other with suspicion. For example, at the time I began attending the school my mother was asked by members of my father's congregation, "Aren't you afraid Glen will grow up to be a little Baptist?" And members of the Baptist church questioned Wesleyan orthodoxy, since Wesleyans were permitted, even encouraged, to read something other than the King James Version of the Bible and were allowed to listen to secular music.

Despite their mutual suspicion, the two churches that shaped my religious upbringing had a lot in common. Both considered most Catholics to be non-Christian idolaters. Episcopalians, Methodists, Lutherans, Presbyterians, and Congregationalists were likewise presumed apostate. Occasionally a member of one of the foregoing could prove their orthodoxy by professing faith in Jesus and denouncing dancing, drinking, and the devil. Those who succeeded in convincing their Wesleyan or Baptist audience of their commitment to these tenets of the faith were then considered missionaries, infiltrating the ranks of the wayward denominations in order to bear witness to Christ and bring some to faith. It was assumed that when these "missionaries" did convert a Presbyterian or Lutheran to the true faith, they would encourage him or her to leave the mainline denomination and attend a Regular Baptist (or Wesleyan) church where they would be surrounded by "real" Christians. And the only reason one would have to consort with Hindus, Buddhists, Muslims, Jews, or atheists would be to convert them to fundamentalist Christianity.

I suppose my departure from this fundamentalist tradition began sometime during my undergraduate career at the University of Michigan, where I majored in philosophy. But the departure did not become self-conscious until my first year of graduate study in a master of divinity program at Gordon-Conwell Theological Seminary. The principal text assigned in the theology class I took in my first semester of divinity school was *Systematic Theology* by the nineteenth-century Princeton theologian Charles Hodge. After a steady diet of Hume as an undergraduate, Hodge's appropriation of Scottish Common Sense philosophy was entirely unpalatable, as was his rant against Darwinian science. I found myself staying up late into the night reading philosophy, attempting to satisfy my hunger for a style of arguing and thinking that was not readily available in the classroom. After the completion of my divinity degree, I continued my study of philosophy, first at Boston College, and then at the University of California, Riverside, during which time I continued my journey away from the religious culture of my youth.

What this journey involved was not a sudden, acrimonious rejection of religion or even of Christianity. The shift was gradual, from the fundamentalist right to the generically evangelical right, from there to the conservative end of the Presbyterian Church (USA), and then into the middle of the Presbyterian spectrum. This trajectory left behind a conception of religiosity defined largely in terms of prohibitions, exclusions, and the continuous conflict with evil. Because most of the changes were gradual, because fundamentalism in America was itself in flux,[1] and because my graduate education separated me geographically from my original, indoctrinating community, my departure from fundamentalist Christianity generated little controversy. It went largely unnoticed by most of those responsible for my initial indoctrination. And when it was noticed, the response it generated was loving and supportive, quite unlike the stereotyped responses we are led to expect in such circumstances. In that sense, my experience may be quite different from that of many: there was no yelling, no threat of excommunication, no ritual of separation.

Although I have rejected much of what I was taught, I shall attempt to offer a qualified defense of religious indoctrination against four common objections. The first argues that indoctrination is objectionable on the ground that it involves coercion or manipulation. The second insists that religious indoctrination involves teaching something that is rationally suspect. The third claims that indoctrination is inconsistent with autonomy, and the fourth that it is inconsistent with authenticity. I shall argue that while particular instances of indoctrination may be objectionable on one or more of these grounds, religious indoctrination per se is not. It need not involve coercion, manipulation, rational confusion, heteronomy, or inauthenticity. And even when it does involve one of these, I argue, it is not always objectionable.

Indoctrination, Coercion, and Manipulation

Indoctrination is often thought to involve one agent getting another to behave in ways the first approves.[2] There are a number of ways an agent might try to do this. They range from types of coercion on one end of the spectrum to types of invitation on the other, with attempts to manipulate or persuade falling in between. It is tempting to assume that all actions near the coercive end of the spectrum are morally objectionable, whereas those nearer the invitation end are morally exemplary. And there is something reasonable about this assumption. In its most obvious form, coercion is the use of force or the threat of force to compel another to act against her will.[3] Recently, Sarah Conly has argued that our understanding of coercion should not be restricted to physical force, but ought to include the use of emotional pressure as well.[4] What is shared by the physical force and the kinds of emotional pressure Conly has in mind is that they undercut the autonomy of the coerced. The resulting action is, in some sense, not her own. Insofar as the nearer an action gets to the coercive, the more it undercuts the autonomy of the agent, we have a reason to frown upon acts that are coercive.

However, undercutting autonomy is not always bad, all things considered. When I interpose myself between my eighteen-month-old daughter and the bright orange berries in the yard that have attracted her attention and tell her that if she puts those berries in her mouth I shall take her inside, I am coercing her. But in this circumstance, coercing her is not only appropriate but even praiseworthy. I would be remiss in my duties as a parent if I allowed her to disregard my (numerous) warnings and eat the enticing orange berries. Morally desirable instances of coercion are not restricted to parental encounters with children. It is a morally good thing, Hobbes argues, when the sovereign employs coercive force to get subjects to honor their contracts. Without such force, in fact, the benefits of a peaceful society could not be enjoyed.[5]

What is distinctive about the instances of good coercion just mentioned is that although overriding the autonomy of the coerced, it is not unresponsive to the value of that autonomy. My removing her from the vicinity of the orange berries is consistent with my daughter's other current or future desires. It aims to increase the scope of her autonomy in future (in this case by keeping her from becoming violently ill). The same cannot always be said for the contract violator the magistrate apprehends. While the magistrate's enforcement of certain laws is a necessary condition for the contract violator's enjoyment of certain liberties, including some of those that made possible this contract, it is hard to see his apprehension as promoting the scope of his future autonomy.[6] Even so, those laws and their enforcement value the autonomy of the agents who make up the commonwealth, including the contract violator, although the latter's autonomy is not given free rein in this instance.

If the foregoing is correct and coercion can be good, then it is conceivable that some instances of religious indoctrination, even coerced religious indoctrination, could be good. The case will be especially strong, if it can be shown that religious indoctrination can expand the scope of the agent's future autonomy.

However, religious indoctrination need not be coercive. Not all threats of sanction will count as coercive.[7] But more important, not all indoctrination need depend on the actual or threatened use of force. It may also proceed by the promise of future benefit. In some cases the role of such a promise may be persuasive, in other cases it will be manipulative. The incentives may be intrinsic to the religious doctrine, as, for example, the promise of heaven for those who faithfully worship God. Or they may be extrinsic, as when parents choose to attend a church with a large number of teenage girls in the hope that it will encourage their teenage son to attend.

If we only think of indoctrination in relation to coercion, we shall overlook several important dimensions of indoctrination. In part this is because indoctrination is not limited to how someone behaves. It also extends to the beliefs she holds and the things she cares about. As Locke noted in *A Letter Concerning Toleration*, coercion is not a terribly effective mechanism for belief formation.[8] So we should not be surprised to find that the most effective forms of indoctrination are not (or are not exclusively) coercive.

In a recent article on indoctrination and freedom of will, Gideon Yaffe defines indoctrination as "causing another person to respond to reasons in a pattern that serves the manipulator's ends."[9] His exemplar is David Koresh, whose aim was to build a following of persons who would give him large sums of money. He accomplished this aim by getting them to believe that he was more worthy than they to have this money because he was the Messiah.

I shall suggest that Yaffe's definition leaves out an important dimension of indoctrination. However, before offering an alternative, it is worth asking whether, even as Yaffe has defined it, indoctrination need be objectionable. In "The Problem with Manipulation," Patricia Greenspan offers a number of examples of "benign manipulation."[10] Among these she includes Tom Sawyer's successful attempt to get his friends to whitewash his aunt's fence by feigning enthusiasm for the chore, a teacher's attempt to generate interest in an introductory class by exuding an "uncritical enthusiasm" for her field, and a person trying to cheer up her melancholy friend by highlighting the good things that have happened to him lately. These cases possess two distinctive features. First, they do not involve "a failure of respect for [the other] as a reasoning agent."[11] Second, they pass what Annette Baier calls "the expressibility test." Were the manipulated to become aware of the manipulation after the fact, and of the manipulator's motives for acting as she did, it would not destroy his trust in her.[12] Nor would such awareness cause him to "regret the [social] exchange" that resulted from it.[13] Instances of indoctrination that meet these conditions, then, will be unobjectionable.

For the purposes of Yaffe's argument, concerned as it is with the relationship between manipulation, coercion, and free will, the definition of indoctrination as a kind of manipulation is adequate. He wishes to discuss one way of manipulating a person and to contrast it with a gun-to-the-head variety of coercion in order to explore how these kinds of cases affect the moral responsibility of the agents involved. The label "indoctrination" provides him with a handy way to refer to the first sort of case. However, if one's aim is to understand and assess indoctrination, per se, to define it in this way is already to begin on the wrong foot. First, it narrows the scope of what indoctrination involves in a way that ends up excluding most of the ways in which people are brought into doctrine. Second, it prejudges the case by attaching to indoctrination a label, namely, manipulation, that already makes it morally suspicious, even if not always objectionable.[14] If we wish to evaluate the activity that includes more ordinary cases of being brought into religious doctrine without prejudging its worth, we shall need another definition.

Indoctrination and Community

To this point we have been looking at indoctrination from the point of view of the indoctrinator. We have been thinking of it primarily as a type of action in which someone engages. Let us, for a moment, shift perspectives and analyze it from the point of view of the indoctrinated.

From the vantage of the indoctrinated, indoctrination involves being brought into doctrine. As such it involves acquiring some set of beliefs. But not just any acquisition of belief counts as indoctrination. A person walking alone in the wood who comes to believe that there are oak trees in the wood, or even that the wood is inhabited by the spirits of oak trees, is not undergoing indoctrination. For indoctrination to occur, another agent must be present, and one's beliefs must result, at least in part, from one's interactions with that agent. It is worth noting, however, that the presence of that agent need not be a physical presence. The indoctrinating encounter may take place through exposure to the agent's writings or their artwork. So perhaps the presence of the other agent should be put in scare quotes. That presence includes their person and the artifacts they have created.

It is tempting at this point to add a further condition, namely, that the other agent must intend for one to acquire those beliefs as a result of this interaction.[15] But this further condition adds both too little and too much. It adds too little insofar as an agent can act with the intention to form beliefs in another and succeed in this action without this amounting to indoctrination. For example, when I tell my students that David Hume was born on April 26, 1711, I intend for them to form a belief about his date of birth, and many of them do. So the presence of such an intentional act together with success in achieving its aim does not yet provide a sufficient condition for indoctrination.

The intentionality requirement adds too much insofar as such an intention is not a necessary feature of indoctrination. A significant part of indoctrination happens quite apart from anyone intending to produce beliefs in others. This is most noticeable when one considers the role of rituals in indoctrination. Indoctrination involves not just being brought to hold particular beliefs and values, but also being brought into a way of life and a community that identifies itself with these beliefs. Thus it involves holidays, rituals, and other formalized or semi-formal practices. When one gathers with others on these holidays and the rituals are observed, no one in the group need intend to produce beliefs in any of the others present. They may each gather with the sole intention of observing the rites, perhaps as an expression of their own religious affections, or as a way of communing with the group, or as a sign of their obedience to God. Those rituals may have originated in an intention to bring others into doctrine, but they needn't. They may have their origin in a spontaneous outflowing of religious affection or self-expression.

The picture of indoctrination that emerges from the vantage of the indoctrinated involves coming to behave in certain ways, hold certain beliefs, and care about certain values as a result of one's interactions with another agent. It also involves being brought into a community and its way of life. If this description captured everything that is distinctive about indoctrination, it would be hard to see why the term had acquired such negative connotations. Something further must be added to make sense out the objections. This further qualification is that one comes to hold these beliefs, values, and so on, through nonrational means.[16] At least some of one's beliefs, values, behaviors, and identifications must have come about through a mechanism other than hearing and responding to reasons.

Adding this nonrational element brings to the fore the principal ethical challenges to indoctrination. If the beliefs and values come to be held as a result of a nonrational mechanism, what is to guarantee that they are true? And even if they are, we don't just care what a person believes or values, how she behaves, and with whom she identifies. We also think it matters how she acquired those beliefs, values, behaviors, or identity.[17] Is her belief in a proposition or her endorsement of a value justified? Did she come to behave in those ways autonomously? Is her identity authentic? We noted above that neither coercion nor manipulation need be objectionable, provided they were responsive to the autonomy of the coerced or manipulated. But if beliefs, values, and so on that are acquired through coercive or manipulative indoctrination cannot be squared with autonomy because they undercut a necessary condition for autonomy, namely, rationality, then while coercion and manipulation can sometimes be defended, coercive and manipulative indoctrination cannot.

Thus three primary challenges to indoctrination emerge. First, it involves causing people to believe something that is false, confused, or in some other way rationally suspect. Second, it is inconsistent with autonomy. Third, it is inconsistent with authenticity.

Beliefs and Doctrines

Antony Flew and John Wilson build the mistakenness or irrationality of what is believed into their definition of indoctrination.[18] Tasos Kazepides' frequent contrast between "worthwhile knowledge" and doctrine, and his likening of indoctrination to exploitation and torture, disclose a similar assumption.[19] However, as this objection is often developed, it simply begs the question against the religious believer. Or it depends upon criteria of certainty or evidence that would preclude the teaching for belief in ethical, metaphysical, political, logical, and historical claims.[20] Further, the objection typically depends for its force on an exaggeratedly wooden and literalistic understanding of religious doctrines that fails to represent their full breadth and nature. It assumes what George Lindbeck and others have called a "propositionalist" picture of doctrine in which doctrines are assertions about the physical and metaphysical world. Such a picture leaves out at least two important alternatives.

For the "experiential-expressivist," doctrines are "symbols of inner feelings, attitudes, or existential orientations."[21] They provide a way of understanding and articulating certain dimensions of human experience, such as what Friedrich Schleiermacher called "religious affections," what William James called "a sense of reality, a feeling of objective presence," what Rudolf Otto called the feeling of "the numinous," and what Paul Tillich called "man's ultimate concern."[22] These kinds of experiences are widespread, if not universal, and religious doctrines provide a language for expressing and contemplating them.

A third approach to doctrine is the "cultural-linguistic" or "regulative" approach. According to the regulativist, religions provide "idioms for construing reality, expressing experience, and ordering life." Religious doctrines "help determine the vocabulary," semantics, and "syntactical rules that guide the use of this material in construing the world, community, and self." Doctrines determine which idioms, expressions, and orderings cohere with the rites, symbols, concepts, and stories of the religious community and which do not.[23]

What these alternatives mean is that even were it possible to mount a conclusive case to the effect that religious propositions were confused or could not be supported by rational arguments, this case would still fail to decide the matter. The expressivist and the regulativist would point out that the critic has misunderstood the fundamental nature of doctrine.[24] Indoctrination is not (or not exclusively) about believing propositions, the expressivist and regulativist would argue. It is about giving expression to certain kinds of experiences and identifying with particular communities and ways of life.

Indoctrination and Autonomy

A more compelling objection to indoctrination is that it undercuts an agent's autonomy. "The idea of autonomy is the idea of self-government. An autonomous political entity is one that is independent of external control; it manages its own affairs. Similarly, individuals are autonomous to the extent that they govern themselves."[25] We value autonomy. We consider it a necessary precondition for moral responsibility. So if indoctrination undercuts autonomy, it controverts one of our most cherished ideals and undermines the conditions needed for moral agency.

There are two cases to be made for the claim that indoctrination undermines autonomy. The first is built around the thought that autonomy involves choosing for oneself, whereas indoctrination prevents choosing for oneself. It is assumed that one is self-governed only when one's will is determined by the force of the available reasons. Since indoctrination involves coming to believe, behave, value, or self-identify through nonrational means, then one cannot have chosen these beliefs, behaviors, values, or identifications for oneself. Therefore, indoctrination undermines autonomy.

The second argument claims that indoctrination prevents people from developing the ability to choose for themselves. Beliefs we hold on the basis of an evaluation of evidence are open to rational revision. If the evidence changes, so will the belief. Beliefs that we hold on nonrational grounds, because they are not held on the basis of reason, resist correction even in the face of overwhelming evidence to the contrary. Thus, according to this line of argument, indoctrination undermines one's ability to revise one's position in light of the available evidence.[26]

The picture of human agency on which the first of these objections depends is overly rationalistic. If we accepted it, very few human actions would be deemed autonomous. As Wittgenstein, Gadamer, Mead, and numerous others have argued, we acquire many of our beliefs, values and "fundamental convictions . . . without rational weighing of grounds."[27] We arrive at them through our interactions with significant others, through the grammar of the language-games into which we have been initiated, through the landscape and horizons of the traditions we have inherited.[28] Being shaped by these languages and traditions is not just common, it is crucial. Without them we could not engage in the kind of rational assessment and weighing of evidence that the objector advances as the ideal mode of belief formation. In an oft-cited passage Wittgenstein observes, "I did not get my picture of the world by satisfying myself of its correctness; nor do I have it because I am satisfied of its correctness. No: it is the inherited background against which I distinguish between true and false."[29]

Not only is the weighing of reasons dependent upon beliefs and values that we have acquired through nonrational means, the choosing of actions is likewise dependent upon such beliefs and values. Our conception of choosing depends upon the experience not just of acting on our desires but of giving some of these greater sway than others. We endorse or identify with some of our desires and we reject others. We can do so in two different kinds of ways. We can engage in what Charles Taylor calls "weak evaluation," in which we look at the options in front of us and try to determine which of them we most feel like pursuing. This is the sort of choosing that takes place when we look at a restaurant menu and decide that we want the green curry rather than the Pad Thai. Weak evaluation is not the only kind of evaluation open to us. "Indeed, we might think of it as a necessary feature of the capacity to evaluate desires that one be able to distinguish the better one from the one that presses most strongly."[30] A second way that we choose involves "strong evaluation." In strong evaluation we assess which of our options is more worthy of our endorsement. In so doing we draw upon a sense of who we are and who we would like to become that, in turn, is shaped by the evaluative language, stories, heroes, and villains we have inherited from our tradition. It is the latter sort of choosing that is so important for autonomy, and it is only possible if one's lifeworld already contains a language for drawing normative distinctions. Thus, reasoning, evaluating, and choosing are made possible by beliefs and values that one acquired through a nonrational mechanism. Without the beliefs and values we have inherited from our tradition, we would fail to develop into autonomous agents in the first place.

Our answer to the first autonomy objection opens a way to address the second. Obviously if all of us first acquire beliefs, values, and the like through a nonrational mechanism, and if some of us are able rationally to revise some of these values and beliefs, then the fact that a belief or value has been acquired nonrationally does not mean that it is not open to rational revision. Further, the doctrines and texts of the historic religious traditions invite their practitioners to engage critically with the tradition in ways that will lead to revision of current practices and beliefs. They do so in a way that will cast a critical eye both on the old and on the new, and in this way can provide a corrective to reified aspects of the tradition as well as to current fads.[31]

At this point one might respond by suggesting that my defense of religious indoctrination depends upon my having helped myself to an overly broad definition of indoctrination. Some might be inclined to incorporate the undercutting of autonomy into the definition of indoctrination itself. There is nothing particularly objectionable about such a stipulation. But it lends itself to a certain kind of confusion. If we begin with such a definition, then we cannot directly begin talking about the objectionable nature of being brought into religious belief, because it must first be established that the latter involves coming via a nonrational mechanism to a belief that will not be open to revision.

A more pressing counterargument would grant that some of our beliefs, behaviors, values, and self-identifications must be acquired through nonrational mechanisms, but insist that once we have reached an age where we are capable of acquiring these things through rational discussion we are obliged to do so and others are obliged not to influence us in nonrational ways.[32] Such a claim would provide a nice explanation of why we find it objectionable when a sales pitch bypasses our capacity for reasonable reflection. It would also suggest that we have an obligation not to let ourselves get carried away by the political rhetoric that fills the airwaves at election time. Its ability to handle these two situations gives it a significant degree of plausibility. Nonetheless, I think it mislocates the problem.

It is not the case that we cease to acquire beliefs and values through mechanisms other than the weighing of evidence and assessing of reasons after we acquire the ability to perform the latter.[33] Nor is it clear that we should. "Everybody's doing it" may not justify joining in, but from the point of view of evolutionary biology it is good that we are inclined to do so. The same is true for the ways in which we respond to scarcity and the trappings of authority.[34] Further, our ability to choose the proper course of action merely by employing our capacity for rational belief formation is notoriously inadequate, which is why people who teach test-taking skills encourage students as a general rule to go with their first answer to a question. If they attempt to reason it through, they are just as likely to talk themselves into a wrong answer as they are to land upon the right one. The inadequacy of our rational capacity to guide our actions was part of what led Rousseau to encourage the maintenance of a civil religion.

> The wise men who want to speak to the common masses in the former's own language rather than in the common vernacular cannot be understood by the masses. For there are a thousand kinds of ideas that are impossible to translate in the language of the populace. Overly general perspectives and overly distant objects are equally beyond its grasp. Each individual, in having no appreciation for any other plan of government but the one that relates to his own private interest, finds it difficult to realize the advantages he ought to draw from the continual privations that good laws impose.[35]

Of course, others can take advantage of these tendencies. But this observation points us toward a different principle to explain what is morally troubling about sales pitches and political rhetoric. What makes the latter troubling is that, ordinarily, it promotes an end that diverges from our best interests. And this divergence is not merely an accident. Typically, our best interests would not appear among the concerns that led the salesperson or the politician to act as she did. Thus, we ought not to trust such individuals, which requires a greater skepticism on our part. In circumstances where we have reason not to trust the other and where something important is in the offing, we have an obligation to be more vigilant and to hold ourselves to a different standard of belief and value formation than we do under friendlier circumstances.

Indoctrination and Authenticity

Even if indoctrination does not lead to someone else literally choosing one's actions in one's place, thus undermining autonomy, one might worry that it does so in a figurative way. The beliefs, behaviors, values, and self-identifications one has come to through indoctrination are the beliefs, behaviors, values, and identifications of others, be they parents, priests, rabbis, or imams. As such they are someone else's beliefs and values, rather than one's own. They are inauthentic.

One response to this objection would be to reject the notion of authenticity altogether. Our discussion of the ways in which our abilities to reason, value, and choose are necessarily grounded in traditions and acquired through nonrational mechanisms might be taken to support such a response. It is not clear whether the agents who create their own values, mold their own behaviors, and craft their own identities *ex nihilo* are gods or monsters. But it is clear that they aren't human. Creatures like us engage in these activities by drawing on a stock of ideals and ways of life that we have inherited. Nonetheless, to reject the ideal of authenticity entirely would be too hasty.

The notion of authenticity gains both its sense and its attractiveness by contrast with a familiar character type.[36] It is the character of the mindless follower. Mindless followers do what is popular among those around them, or among an authoritative or charismatic subset of those around them, more or less without thinking. This following extends from the style of clothing they wear and the athletic team they support to the highest moral and political ideals they espouse. And they remain comfortably oblivious to the conflicts that exist between some of their values, beliefs, and behaviors. What results are lives of unnoticed contradictions, more or less identical to the lives of those around them. These are lives to which, from the outside, it is difficult to ascribe agency because they seem so thoroughly conformist and entirely predictable. The critic is right to suggest that this kind of inauthentic existence could not take place apart from indoctrination. It is just that the desirable kind of life to which this caricature stands in contrast could not take place without it either.

It is important to notice that the ideas around which the caricature of inauthenticity is built do not all carry the same weight. The notions of predictability and originality, for example, have a penchant to mislead. This confusion is especially evident in the angst of teenage rebellion, but it can be found in older and wiser heads as well. Agents who were truly unpredictable would not be heroic, they would be horrific. Our day-to-day interactions depend upon our ability to predict the actions of others, and it is on account of our ability to do so that we ascribe rationality to them.[37] When we encounter someone who is truly unpredictable, we are unable to interact with them and are forced to treat them not as agents but as aberrations from whom we seek to insulate ourselves, often by removing them from society. Likewise, actions which were truly original, truly unprecedented, would remain opaque to us. We would be unable to understand or appreciate them. Again, it would be difficult for us to see them as the result of reason or agency, rather than as a consequence of malignant physiology.

What, then, do we look for in persons who are not inauthentic? We look for individuals who have taken a certain kind of ownership of their lives. They have endorsed certain values as more important in their lives than others, and they resist influences that would subordinate higher values to lower ones. This resistance will include a rejection of the movement of the masses when it is out of step with the values they have endorsed as highest. Either that or it will require a revision of their value rankings.

Ordinarily their departure from the movements of the masses will happen for one of two reasons. Either they will recognize a conflict between current practice and the values of the tradition with which they identify or they will have been socialized into a different tradition. The former is what takes place when the prophets of Israel upbraid the people for ignoring the plight of the most vulnerable in their society, namely, the widows, orphans, and strangers in their midst. The philosophy student who rejects what are offered as reasons to support a marriage amendment by the community in which he was raised exemplifies the latter.

There are two strands in the ideal of authenticity that emerge at this point. According to one, the ideal of authenticity does not stipulate the conclusion the "authentic" individual will reach when confronted with a conflict in values. Rather, it requires that whatever way they end up going, they do so self-consciously.[38] They become aware of the contradiction, and they do not resolve it by ignoring it. They resolve it by seeking greater clarity regarding the values they hold and the sort of persons they take themselves to be. As a result, they are not seen as passive, as merely going along with the crowd, even though the values on which they draw in the process of clarification were acquired nonrationally from the tradition and even if the values they end up endorsing are the values of their contemporaries. According to the other strand, authenticity is incompatible with "false consciousness." It requires an orientation to the ideal of human flourishing. According to the second, since it is possible to be both self-conscious about one's values and deluded about what leads to human flourishing, one can be both self-conscious and inauthentic. According to the first, one is authentic merely by taking ownership of one's values, so one may be simultaneously authentic and a fool.

If we adopt the former understanding of authenticity, there are practices within many of the religious traditions that work to combat the thoughtless adoption of values and identities and thus work to promote authenticity. This is part of the function of confirmation and first communion in mainline Protestant and Catholic traditions, baptisms and testimonies in Anabaptist traditions, bar and bat mitzvahs in various Jewish traditions. It plays a significant role in the development of the notion of a vocation or a divine calling, especially in the nineteenth and twentieth centuries.

If we adopt the latter understanding of authenticity, then it is an open question whether religious indoctrination is compatible with authenticity. It depends on the adequacy of the conception of human flourishing in question. Obviously this is not something we can decide a priori. Or if we can decide it, the decision will be presumptively in their favor. For any position which a thoughtful person upon reflection advances as true is likely to be true at least in part.[39] Taylor points out that the case is even stronger in the case of traditions than it is in the case of individuals: "It is reasonable to suppose that cultures that have provided the horizon of meaning for large numbers of human beings, of diverse characters and temperaments, over a long period of time—that have, in other words, articulated their sense of the good, the holy, the admirable—are almost certain to have something that deserves our admiration and respect, even if it is accompanied by much that we have to abhor and reject."[40]

This supposition may prove wrong. Or what the tradition gets right may be so intertwined with values and ideas that we find confused or perverse that in the end we give up trying to extract them. But as a starting point there is a presumption in favor of the compatibility of indoctrination and authenticity.

Conclusion

The upshot of the foregoing argument is that religious indoctrination per se is not objectionable, at least not for the reasons commonly marshaled against it. It need not involve false, confused, or otherwise rationally suspicious beliefs. It need not involve manipulation or coercion, and even when it does that need not make it morally objectionable. It need not undermine autonomy. Nor is it inconsistent with authenticity.

Of course, that is not to say religious indoctrination is never objectionable. On the contrary, I have suggested two criteria for determining when religious indoctrination is morally objectionable. It is objectionable when it is inconsistent with the autonomy of the indoctrinated. It is also objectionable when it violates the conditions of trust the indoctrinated assumed held between herself and the indoctrinator(s). But quite often religious indoctrination will be compatible with trust and autonomy and will even foster them. Thus, rather than viewing religious indoctrination as suspicious until proven innocent, I have suggested we ought to presume it innocent until or unless, on particular occasions, it is shown to subvert autonomy and trust.

NOTES

1. For example, whereas my grandparents would have identified themselves as fundamentalists, my parents would now identify themselves as evangelicals. And many of the activities that would have been prohibited in my grandparents' generation and even in my own childhood (like dancing) are no longer tests of orthodoxy for Wesleyans.

2. Gideon Yaffe, "Indoctrination, Coercion, and Freedom of Will," *Philosophy and Phenomenological Research* 67 (September 2003): 340–41.

3. "Coercion occurs if one party deliberately and successfully uses force or a credible threat of unwanted, avoidable, and serious harm in order to compel a particular response from another person." Tom Beauchamp, "Manipulative Advertising," *Business and Professional Ethics Journal* 3 (Spring–Summer 1984): 4.

4. Sarah Conly, "Seduction, Rape, and Coercion," *Ethics* 115 (October 2004): 96–121.

5. Thomas Hobbes, *Leviathan* (1668), ed. Edwin Curley (Indianapolis: Hackett, 1994), chaps. 14 and 15.

6. Although Kant and Seneca show that it may not be impossible to see it in these terms.

7. For example, the university administrator who tells students they will not be allowed to attend classes or take exams unless they are clothed at the time they sit the exam or attend the class is threatening a sanction (removal from class) but does not appear to be coercing her students.

8. John Locke, *A Letter Concerning Toleration* (1689), ed. James Tully (Indianapolis: Hackett, 1983), 27 and 46.

9. Yaffe, "Indoctrination, Coercion, and Freedom of Will," 335.

10. Patricia Greenspan, "The Problem with Manipulation," *American Philosophical Quarterly* 40 (April 2003): 155–64.

11. Ibid., 159.

12. Annette Baier, "Trust and Antitrust," *Ethics* 96 (1986): 231–60; reprinted in *Ethics and Personality: Essays in Moral Psychology*, ed. John Deigh (Chicago: University of Chicago Press, 1992), 11–40, esp. 33–38.

13. Greenspan, "The Problem with Manipulation," 161.

14. Of course, "indoctrination" itself carries a pejorative connotation. But this is the very thing I intend to challenge. As Mary Anne Raywid observes, this connotation is comparatively recent. Prior to the 1920s, "indoctrinating" was generally taken to be synonymous with "teaching." "The Discovery and Rejection of Indoctrination," *Educational Theory* 30 (1980): 1–10.

15. R. M. Hare, "Adolescents into Adults," *Aims in Education: The Philosophic Approach* (Manchester: Manchester University Press, 1964), 47–70; Ivan Snook, *Indoctrination and Education* (Boston: Routledge and Kegan Paul, 1972), 46–67.

16. C. J. B. Macmillan, "*On Certainty* and Indoctrination," *Synthese* 56 (1983): 369–70; James W. Garrison, "The Paradox of Indoctrination: A Solution," *Synthese* 68 (1986): 263–64.

17. Perhaps this concern stands behind Tasos Kazepides' tendency to define indoctrination in contrast with ways in which students come to knowledge and understanding. Kazepides,

"Socialization, Initiation, and Indoctrination," *Philosophy of Education* (1982): 309–18, and "Indoctrination, Doctrines, and the Foundations of Rationality," *Philosophy of Education* (1987): 229–40.

18. Antony Flew, "What Is Indoctrination?" *Studies in Philosophy and Education* 4.3 (1966): 281–306; John Wilson, "Education and Indoctrination," in *Aims in Education: The Philosophic Approach*, ed. T. H. B. Hollins (Manchester: Manchester University Press, 1964), 24–46.

19. Kazepides, "Socialization, Initiation, and Indoctrination," 311 and 314, as well as "Indoctrination, Doctrines, and the Foundations of Rationality," 230.

20. Hare, "Adolescents into Adults," 48–50, 53–54.

21. George Lindbeck, *The Nature of Doctrine: Religion and Theology in a Postliberal Age* (Philadelphia: Westminster Press, 1984), 16.

22. Friedrich Schleiermacher, *The Christian Faith* (1830), ed. H. R. Mackintosh and J. S. Stewart (Edinburgh: T&T Clark, 1999), 76–78; William James, *Varieties of Religious Experience* (1902), in *William James: Writings, 1902–1910* (New York: Library of America, 1987), 59; Rudolf Otto, *The Idea of the Holy* (New York: Oxford University Press, 1923), 10–11; Paul Tillich, *Systematic Theology* (Chicago: Chicago University Press, 1967), 211.

23. Lindbeck, *Nature of Doctrine*, 47–48, 80–81.

24. In a generally careful and well-argued article, Michael Hand dismisses this response on the ground that nonpropositional interpretations of religious speech "are quite unrecognisable to those who actually hold religious beliefs" and are thus not even "remotely plausible." Hand, "A Philosophical Objection to Faith Schools," *Theory and Research in Education* 1.1 (2003): 94. Were he primarily concerned with Southern Baptists or the Assemblies of God, such a claim might make sense. But insofar as his argument is directed at the Church of England and the Catholic Church, it is quite bewildering. Regulativist and expressivist approaches to doctrine are quite widespread in Anglican and Catholic circles, as well as within Presbyterian, Methodist, Lutheran, and Congregational churches, to name just a few. And they are the dominant approaches to doctrine among Reformed Jewish communities.

25. Harry Frankfurt, "Autonomy, Necessity, and Love," in *Necessity, Volition, and Love* (Cambridge: Cambridge University Press, 1999), 131.

26. Wilson, "Education and Indoctrination," 27–29; Hare, "Adolescents into Adults," 51–54; Hand, "Philosophical Objection," 95.

27. Macmillan, "On Certainty and Indoctrination," 370.

28. George Herbert Mead, *Mind, Self, and Society* (Chicago: University of Chicago Press, 1934), 135–64; Ludwig Wittgenstein, *On Certainty*, trans. Denis Paul and G. E. M. Anscombe (Oxford: Blackwell, 1969), 34, 94, 139–56; Hans-Georg Gadamer, *Truth and Method*, 2nd rev. ed., trans. Joel Weinsheimer and Donald Marshall (New York: Continuum, 1989) 302–7; Charles Taylor, *The Ethics of Authenticity* (Cambridge: Harvard University Press, 1991), 32–41.

29. Wittgenstein, *On Certainty*, 94.

30. Charles Taylor, "What Is Human Agency?" *Human Agency and Language: Philosophical Papers 1* (New York: Cambridge University Press, 1985), 28.

31. Given the fundamental role played by sacred *texts* in Judaism, Christianity, and Islam, one could argue that some degree of critical reflection and rational revision is inevitable within these traditions simply by virtue of the need to (a) interpret the texts and (b) decide upon their relevance to the religious practitioners' current circumstances. John Kelsay advances such an argument in the context of Islam in "Democratic Virtue, Comparative Ethics, and Contemporary Islam," *Journal of Religious Ethics* 33 (2005): 697–707. Francis Schüssler Fiorenza and David Tracy do so in the context of Christianity in Schüssler Fiorenza, "The Church as a Community of Interpretation: Political Theology Between Discourse Ethics and Hermeneutical Reconstruction," in *Habermas, Modernity, and Public Theology*, ed. Dan Browning and Francis Schüssler Fiorenza (New York: Crossroad Publishing, 1992), 66–91, and Tracy, *Blessed Rage for Order* (Chicago: University of Chicago Press, 1996). The claim that these traditions invite critical engagement and the rational revision of belief is reinforced by the *contents* of these texts. This sort of engagement is modeled in, among other places, the prophetic tradition in Jewish scripture. It is prominent in the "You have heard it said . . . but I say" sequence in the

Sermon on the Mount and also plays a significant role in the parables of the Gospels. For an argument regarding the self-critical nature of the parables, see Rowan Williams, "The Judgment of the World," in *On Christian Theology* (Oxford: Blackwell Publishing, 2000), 29–43. Even a verse like Sura 3:7 in the Qur'an, which is sometimes cited as a justification for unquestioning belief, has a long tradition of encouraging debate and revision as a result of the distinction it draws between verses with "definite" meanings and those with "ambiguous" or "allegorical" meanings. Finally, Hans Georg Gadamer and Seyla Benhabib have argued that it is in the very nature of these religious traditions as *traditions* that they are open to critical reflection and the revision of their constituent values, beliefs, and actions. See Gadamer, *Truth and Method*, 373–79, and Seyla Benhabib, *The Claims of Culture: Equality and Diversity in the Global Era* (Princeton: Princeton University Press, 2002), chap. 1. Of course, none of these arguments guarantees that any particular indoctrinating community will encourage critical reflection and rational belief revision. As many of the other chapters in this collection make painfully clear, some indoctrinating communities discourage such reflection. My point is simply that the resources for reflection and revision are present within each of these historical religious traditions. Thus, one might be indoctrinated into any one of them and *precisely as a result of this indoctrination* be equipped with the tools and temperament needed to engage in the kind of reflection the critic deems crucial.

32. Wilson, "Education and Indoctrination," 29.

33. Robert Cialdini, "The Science of Persuasion," *Scientific American* (February 2001): 76–81.

34. Insoo Hyun, "Authentic Values and Individual Autonomy," *Journal of Value Inquiry* 35 (2001): 198–99.

35. Jean-Jacques Rousseau, *On the Social Contract* (1762), in *Basic Political Writings*, trans. Donald Cress (Indianapolis: Hackett, 1987), 164.

36. On the primacy of "inauthentic" for our understanding of "authentic," see Theodor Adorno, *The Jargon of Authenticity*, trans. Knut Tarnowski and Frederic Will (Evanston: Northwestern University Press, 1973), 7–8.

37. David Hume, *A Treatise of Human Nature* (1739–40), ed. David Fate and Mary J. Norton (New York: Oxford University Press, 2000), bk. 2, pt. 3, sec. 1, pars. 13–15.

38. This account of authenticity is similar to what Robert Young calls "global autonomy." Young, "Autonomy and Socialization," *Mind* 89 (October 1980): 566–67.

39. For a defense of this claim, see Mill, *On Liberty* (1859), in *On Liberty and Other Essays*, ed. John Gray (New York: Oxford University Press, 1991), 51–54.

40. Charles Taylor, "The Politics of Recognition," in *Multiculturalism: Examining the Politics of Recognition*, ed. Amy Gutmann (Princeton: Princeton University Press, 1994), 72. In a similar passage, Mill observes, "The traditions and customs of other people are, to a certain extent, evidence of what their experience has taught them; presumptive evidence, and as such, have a claim to his deference." Mill, *On Liberty*, 65.

PART 3

EMBODIMENT, FAMILY, AND CONFLICT

8

FROM REVELATION AND FAITH TO REASON AND AGNOSTICISM

Paul H. Hirst

The Formation of Faith: Upbringing and Schooling

I was born in 1927, the second child of a young couple who had recently joined a small group of some thirty fundamentalist Christians meeting regularly in an upper room in the center of an industrial town in the north of England. The group, referred to as a "Meeting" of the Glanton Brethren, was a strict and exclusive subgroup of the so-called Plymouth Brethren, who had broken away from the Church of England in the mid-nineteenth century seeking to be true to the teaching of the New Testament in all matters concerning personal salvation, the ordering of Christian living, and the conduct of Christian worship. The Meeting dominated my parents' life, as my father considered he had at last, after several years of searching, found a group of Christians totally committed to the teaching of Scripture as originally given to its writers by direct divine inspiration.

Both my parents had grown up within a branch of the Christadelphians, a sect with much the same ideals as the Plymouth Brethren but whose denial of the full deity of Christ my father had come to consider a gross doctrinal error. At grammar school he had taken readily to the study of both French and Latin, and this strong interest in languages led on his leaving school to take a job as a clerk in the office of a firm of cloth exporters. It led too to his evening study of other European languages for commercial letter writing while at work, and to his privately learning Greek, so that with his knowledge of Latin he could read the major texts behind the then almost universally used King James English translation of the Bible. By his early twenties this Bible study led him to seek a Christian denomination whose teaching and practice adhered more strictly to his personal interpretation of the New

Testament than that of the Christadelphians. He found what he was looking for among the Glanton Brethren, a loose confederation of Meetings whose activities of Bible study, preaching, extemporaneous prayer, and worship were organized and conducted by all the male members of the group under the leadership of the more senior "brothers." The teachings of the confederation were those set out primarily in the writings of a scholarly Anglican cleric, John Nelson Darby, who had eventually left the Church of England.

An able student, my father when still young soon became a prominent member of the local Glanton Meeting, having embarked on a pattern of life in which he henceforth devoted nearly all his nonworking time to personal Bible study, the Meetings, and the support of less able and fortunate members of that community. The interpretation of biblical teaching to which he became passionately devoted saw the whole of God's creation as deeply corrupted, infected by evil and sin, and destined for final destruction. Personal salvation for individual human beings as unique spiritual entities had been made possible through the incarnation, life, and sacrificial death of Christ, and was available only by the grace of God to those who repented from their sinful, natural lives, trusting for their salvation only in God's free grace. Under God's grace they could then come to see that they must give their lives above all to the spiritual service of God in obedience to his teaching as set out in the New Testament. The Old Testament was understood as outlining the dealings of God with his creation preparatory to the incarnation of Christ, and was therefore regarded as indicative of what was to come.

My father then sought to live as completely as he possibly could as a "redeemed" spiritual being, the conduct of his own life and that of his family following strictly the commands and teaching of the New Testament. He considered he should live as "in the world but not of it," seeking to witness to the gospel of redemption while seeing the whole of the material world and all human social, political, and cultural activities as ruined by sin, to be engaged with only in so far as one's spiritual activities made that necessary. He saw having a family as an ordained part of God's order, which required human lives as redeemed beings for his ultimate spiritual new creation. In keeping with this view my father had the lowest level of job that would provide him and his family with the means to live simply and responsibly while devoting themselves to the demands of their spiritual lives. He saw all participation or advancement in education, a career or any social community other than the Meeting—seen as an expression of the true church and the Body of Christ—to be justified only as promoting spiritual development, and otherwise as an undesirable involvement in the life of a fallen world. He considered certain elements of education to be directly necessary for any deep understanding of spiritual truths. All other forms of knowledge and understanding he saw as incredible insights into God's amazing power and glory, but when pursued for their own sake by sinful men as full of error and inherently liable to corrupt those who pursued them.

This view of life both implicitly and then increasingly explicitly shaped almost the whole of my existence from my birth until I literally left home at seventeen to go to university. I had a sister only seventeen months older than me, but she figured little in my life except as the only readily available child model for me to emulate. My father was clearly the head of the household in all matters, and I accepted until well into my teens that his decisions had an indisputable authority over the whole of our lives. He delegated all responsibility for the running of the home and the nonreligious activities of us children within a specified financial budget to my mother, though she would defer to my father on matters where she was uncertain what was to happen. He had almost nothing to do with his children directly except by way of our religious activities and matters of strict discipline and severe punishment. For major misdemeanors I was of course spanked and later, until I was fifteen, beaten or strapped. My model sister needed no such punishment. I can recall no occasions when my father looked after me personally, ever played with me, ever took me individually anywhere other than to Meetings, or showed me any affection in any way whatever. Indeed, affection figured hardly at all in my relationship with my parents or anyone else in my life until well after I left home. Apart from the odd peck on the cheek that my father gave my mother when leaving her for an away preaching visit, I recall no show of affection at home. Love and affection, it was made quite clear, were to be understood as the doing and wanting to do of whatever was right and good. They had nothing to do with feelings or emotions, which in any case should have no place in our daily lives. Just occasionally some limited expression of emotion seemed to be acceptable during prayer or preaching at a Meeting.

I was looked after quite adequately in all basic ways though there were no luxuries of any kind. Money was always very tight and must never ever be wasted or spent on matters of self indulgence. There were a few toys, simple games, and suitable children's books. Reading was encouraged along with being resourceful in making things. I never felt in danger or insecure and indeed was extremely overprotected, being allowed only strictly necessary out of school-hours contact with other pupils at my local state-run schools and with a few neighborhood friends at home. There was very little "play." All children and adults outside the Meeting were clearly a danger with whom contact should be minimal and carefully supervised. Just why this was so one simply picked up like everything else, as part of the demand of living as God wished in a sinful world. That we were privileged to understand this was made very clear. There being no other children of my age in our Meeting, I was an extremely isolated child, and felt that all the more so after age five, when I became seriously ill for several months with diphtheria and following complications. I had to spend many weeks in solitary confinement in an isolation hospital, seeing my parents rarely, and only through a glass door, before eventually returning home to a long convalescence and the ordeal of learning to walk again. Life as a young child always seemed difficult, significantly different from that of others at school and around home, only rarely joyful or happy. It was full of external controls for reasons I was told and expected to accept. That my parents might often be displeased with me seemed inevitable and something I must accept as a sinful child in an evil world.

Yet there were windows that from time to time opened briefly onto a different world. My maternal grandmother, from a family with a successful small business, had been to a newly established teachers' training college, had married the owner of a local shop, and with a resident housekeeper had taught school while bringing up seven children. By the time I really became aware of her my grandmother was widowed, still teaching, and still living locally with the housekeeper. All her children, apart from my mother, had left home to go to university and thereafter lived far away though two came back to live with her for longish spells, and others came back from time to time on brief visits. Though brought up as Christadelphians, all of these relatives but my grandmother and one son had severed all connection with religious beliefs and practices. That my father disapproved of all these relatives, and our having much contact with them, was axiomatic in our lives, but my mother took me and my sister to visit her mother from time to time and particularly when one or more other relatives might be there. Just occasionally too an aunt would even visit us for an afternoon bringing sweets and presents, delights we otherwise never came across except at Christmas and on birthdays. I understood that, by and large, these relatives, their children, and all my father's family belonged to a world that had nothing to do with us. I learnt very early that though there might seem to be much of interest in their lives it was of only transient, superficial value and not for those who understood the ultimately serious purposes of life. Nevertheless, they were interested in music, literature, art and travel; and it was not completely obvious to me why these could not be part of our lives except that we lacked the necessary finance.

Music, however, did become a distinct permitted window into another world. Both my parents had learned to play the piano as children. From somewhere they had on marriage acquired a piano, and though my father in my hearing never played anything but hymns, my mother played some of the simpler piano classics, and my sister and I from the age of seven had piano lessons with a Christadelphian lady. This, in part presumably for being a quite individual pursuit with little associated worldliness, was allowed us as our only major form of relaxation, and it became for me in my teens a very slowly increasing link to the world of secular pursuits and symbolic of other possibilities.

With little by way of other nonreligious activities available to me, I not surprisingly, even as a quite small child, found schoolwork more interesting than almost anything else in my life. I was reasonably good at most of the things that went on at school; and if not overly encouraged by my parents, I there found pursuits that gave me some sense of achievement and satisfaction. I easily passed the tests to enter the local boys' grammar school at eleven, and though I had nothing of my father's flair for languages I took quite readily to the sciences and mathematics. From the age of fourteen I was therefore encouraged by the school to drop all other subjects of study but physics, pure and applied mathematics, and subsidiary English, the last being necessary for the examinations that might get me to a university. The school had a tradition for excellent teaching in mathematics; and there I came under the tuition of a brilliant schoolmaster, who by the time I was seventeen had prepared me sufficiently well for me to gain early entry to Trinity College, Cambridge, with enough in scholarships to cover all the costs for my studying mathematics there.

During my time at grammar school my father did nothing to overtly encourage or discourage me from the desire the school explicitly built up in me that I should in due time go to Cambridge. My sister, with a flair for languages, had similarly made her way before me to study French at university. But our home throughout remained a stern training ground in religious devotion. We had no books in the house but those for my father's biblical and linguistic studies plus a few works of reference and the works of Shakespeare. We brought home, solely for our temporary use, school books in our areas of study. We used our school libraries and the local public library a little, but with no encouragement from our parents for wider reading. Until two years into World War II, when I was fourteen, we had no radio, and it was for the next two years used only for listening to the news. Around the same time we first had a daily paper, which my father took with him to work and which we were never encouraged to read. Apart from school and domestic activities, religious activities were the dominating concern of the whole of life, with much piano practice and, for my sister, sports at school, the only significant diversions.

Throughout all this period in matters of religious beliefs and moral teaching and practice I was acquiescent in all that the whole context of my life instilled in me. My respect for my father's careful study of the Scriptures, his scholarly knowledge, and concern for seeking the truth was unquestioning. He became an accomplished and highly regarded speaker in nearby Glanton Meetings. His pastoral devotion to the congregation of our own Meeting, of which he was now the "leading brother," was unsparing. He was a man of stern faith and discipline and complete moral integrity. I simply had neither grounds nor the will to seriously question the position he took, which was overtly contradicted by little that came my way at school or at home, though I realized that it was extremely narrow in its outlook. Asking about the future salvation of my aunts, uncles, and cousins, of my greatly admired mathematics teacher, and of the many other seemingly kind and good adults I came across, I was able to accept with only minimal questioning that "God would righteously judge them according to their response to His gospel." It was forcefully made clear that it was my responsibility to see to my own commitment to the truth and to bear witness to it as and when that was appropriate. I increasingly looked forward to my leaving home for university, with a firm desire to use my freedom to carefully explore the wider world for myself, but I was in no way wishing to explicitly rebel against anything I had absorbed of the faith of my parents.

The seeds of serious philosophical questioning were, however, being sown in my mind. My mathematics teacher had conveyed to me something of his wonder and delight in the achievements of mathematics and of the enormous power of truths once established by mathematical proof. He also made me only too aware of the crucial difference between the grounding of mathematical truths and that of the empirical truths of the physical sciences. What then, I slowly began to wonder, could be the equivalent basis of the truths of religious beliefs about God as set out in the Bible? The confident claim of the Bible to truth by revelation I sensed was strangely circular, and much of the teaching to be distinctly not empirically testable as in the sciences. Somewhere I thought someone must have sorted all this business out when

Christianity was manifestly full of the most excellent practical moral teaching and in some form or other accepted by so many of the world's greatest thinkers. That I would find answers to these questions while at university I felt pretty confident.

There was one other unresolved and not insignificant matter privately tucked away in my mind that I also wanted to get sorted out. At thirteen I had no clear understanding of sex from what I had picked up from the Bible and from the odd biology lesson I had had at school. Nothing at all had ever been mentioned about sex at home. Then out of the blue we were suddenly visited at home one Saturday afternoon by an aunt from far away and her son of sixteen, whom I had never met before. While our parents chatted, he to my amazement and alarm took me into the bathroom, locked the door, and proceeded to masturbate while giving me a graphic crash course in sex education. In inner turmoil on my part we then joined our parents for tea before away the visitors went. From that day I started my own private active and enjoyable sex life, determined to find out quite secretly all I could about this whole new world. Biblical teaching about sex seemed brief and obviously against all sex outside marriage. But why my own solo activities might be wrong seemed curious, particularly as my cousin had said they did no harm to him or anybody else. No way was I going to forgo them in a hurry, and I didn't feel particularly guilty about them either. But here for sure was another dilemma of at least a strange kind that also needed sorting out.

The Transformation of Beliefs: Philosophy and University Life

When I arrived in Cambridge in 1945, I knew only three other people there, all having already spent one or two years at the University. Two were from my old school, but I was to see very little of them. The third was from the Glanton Brethren, and I had met him at a conference for Glanton young people a year earlier. The guidance of this other "brother" was to be significant in introducing me to Cambridge life, though he was from another College in the University and clearly did not want me around too much. Above all right at the start of my new life he took me to the Glanton Meeting in Cambridge to anchor me there and also to meetings of the evangelical Christian Union of the University. At the Christian Union I was immediately welcomed into an impressively large community of extremely able and mostly older students studying every major university discipline, yet meeting for daily extemporaneous prayer and for regular Bible study of just the sort the Glanton

Brethren engaged in. Any idea that I might find myself lost in an alien society was soon gone, and in the circles I began to move in the faith I brought with me from home was nowhere under any serious overt challenge.

I was of course shaken to discover the extreme narrowness of my own background intellectually, culturally, and socially, so I immediately set about trying to remedy that, particularly as in my first year I had little difficulty with any of the areas of mathematics that formed the whole of my official studies. I had little or no money, but using the many available libraries I started to privately read widely in the classics of English literature, in history, but above all now for the first time in philosophy. Bertrand Russell was in residence in my College and lecturing regularly to huge audiences. His *Problems of Philosophy* and, soon, his *History of Western Philosophy* were in the bookshops and were a provocative stimulus to my solitary efforts. I also started reading in the philosophy of mathematics and logic. But it was A. J. Ayer's *Language, Truth and Logic* that directly challenged me to think hard for the first time about the relationship between meaning and truth, for the book said much that seemed to me manifestly quite right about the sciences while being equally obviously mistaken in its attack on all religious claims as meaningless, and moral principles as mere expressions of emotion. The "verifiability principle" of his Logical Positivism—that "the meaning of a proposition lies in the method of its verification"—I thought brilliantly clear, but why then should one not expect religious beliefs and moral principles to be perhaps different but parallel forms of at least putative propositional understanding, alongside the well-established domains of science and mathematics? They might even be closely related to each other in a parallel fashion to the relationship between science and mathematics. Just how moral or religious truths might be "verified," however, I had no clear idea, though I hoped surely to get much nearer to the answers in due course.

In my following two years at Cambridge I read much in theology that made me take a much more liberal view of biblical interpretation, accepting that some biblical writings must be read analogically and some be seen as expressing spiritual and moral truths in ways applicable only in their original social contexts. But I was no nearer to finding the spiritual experience or philosophical understanding of religious concepts that might ground my beliefs more adequately. My readings in moral philosophy led me to flirt for a time with utilitarianism and then the intuitionism of Moore's *Principia Ethica*. But I found neither provided an account of moral truths that satisfied me. I might have gotten much further much faster in my intellectual explorations had I had the guidance and help of others asking the same philosophical questions, but found none among the few strongly evangelical, music-loving, and mathematical friends I made. I became aware at this time though that the religious and moral influences of my upbringing and education had left me emotionally very repressed, compared with others, in that I was not personally as concerned as they were about moral and social issues. I entered into no close personal relationships of any kind that might have disturbed or challenged me. I did begin to wonder a little about my sexual orientation, but I felt secure in my pattern of life, and was able to stay happily among the Glanton Brethren even if slowly my acceptance of their teaching was thinning out on intellectual grounds.

After university I went immediately into six years of school teaching, teaching mathematics to sixteen- to eighteen-year-olds, with two terms in the middle back at Cambridge, officially to obtain a professional qualification in education. In my circumstances I could again use much of my time at university, if only for a relatively brief spell, for much more intense philosophical exploration, which ended in my starting part-time doctoral research into the significance of work in the philosophy of mathematics for the teaching of the subject in schools. But exciting new philosophical books were fast appearing, like Ryle's *The Concept of Mind* and Hare's *The Language of Morals*, which, whatever their author's intentions, only strengthened my view of the autonomy of distinct areas of understanding rooted in logically distinct conceptual schemes and related methods of verification. Even Wittgenstein's *Philosophical Investigations*, with its talk of "forms of life" and "language games," I read as supporting my view of logically distinct domains of knowledge and understanding. What I now wanted above all though was to find a satisfactory account of the verification of moral and religious propositions.

It was therefore with great anticipation that I accepted an unexpectedly offered lectureship at Oxford, to work with graduate students training to teach mathematics but also to explore more widely the significance of contemporary British analytical philosophy for our understanding of educational aims and practices. I could not have had a more opportune appointment, for when I moved to Oxford the place was alive with nearly a hundred teachers of philosophy, many now deeply influenced by the work of Wittgenstein to become his disciples or his critics or both. Lectures and postgraduate seminars in philosophy were being given in many areas by many distinguished academics like Ryle, Hare, Hampshire, Urmson, Austin, and Strawson, and these, as a senior member of the university, I could freely attend. For the first time also I read seriously in the history of philosophy and was swept off my feet by Kant's analysis of the a priori elements in our understanding in his *Critique of Pure Reason* and his *Critique of Practical Reason*. Strawson's work in "descriptive metaphysics" only enthused me further along the same lines. I realized, however, that coming to terms with Wittgenstein's *Philosophical Investigations* was crucial if I was to be able to confidently defend any position I might take on the nature of human beings, the character of mind and of reason, the nature of knowledge and understanding, and in particular the nature and justification of moral and religious truths. What was more, these were now not only issues of concern for me personally but clearly central to areas of my new professional work in seeking to clarify the nature of educational aims and practices.

What I took from Wittgenstein in particular were essentially three theses that I adapted to my own purposes. First, that philosophy is concerned with seeking to help our understanding in all our forms of discourse by mapping carefully the concepts and their relationships embedded in our use of language, thus helping us to remove confusions and contradictions that distort our understanding. Second, that concepts in any area of understanding are to be found in the rules for our use of words rather than any notion that they must be labels of objects of any kind, physical, mental, spiritual, or whatever. Third, that the "private language argument" shows that all understanding, let alone all judgment of truth, is dependent on agreement in the application of the concepts in public discourse. In particular it seemed to me clear that our knowledge of our own and other minds, and our claims to moral and spiritual knowledge, cannot be based solely on episodes of individual private experience. What I did not begin to take from Wittgenstein was that he was radically challenging my claim that all understanding is at least fundamentally propositional in character. I was now, however, distinctly neo-Kantian in my outlook, no longer seriously worried about the justification of moral principles, but increasingly concerned about the Glanton Brethren's claims for the truth of "revealed" religious doctrines, verified on the basis of our experience following mere acts of belief in them. Nothing in contemporary philosophy of religion seemed to me to begin to provide any justification for such a position.

After five years at Oxford my philosophical interests were in fact now expanding so much that I no longer wished to devote the majority of my time to work with future teachers of mathematics. I therefore accepted with some anticipation an invitation extended by the University of London Institute of Education to a lectureship entirely in philosophy of education. Soon I was working closely there with the new holder of the chair in philosophy of education, Richard Peters, in a collaboration that was to determine the shape of my future career. With his strong background in classical studies, followed by work in the history of philosophy and recent writings in philosophy of mind, ethics, and social philosophy, he was able through his support to encourage my confidence in my own philosophical work. Our areas of interest complemented each other; indeed, his position on many matters was even more Kantian than mine. But above all, his firm critical confirmation of my propositional approach to all knowledge and understanding encouraged me to explore the implications of such a view for many fundamental issues in educational theory and practice. Under his leadership we together did much to develop the philosophy of education in analytical terms within Britain, and I for a long period argued hard as part of that for the centrality in the education of all of at least some minimal understanding in mathematics and the sciences, of persons and society, morality, religion, the arts, and philosophy.

That Peters was a practicing Quaker also helped, if only temporarily, to keep my now fading religious adherence alive. With wider academic and professional responsibilities, especially after being appointed to a chair in the university, my attendance at the Meeting became less regular, as other things now seemed more pressingly important. I had come to be quite well known among Glanton Brethren as a speaker, but was now increasingly uncomfortable with my institutional involvement with them. The very nature of my work in recent years had also introduced me to a much wider lifestyle. I had slowly become less emotionally inhibited and socially much more involved with many diverse groups, enjoying also a number of quite close personal relationships. Wider personal experience as well as philosophical study had served to strengthen my conviction that moral judgments are indeed of their nature autonomous and independent of any religious beliefs, and indeed that no religious beliefs could possibly be justified if inconsistent with rationally defensible moral values. The content of my moral beliefs, if still viewed as in their nature basically matters of propositional understanding, was in fact now moving well away from the letter of New Testament teaching on numerous personal matters.

My parents and all my close relatives through my sister had strong Glanton Brethren connections still, but I had lived at some distance from them all for some time, and though I am sure they were aware of certain changes in my pattern of life, and that some areas of it I was keeping private from them, none of them ever challenged me about the situation. My father I sensed saw me as inevitably succumbing to the "worldly" temptations of my academic life and career, but he said nothing, judging I am sure that this was now my own responsibility. He had done all that he felt proper in his witness to me of "the truth." My association with the Meetings was now growing very thin, and the overall sense of personal fulfillment I was now experiencing elsewhere was such that I no longer felt constrained by any of the teaching and moral and social values I had when young accepted without question. By the time I was invited back to Cambridge as professor of education and head of the department of education in 1971 I was no longer able to accept either the moral or the religious teaching of the Glanton Brethren, even if I was still firmly committed to a propositional view of the nature of all justifiable moral beliefs and of any religious claims that must be taken seriously. Both commitments had been fundamental presuppositions within my earliest understanding, and were influencing me still as being foundational in my overall philosophical position on all epistemological and ethical questions and in my whole professional approach to educational aims and principles.

My early professional philosophical work in Cambridge I spent largely on analytically seeking to clarify more adequately the nature of educational theory and practice. But the more I explored these issues the more dissatisfied I became with my basic commitments to the propositional nature of all knowledge and understanding and to the Kantian justification of moral principles. I began to see too that my use of Wittgenstein's later work to bolster up these views was at the expense of my getting to grips with his much more radical challenge to my positivistic presuppositions about meaning and truth. There was also important work now by others like Rorty in his *Philosophy and the Mirror of Nature* and Habermas in *Knowledge and Human Interests* that made me aware as never before of the true significance of the social construction of all knowledge and understanding. But it was the work of Alasdair MacIntyre in *After Virtue* and *Whose Justice? Whose Rationality?* that led me to radically rethink, first, my whole view of the role of reason in human life and morality; second, the significance of social practices in the determination of ourselves and our lives; and third, how best to conceive the good life for each of us.

First, it became clear to me that our understanding of our world is fundamentally practical rather than propositional and theoretical, concerned with the achievement of practical ends in the satisfaction of our natural desires of great variety rather than the achievement of true propositions. In the exercise of theoretical reason the outcome is the formulation of bodies of propositions on which we can agree in our judgements of truth according to appropriate publicly shared criteria and evidence. But in practical reason the outcome is rather agreed bodies of actions and practices in the doing of which we achieve certain complex forms of individual and social good in the satisfaction of our desires. Both exercises of reason employ concepts and language. But the nature of action itself is such that what it is rational to do, what constitutes our good, can be discerned only in the doing itself, and the concepts and propositions of practical discourse are only inadequate indicators and generalizations of what practice involves and entails. Practical discourse and its patterns of reasoning must therefore be developed in practice itself if it is to be adequate to its purpose.

On this view the notion I had subscribed to, that rational moral action is achieved by the application in actions of propositional truths and principles justified by theoretical reason, is seen to be just a fundamental misunderstanding of how our capacities for reason operate in relation to our other capacities and to those of action in particular. To see reason as always proposition-seeking leads to seeing rational action as stemming from some basic power of an autonomous will to act on propositional principles rather than to see it as anchored firmly in the satisfaction of naturally given needs, wants, and desires. In the moral teaching in which I had been brought up moral action had nothing to do with natural desires. It was seen as stemming from adherence to revealed propositional principles, and from the assertion of a will which in our "fallen" natural state must prove inadequate to the task of acting morally unless spiritually empowered. Even when spiritually led, our desires needed to be confirmed, as leading to our ultimate good, by revealed biblical propositional teaching. In changing my approach to the whole character of moral reasoning, I was in fact now rejecting on philosophical grounds a philosophical doctrine presupposed in my early religious faith. I was cutting a very fundamental link with my past. In my personal life I was in fact still living publicly very much in conformity with the moral principles from my religious past. But my more private life and my whole outlook and priorities were undergoing a radical change.

But second, provoked by MacIntyre, I also came to hold the view that we are not constituted as individual persons simply by what we are by nature. We become who we are as persons only through the exercise of our individual natural capacities in relating to others and by participating in, or in reacting to, linguistically socially constructed conceptual schemes and all manner of other socially patterned practices. As persons we are not fundamentally separate atom-like individuals for whom social relationships are secondary and of significance only because of their contingent value to us. To be a person is to think, feel, and act in relationships with others which are constitutive of us as the individuals we are. We individually are our seemingly private thoughts, beliefs, feelings, and desires, but we are also our actions, skills, habits, patterns of behavior, dispositions, and so on; and the specific character of all our exercising of all our capacities, even the seemingly most private, stems significantly from our response to the features of the public social practices to which we are heirs. On this view, though individually we are in part necessarily the product of our naturally given characteristics and capacities, we are also necessarily socially constructed from birth by the conceptual schemes and social practices in the society we encounter.

For such a view there was no place in the strictly individualistic teaching of the Glanton Brethren in which I was brought up. One's individual character and capabilities were considered to be determined by God and simply to be exercised individually in obedience to His teaching alone. One's personal involvement with others beyond that needed for the basic necessities of life was to be minimal and not at all for the satisfaction of one's natural desires in general. The goal was that of individual salvation in a direct relationship with God. Once again my philosophical investigations had led me to finally reject completely a fundamental philosophical presupposition in the teaching and practices of my upbringing.

In keeping with these earlier changes MacIntyre not surprisingly led me in the third place to a totally different idea of the good life for each of us. If human societies are seen as progressively developed in practical experience by the creation of practices developed precisely for the satisfaction of our interrelated fundamental human needs, wants, and desires, they have done this in complex structures of practices that range from those of simple common skills to patterns of eating and farming and industrial production, of pursuing knowledge and understanding, of creating family life and economic and political systems, and of medicine, music, the arts, and games of all kinds. With some simple practices it is easy to see how far they are rational in the sense that they satisfy successfully clearly specifiable needs or desires, or fail to do so. But many of our desires relate closely to other desires that we also wish to satisfy, and many involve relationships with people who differ from us in many significant respects.

The success of societies in developing major practices that are widely acceptable, and that maximize the satisfactions of all those they involve, is a highly complex experimental and pragmatic matter and can result in organizational structures and principles that may or may not be widely applicable. But a good life for each of us must, I think, necessarily be seen as a life composed in relation to the practices in the society in which we are placed, which maximally satisfies our desires across the whole trajectory from birth, development, through flourishing maturity, to decline and death. It is one in which our individual natural capacities, which are shared with others to varying degrees, and which grow, mature, and decline, are exercised to provide the fulfillment of our potentialities and our fullest satisfactions across the whole of our individual natures and across our whole lives. The possibilities for any one life are clearly very wide ranging, and there seems no reason to think there is for any one of us only one pattern of a good life in relation to the practices available in a modern society. With the great expansion of knowledge and understanding, the development of new technological practices, and the development of complex social institutions, it seems that the maximum freedom of informed choice for each of us is the only way we can each hope to achieve a good life that matches our own individual capacities and desires. But that is only possible if we fully recognize our necessary interrelatedness with and dependence upon others who are equally seeking their own good lives. A truly good life, for this and other reasons, is only possible in a good society.

The Morality of Religious Upbringing, Indoctrination, and Education

From all I have come to understand about the nature of good lives, it seems to me that the upbringing and education of the young are best understood as the means whereby developing children are, from birth, intentionally introduced to the practices surrounding them in their society, in relation to which their good is to be found both in the present and for their future lives. Some of those practices and their influences might, however, be highly damaging, not only in relation to children's immediate good but also in restricting their future choices of practices, and indeed in their deciding adequately their whole pattern of life. There is, however, as I see it no escape here from the responsibility that parents, educators, and other adults have during the early years of children and young people committed to their charge. The proper exercise of their responsibility must surely be seeking to initiate those in their care into those practices which are appropriate to their individual maturing capacities, and the development to the full of their capacities to themselves make informed choices about those practices which will together constitute the "narrative" of a good life throughout all their adult years.

But what then of the significance in the upbringing and education of children of the social practices of religions, and in particular in my case what of the religious beliefs and practices of the Glanton Brethren into which I was initiated when young? My coming to realize the importance of social practices in our understanding and the making of good lives led me to think again about the nature of all religious beliefs and practices, particularly those concerned with a comprehensive view of what constitutes a good life. As with all beliefs and social practices, I now came to see those of religions as conceptual and practical social constructions seeking to satisfy certain desires we almost universally seem to develop, and to know about and come to terms with the ultimate and fundamental character and purpose of our own existence and that of our given context. But then one has to face directly the justification of any claims to truth that any religion makes, and whether or not its practices satisfy our desires in ways that constitute our individual and social good in all their achievements. On the basis of my own knowledge of religions and my philosophical explorations the answer seems to me that there are at present no good reasons for accepting the truth of any of the dominant bodies of religious claims or the practices they support on the grounds that they offer for them.

We are in fact unable to understand many matters in our experience, and the satisfaction of some of our intellectual, psychological, and material desires seems well beyond our achievement. But it may also be the case that certain forms of understanding and the satisfaction of desire are in principle unachievable, granted our given natural capacities, and that religious concerns fall into that category. My own judgment is that that is indeed the case. But be that as it may, the only position I think it now reasonable to take on all religious claims is one of skepticism or agnosticism, until such a time as there is altogether more convincing evidence for their justification than we have been able to discover to date. Maybe evolution will eventually result in beings with more advanced spiritual capacities than we seem to have at present, and that will make possible agreement in judgments of truth concerning the spiritual realities that figure in most major religions. Time will tell, and I will speculate no further.

As I have indicated earlier, the religious beliefs of the Glanton Brethren, which determined my own upbringing, are seen by them as propositional truths about spiritual realities and historical events whose validity rests on their revelation in written Scriptures and our coming to see them as true in our own experience if we submit ourselves to their claims. As my grasp of human knowledge, understanding, and experience in all other areas has increased, and particularly my philosophical understanding of the demands for establishing propositional and practical knowledge in all other areas of human experience, the claims made in these beliefs I judge to be purely speculative in character and to be partly circular in argument. In many minor matters they also seem to be inconsistent with our advanced and well-established knowledge in certain nonreligious areas, particularly in the sciences and history.

Reaching that conclusion about these claims has meant my finally freeing myself from the intellectual constraint of many of the basic beliefs and practices that composed the life into which I was initiated as a child. Many other beliefs and practices originally linked to those religious beliefs I have retained, seeing them now as justified on other grounds. They are of course still therefore an essential part of who I now am and play their part in the good life I now seek to lead, a life in which at least all conscious elements of faith in revealed religious claims no longer figure. Their place has, at least consciously, been taken now by my overall desire to live by the achievements of practical and theoretical reason, which I consider clearly entails being agnostic where all specifically religious matters are concerned.

But how far was I religiously indoctrinated? The notion of indoctrination is to some extent controversial, though in its central use it is generally taken to be the intentional teaching of beliefs, considered by some to be dubious, for acceptance as true without attention to the evidence for and, more important, against them. There are weaker uses which partially satisfy those criteria, and in my own judgment my upbringing until I was seventeen was in fact a somewhat weakened form of indoctrination. Certainly the religious and moral doctrines held by Glanton Brethren exclusively determined the discourse and related practices of all the moral and religious elements in my life at home and at the Meeting, and effectively determined almost all my attitudes, beliefs, and behavior. This was undoubtedly the intention of my parents. That these beliefs and practices were not those of others I was well aware, and I accepted that those others were thus guilty of serious errors of judgment, as the doctrines made plain.

The ground for my accepting the beliefs of my parents was in part just that I trusted their judgment, particularly that of my father, who cared so much always about the truth and devoted hours almost daily to Bible study. But there was much made of the Scriptures' own direct claim to be revealed truth, plus the promise of proof in my own experience in due course as a result of accepting what was being taught. No alternative doctrines or practices were ever given serious consideration, as they were simply not the teaching of Scripture, and questioning the truth of Scripture was never even contemplated. I recognized when very young the moral integrity, consistency, and discipline of my parents, and knew of no other basis for these virtues than the teaching of the Bible. Public witness to the truth of the claim that the saving power of Christ delivers from sin in personal experience was significantly a regular element in the evangelistic preaching of members of the Meeting. True, our way of life seemed rather unnecessarily restricted, but for the early years of my adolescence we were in a country at war, and in any case we had no money for the things some other people had or did. Only in my last two years at school were there any misgivings in my mind about the truth of the basic teachings underpinning our life, but even then I wanted to understand more of that basis and more of "the World" outside, rather than to reject or rebel against anything I had been taught. To what extent my basic acceptance of the Meetings' teachings was due to the severe inhibition of all expression of emotions in our lives it is hard to say, though that has proved in the end to be the most lasting legacy of my upbringing.

Was I then indoctrinated? I think the answer must be yes. Though there was never any attempt to suppress my questioning of the doctrines on which our life was based, no attempt was made to introduce me to the legitimacy and importance of such questioning, nor as I have said, were any alternative beliefs ever given serious consideration. The powerful influence over me of our whole way of life implicitly and explicitly put me in no position to seriously entertain the fundamental questions, which only philosophy was to awaken in me after I had left home for university. Indoctrination I see as of its nature at least limiting consideration of the proper justification of beliefs even when it does not intentionally inhibit such consideration. I suggest therefore that my own experience might be considered a somewhat less than paradigmatic case of indoctrination, as I consider my parents had no intention whatever to deny me any questioning of their beliefs and practices. I think they genuinely believed that they had found the most basic truths of the good life—the spiritual life—and that all serious doubting of that was impious evil from which no good could possibly come. They therefore felt they were protecting me from that evil in my growing up, after which I must make my own decisions and answer to God for all I pursued.

But what then of the morality of my religious upbringing? Whether or not it is to be described as a form of indoctrination, I certainly now regard it as a morally unsatisfactory form of upbringing in certain very important respects. Fundamentally, this is because if upbringing is to be concerned with each child developing from the very start the narrative of a good life, as I have suggested earlier, then those lives must from the very beginning be determined, by practical reason, for the progressive development of their own exercise of practical reason at every stage to maturity. Until their own capacities for reason develop, children need to be cared for and taught by their parents or carers in the light of the best possible rational practices we have for that progressive development of the child's own rational thought and actions. That certainly seems to necessitate establishing early a firm pattern of moral understanding and behavior with explicit expression, even from the start, of the reasons why these actions are required. The necessity for parental control and authority, and the building of rational practices for the structuring of their lives and relationships, needs justification to children in the simplest terms just as early as they can begin to make sense of it. And the introduction of alternatives and choices as soon as they are appropriate and meaningful must become ever more open to children in their steady progress toward maturity. To give inadequate grounds for alternative moral and religious beliefs and practices in alternative lifestyles, or to deliberately delay a child's concern for these without good reason when they can become meaningful and significant elements in their lives, is to distort their development. It is to fail to equip them to progressively develop their own good lives in major respects within the society in which they will live.

My parents rightly sought, as all parents should, to bring me up within the web of moral and religious beliefs and practices which they held to be true, and within that web they sought the best formation of my life that they could. They clearly wanted me to understand how what they taught me and asked me to do was justified within that religious system. But they protected me tightly from any alternative systems; and though they did not deliberately prevent me from raising fundamental questions about their own system, they clearly considered that the answers within that system of revealed truths must be adequate, further enquiry being a dangerous expression of merely natural intellectual speculation. Such a situation, even if defensible within their own beliefs at the time, I now judge to be morally unacceptable. Not that I would blame them morally for doing as they did, as to do otherwise they could not but judge to be morally wrong and serious sin. If "ought" implies "can," then I think they must be ultimately be judged as incapable of acting otherwise because of limitations in the development of their own rational capacities rather than any flaw in their deep commitment to the good of their children as they understood it. In their own terms my parents lived good lives, but in wider, more rigorously rational terms those lives, and those of their children, were unjustifiably impoverished.

Their considerable restriction of my upbringing, in terms of the areas of knowledge and understanding and of the rich pattern of social activities of the world outside the family and the Meeting, was surely equally undesirable, particularly as I passed through adolescence. This was to deny me early exploration and development in areas of living in which my capacities and interests might have found quite different and perhaps greater forms of personal fulfillment than those of which they approved after their radical condemnation of "the World." That in my later education and experience I could overcome some of these early deprivations was fortuitous—I was certainly denied choices and opportunities that I otherwise might well have had. The restrictions on me were thereby also denials of my legitimate freedom and restricted the development of my capacities to make rational choices for my life. They frustrated rather than promoted the development of my autonomy. In addition the doctrines they understood as teaching the need to inhibit the expression, and thence the occurrence, of natural emotions was in fact to distort my experience and understanding of myself and others in ways that persisted well into my adult life. All these restrictions might be seen as further forms of or consequences of indoctrination in my upbringing. Whether that is formally so or not, they seem to me clearly morally undesirable.

Upbringing, I have maintained, should seek to launch every child into the development of a good life, as a life structured maximally by the person's own exercise of practical reason. Religious indoctrination, like all other areas of indoctrination, can have no place in such an upbringing, as its consequences are by definition antipathetic to the development and exercise of reason. Education I consider is best understood as continuous with upbringing, and to have the same overall aim—namely the development of each pupil's good life. It is the formal institutionalization of initiating pupils into those practices, essential or desirable for most members of a given society on their journey to maturity, for which the home and parents alone cannot adequately provide. Religious education in those terms is of its nature not indoctrinatory; it concerns itself with initiating pupils into the beliefs and practices of religions so that they can come to understand the concepts and activities involved, while enabling them to rationally assess claims to truth and to the satisfaction of desires concerning our ultimate questions about human life and its context. Such religious education is not incompatible with the upbringing of children in some particular faith, but it is a necessary complement to any such upbringing if pupils are to be helped to achieve good lives as lives determined above all else by the exercise of practical and theoretical reason. For me my study of philosophy was the means to my slowly but finally escaping from the doctrines and practices that formed my early life. It was a pity that the upbringing I judge my parents had the right to give me was not complemented while I was still at school by serious religious education, something I consider crucial within the education of all children in our present religion-dominated societies.

References

Ayer, Alfred J. *Language, Truth, and Logic*. London: Faber, 1936.
Ferré, Frederick. *Basic Modern Philosophy of Religion*. London: Allen and Unwin, 1967.
Hacker, P. M. S. *Wittgenstein's Place in Twentieth-Century Analytic Philosophy*. Oxford: Blackwell, 1996.
Hampshire, Stuart. *Thought and Action*. London: Chatto and Windus, 1959.
Hare, R. M. *The Language of Morals*. Oxford: Oxford University Press, 1952.
Hirst, Paul H. *Knowledge and the Curriculum*. London: Routledge, 1972.
Hirst, Paul H., and R. S. Peters. *The Logic of Education*. London: Routledge, 1972.
Kant, Immanuel. *The Critique of Practical Reason*. Translated by L. W. Beck. New York: Bobbs-Merrill, 1956.
———. *The Critique of Pure Reason*. Translated by N. K. Smith. London: Macmillan, 1968.
MacIntyre, Alasdair. *After Virtue: A Study in Moral Theory*. London: Duckworth, 1981.
———. *Dependent Rational Animals*. London: Duckworth, 1999.
———. *Whose Justice? Which Rationality?* London: Duckworth, 1988.
Peters, R. S. *Ethics and Education*. London: Allen and Unwin, 1966.
Rorty, Richard. *Philosophy and the Mirror of Nature*. Oxford: Blackwell, 1980.
Russell, Bertrand. *A History of Philosophy*. London: Allen and Unwin, 1946.
———. *The Problems of Philosophy*. London: Williams and Norgate, 1912.
Ryle, Gilbert. *The Concept of Mind*. London: Hutchinson, 1949.
Strawson, P. F. *Individuals: An Essay in Descriptive Metaphysics*. London: Methuen, 1959.
Wittgenstein, Ludwig. *Philosophical Investigations*. Trans. G. E. M. Anscombe. Oxford: Blackwell, 1953.

FOR THE LOVE OF PARADOX:
MENNONITE MORALITY AND PHILOSOPHY

Diane Enns

> Either ethics makes no sense at all, or this is what it means ... not to be unworthy of what happens to us.
>
> —Gilles Deleuze, *The Logic of Sense*

The Russian Mennonite community in which I was raised during the 1960s and 1970s shared a past that we children absorbed like the humid air of our southern Ontario summers.[1] The stories that emerged in fragments at family gatherings did not seem out of the ordinary. We assumed, with the indifferent innocence of children, that all families had such stories to tell—of refugee compounds, labor camps, curfews, and dramatic escapes to freedom. Some words opened a vast silence with their chill—Siberia, communism, Makhno—but only much later did we grasp the significance of the grim faces in faded photographs, sudden emotion escaping a stoic eye, and the stern disapproval of frivolity.

Most of the older members of our church had been born in the Soviet Union, descendants of the Mennonites Catherine the Great invited from Prussia to farm the fertile land of Ukraine in the late eighteenth century. This they did with great success—a success they could not know would seal their fates when Stalin began the collectivization of farms and instigated the purges responsible for the death and destruction of the 1930s and 1940s. It was a terrible page of history, with stories not unlike other twentieth-century episodes of violent repression—telling of murder and rape, dispossession and flight, poverty, illness, and starvation. In the end, those who managed to escape to Germany and from there to Paraguay, Canada, or the United States

---

The author would like to thank Karen Enns for her careful and insightful comments on this chapter.

were immeasurably more fortunate than those who chose to retreat in the opposite direction, many of whom died miserably of hunger and exposure.

Why is the legacy of such a past a collective moral attitude characterized in part by intolerance, exclusivity, hypocrisy, and self-righteousness? For while the Mennonites are known internationally for their pacifism and humanitarian aid,[2] and their work for global peace and social justice, at the level of everyday life in small communities a dogmatic adherence to the centuries-old edict of separating oneself from the world and all that is considered worldly prevails. An obsession with purity ensues: with the pure body, which admits the body of the other only under the proper conditions of marriage and within the bounds of community; the pure community, founded on blood ties and the acceptance of the moral authority of the church; and the pure mind or soul, uncontaminated either by desire or passion—of a sexual or intellectual nature—and motivated by an unquestioning obedience to the will of God. It is an obedience—*all we like sheep*—fundamentally at odds with philosophical inquiry.

The moral world of the Mennonite faith I fervently embraced as a girl was a narrow place. It did not permit exceptions or admit paradoxical predicaments without solutions, and fostered a community of judgment and punishment that I have spent years fleeing, both literally and figuratively. It provided only black-and-white platitudes that could not equip me to deal with the ethical questions raised by violence, revolution, and oppression, despite the fact that these phenomena weighed heavily on our consciousness as a community. My flight from moral absolutes and the prohibition of dissent eventually propelled me to those European thinkers of the twentieth century who were also haunted by violent political events. They wondered how to speak of ethics after Auschwitz, how to understand community beyond an inclusive/exclusive binary, and how to rethink politics after totalitarianism. These have become my questions. To get to a place where I could ask them, and could think about them philosophically, however, I first had to reject the faith and community that provided me with meaning for the first twenty years of my life.[3] I left the Mennonite world in order to discover the "foreign"—the material alterity manifest in dissent and critique that we were not allowed to encounter or indulge—and for the love of paradox, the kind of paradox we cannot live without morally or politically. The religion I embraced could neither admit nor negotiate this paradox.

In this chapter I will describe the stringent limitations on thought that the Mennonite faith imposed, as well as the tiny cracks in the edifice that enabled me—slowly and at some sacrifice—to extricate myself from these constraints. That the activity of critical, philosophical reflection itself was considered dangerous for Mennonites, at least in the time and place in which I lived as one, posed a formidable obstacle for anyone who indulged an intellectually curious spirit. The consequences of a moral authority that prevents thinking in the name of securing one's faith are debilitating, for such an authority prohibits the trust in one's own moral intuition and response—substituting blind adherence to rules for the compassion and critical deliberation that is required of us in our relations with others. In the process of this exploration, I will reflect on how the residues of such a profound experience have affected my own thinking: inescapable conflicts or tensions that inadvertently arise, often between the lines; ghosts that haunt and drive my interests; a keen sense of justice and an anxiety regarding violence that propels me toward questions of politics and ethics; and finally, an ongoing struggle—despite having left the Mennonite Church some twenty years ago—to forge my own path as a woman with a penchant for philosophical inquiry and political critique. In the process I hope to demonstrate the necessity of rethinking our ethical and political ideals. There are other ways of cultivating a community bound together by compassion and justice, and we need to find them.

The Question

As an ethnic group, the Russian Mennonites have traditionally been marked by a pronounced schism between intellectual interests and an extremely practical bent, a schism my own family embodied rather well. My paternal great grandfather was an exceptional businessman in Ukraine, responsible for railroad construction and flour mills, whose son became a farmer in the new country, passing on his skills, land, and ambition in turn to my father, who took charge of their small farm at the age of fourteen and turned it into a successful major business operation. Philosophical pursuits—from the perspective of Mennonite farmers who live and breathe a pragmatic stoicism that renders the Protestant work ethic mere child's play—are far beyond anything that could be recognized as legitimate "work." Furthermore, to *question*—as I was repeatedly instructed by my church community—was to doubt God's omnipotence and gift of grace.

It was my mother who dared to open Pandora's box and let fly the demons of philosophical thinking. Her family represented the Mennonite predilection for book-learning and teaching. My mother's grandfather was a professor of German literature and a religious leader, eventually imprisoned during the worst of the Stalin purges, and executed in 1941 (although this was not known until decades later). His letters from various prisons or camps—Butyrka, Lubyanka, Solovetsky—urged his children, who he did not know were barely getting enough to eat, to be diligent in their studies. Only one of his sons was fortunate enough to be able to pursue an education. But the turbulence of the time, the experience of flight, imprisonment, and torture alongside his father, took a heavy toll on this great-uncle of mine. Becoming ill while a student in Göttingen after the war, he left for Canada in 1962, spending the rest of his life in the care of my grandparents, forever imprisoned by his schizophrenic terror of the Russian communists he believed were watching him. It is his response to trauma that haunts me now as I contemplate the psychic and political effects of a community's experience of violence and explore the process of survival.

The split embodied in my own family led to unusual departures from the Mennonite culture in which I was raised. While in the church pews we listened without speaking, trusting a faith that prohibited doubt, at home an inquiring mind was encouraged (within certain acceptable political parameters). My mother would frequently leave the table to consult an encyclopedia or dictionary for answers to our unresolved dinner arguments. Her passion for debate and her enthusiasm for learning were irrepressible. When my younger brother, her fourth child, entered school, my mother decided to pursue a university education despite the protests of my pragmatic and old-fashioned father. She would come home from her philosophy class animated in a manner we could not then understand, and ask us a startling question: are we really humans dreaming we are butterflies or butterflies dreaming we are humans? Years later in my own first philosophy class, this inversion of reality remained thrilling, as though turning the world as we understand it upside down and suspending all judgments and presuppositions in order to *dwell in the question*, as Gilles Deleuze would put it, were the very indispensable task of philosophy.

My father's pragmatic approach to life was also enabling in ways I could not know at the time. His intolerance of hypocrisy and the underhanded business practices of some of the Mennonites in our community was the subject of many dinner-hour diatribes. His difficulty accepting bell-bottom jeans or long hair on young men when they came into fashion, and his vehement arguments with me against "women's libbers," organic farming, and the welfare system were signs of the inflexible, conservative politics I rebelled against, but his intolerance of those who prayed fervently on Sunday and engaged in suspect business dealings on Monday thankfully immunized us against the belief that was otherwise easily absorbed: that Mennonites were God's chosen people. My father taught me the meaning of integrity, which he would argue now had nothing to do with growing up Mennonite, but he also conveyed the importance of "suspicion." He would laugh to hear me say it, but it is a suspicion that has much in common with an attitude underlying the work of my most-loved philosophers.

To dwell in the uncertainty of the question, let alone summon the courage to express it in the first place, was for a Mennonite girl in my time and place a radical, heretical act. I showed no signs of acquiring such a voice as a young, emotionally impressionable girl in a Mennonite high school, intense about all my pursuits and therefore, not surprisingly, utterly devoted to discovering God's will for my life—a God whose image occupied my thoughts constantly, a transcendent other whom I imagined to be listening to all the longings of my heart. An aura of the forbidden enshrouded the question, somewhat akin to the mystery surrounding sex. Somewhere around the age of ten I innocently asked my Sunday School teacher what "circumcision" meant, having encountered the term in a Bible passage. Visibly flustered, eyes to the floor, she quietly told us to ask our parents. I did so, naturally, while they sat in the family room, my father watching television, my mother reading, and suffered that bald shame of exposure on hearing the words "penis" and "foreskin" in front of my father, who fixed his gaze on the television throughout the brief ordeal. I decided not to ask what a foreskin was.

A philosophical question evoked a similar sense of the forbidden (if not the shameful). C. S. Lewis's *The Screwtape Letters* made a significant impression on me as a teenager. The fact that a demon—in my mind, Satan—was constantly introducing questions and doubts in our minds, whittling away persistently at our fragile faiths, caused more than a little torment when indulging in the act of reflection. Indeed, it was a powerful disincentive for thinking at all, for one was always wondering whether it was God or Satan who introduced thoughts into our minds. The only way to tell was to submit blindly to the moral grid imposed on every facet of our lives: anything to do with sexual desire was being introduced by Satan; anything that made us doubt the omnipresence or omniscience of God, the authority of the Bible and of the pastor who told us how to interpret it, the wisdom of the Sunday School teacher, and the good intentions of our parents, came from Satan. For a serious, introspective teenager, this spelled a schizoid existence: a hatred of the body, distrust of the mind, fear of desire, profound suspicion of one's own emotions and intuition, and implicit trust in church leaders—

the elderly men who were supposedly shepherding the flock on our meek and obedient way to the Kingdom of God.

It is this conflict between blind obedience and trust in oneself, and between the "dangerous" flesh of the body and the rational workings of the mind, that manifested itself in one particularly heinous manner in my teenage years, although I did not hear of it until sixteen years after I had left the church. At a cousin's wedding reception I was informed by an old acquaintance from the youth group to which I belonged during high school that two of my close friends at that time—girls with whom I had planned social events, Bible studies, singing engagements, and youth retreats—had been subjected to repeated sexual assaults during the very years we knew each other. Both were victimized over a number of years, one by an uncle, the other by a well-respected youth minister whom we admired and trusted implicitly to be accomplishing God's work.

In the weeks after hearing this tragic news I agonized over my memories of conversations with these friends, wondering how I could not have known, how anyone could not have known, and how it could happen that youth learn to mistrust their own perceptions, learn to keep silent about torment and violation. While no community is without betrayal, and the victimization of its most vulnerable members, there is something particularly twisted about the violence that occurs in the name of God, and about a moral system that unintentionally solicits such silence. I don't know what the knowledge of these crimes would have done to my faith had I known about them as they were occurring; in hindsight they confirmed what I have learned in the years since: that there is no good without the taint of evil, no inside without an encounter with the outside, no holy without the unholy. This is what renders ethics far too complex for moral templates such as the one we were given as Mennonite children.

The World

The beginning of my extrication from the stifling conformism of my community and its prohibition of questioning ironically occurred at a Mennonite Bible college in Manitoba. It was a school to which the people of my church were afraid to send their children, for they often returned seriously confused if they returned at all.[4] While many suffered from the doubt introduced by higher education for a brief, tormenting period and then returned to the security and comfort of the fold with relief and resignation, I was among those few who never returned. The first crack in the foundation of my faith came in the form of an exegetical exploration of biblical and sacred texts—examining their inclusion or exclusion from the canon, their multiple translations, omissions, and errors, as well as their infinite interpretations—that eroded any vision of God breathing words into the writing instruments of his prophets and disciples. Though it entailed a painful, irrevocable loss—not only of my community but of all that had given a deep and satisfying meaning to my existence—there was no turning back after experiencing what I did not recognize at the time to be an introduction to philosophical inquiry.

A particularly astute and intrepid professor taught an inspiring course on the letters of Paul that introduced me to the marvelous world of hermeneutics. I did not realize at the time that the excitement of looking up passages in the original Greek and finding inconsistencies in translated texts or blatant omissions (not without their political import) would be the catalyst for leaving the Mennonite Church and the God I had loved. Most significant, it sparked an interest in the historical contingency of texts and ideas, and concern with the human tendency to crave certitude and absolutes in the face of the indeterminacy of quotidian life. Ironically, "Letters of Paul" was the only course I ever failed, having suddenly decided to exchange my books for a backpack. The disembodied "ivory tower" nature of higher education and what I perceived to be an attitude of self-righteousness and academic arrogance became intolerable for me that spring of 1983. I vowed never to return to an academic institution.

It was still a long time before I would find my way to the philosophical texts that changed my life and to the parallel operation of extricating myself from the moralism of my Mennonite upbringing. My faith had already been seriously undermined by a historical and scholarly reading of biblical texts, but it was ultimately my encounter with other equally fervent faiths and diverse ways of life while traveling in North America, Europe, Latin America, the Middle East, and Asia for months at a time over several years that enabled me to say finally that I did not believe in the God or morality of my childhood. It was not a matter of refuting arguments for the existence of God and rationalizing away my belief system. It was my encounter with the *world*—that world we had been taught to distrust and even to despise because it was fallen and imperfect, full of the evil we had to fight to keep at bay. I discovered this world with breathtaking surprise and childlike fearlessness. There was beauty and goodness in the family from Iowa who took me and my traveling companion in for a weekend while hitchhiking to Latin America; in the cheerful Hispanic farmer who drove us forty miles out of his way to show us a raisin factory and load us with ten-pound bags of California raisins; in the extraordinary resilience of the Tibetan monks who led us through the two-thousand-year-old palace of Yambulakang; in the Tibetan people who prostrated themselves, weeping, in the Potala Palace where the Dalai Lama once slept; and in the old Chinese men of Xian gathering in the park at dawn with elaborate birdcages balanced on their knees, smiling at us proudly as we stopped to listen to the noisy birds, delighted to be disturbing the stillness of a chill morning.

Leaving my church and my faith was not therefore only or even primarily an intellectual process, but a deeply phenomenological and emotional one (although these are difficult to separate). This exceptional and foreign world could not be accommodated by the narrow framework of my childhood beliefs, and neither could its moral dilemmas. It was an experience of something I would later encounter in theory: an understanding of the world as given, as lived moment by moment, and spectacularly (rather than dangerously) susceptible to change. Five years after my final backpacking adventure I would read Maurice Merleau-Ponty's beautiful phrases: "I am thinking of the Cartesian cogito, wanting to finish this work, feeling the coolness of the paper under my hand, and perceiving the trees of the boulevard through the window. My life is constantly thrown headlong into transcendent things, and passes wholly outside me."[5] These words opened the floodgates to a kind of thinking and writing in which intellect and affect, transcendence and immanence, mind and body, philosophy and poetry, were inextricably entangled.

It took some time, however, to understand and negotiate the void that leaving God opened up in my life. I struggled periodically with a profound sense of meaninglessness in my twenties, something I would later understand—reading Simone de Beauvoir and Jean-Paul Sartre—as simply the human condition. I had, for about five years, relished being a servant of God, constantly begging him to tell me his will for my life, acting out of sincerity and compassion, I believe, but nevertheless with one ultimate goal in mind: to please God. It was an experience probably incomprehensible to one who has never believed in a God, or has only nurtured a faith tangential to the rest of one's life, but many will understand why the language I use here evokes the intensity and intimacy of the relationship between lovers. When I encountered the texts of medieval mystics such as Mechtild of Magdeburg and Hildegard of Bingen during my graduate studies, the ardent sentiments these women expressed were not unfamiliar. "Ah, Lord, love me passionately, love me often, and love me long," Mechtild writes, "For the more passionately you love me, the purer I shall become. The more often you love me, the more beautiful I shall become. The longer you love me, the holier I shall become here on earth."[6] Anyone who has lost God must accomplish the work of mourning Freud describes as the painful coming to grips with the loss of a beloved object; an object to which our libido is firmly attached, and which we are reluctant to abandon even if we accept that it no longer exists.[7]

I tried to fill this void in a number of ways. Despite my earlier promise never to darken the door of a university again, I discovered a field that spoke to my need to think starting from the basis of experience, and returned to school to complete a B.A. in Women's Studies. Finding myself in the unexpected situation of being divorced and the sole caregiver of a young child, and quite suddenly realizing my need for intellectual engagement, I was drawn to those women writers who introduced me to the social construction of mothering, who made the familiar *unfamiliar*, wreaking havoc with my assumptions and awakening me to a political world of which I knew nothing. I met Virginia Woolf's Mrs. Ramsay, who braces herself to meet Mr. Ramsay's demand for sympathy, his desire to be assured of his genius, and pours her energy into this task, "as a nurse carrying a light across a dark room assures a fractious child," until "there was scarcely a shell of herself left for her to know herself by; all was so lavished and spent."[8] I read Simone de Beauvoir asking the radical question, what is a woman?—"Are there women, really?"—and understood implicitly her description of the "independent woman" who feels tied to her body, and longs to lose herself in the intellectual life reserved for men.[9] I encountered psychoanalysis and became fascinated by the development of the sexed subject and the relation between self and other, which later brought me to the work of Michel Foucault, Jacques Derrida, and Emmanuel Levinas.

My discovery of feminism *as a cause*, however, to replace the purpose religion had given me, only provided a short-lived excitement. I encountered in our women-only events, in our celebration of some unnamable feminine essence and a concomitant exclusivity and moralism, and in our unwillingness to engage in self-critique (though this was not acknowledged), echoes of my Christian past. This was my introduction to the workings of ideology, and to the beginnings of a critique of identity politics that preoccupies me still. The dogma and moralism I had tried to flee seemed to cling to me. I heard it in my own voice as an enthusiastic feminist, unable (for a time) to recognize the self-righteousness of the platform from which some of us spoke.

It was not long before my attraction to the work of Beauvoir and Merleau-Ponty, with their emphasis on the contingency of ethics and politics, and to the feminist and postcolonial criticism that nurtured my growing interest in political struggle, led me to the fields we call poststructuralism and critical theory. In the work of Foucault and Derrida, Hélène Cixous, Gilles Deleuze, Frantz Fanon, Edward Said, Homi Bhabha, and Gayatri Spivak, among others, I found my first philosophical home.

Paradox

It was a flight from the necessity of foundational thinking and moral absolutes that drew me to those European thinkers of the twentieth century who were affected by the events of fascism and the Shoah, and whose work never forgets this history. It made sense to me that the lessons of such a history would point to the impossibility of normative ethical and political precepts. Wouldn't an encounter with fascism, totalitarianism, and genocide, however directly or indirectly experienced, result in an understanding of ethics as contingent, as fundamentally constituted by ambiguity—a notion Beauvoir elaborated in her own response to the events of this history? A paradox is introduced to the destiny of humankind, she writes in the opening to *The Ethics of Ambiguity*; man escapes from his natural condition without freeing himself from it: "He asserts himself as a pure internality against which no external power can take hold, and he also experiences himself as a thing crushed by the dark weight of other things."[10] While men have always felt this tragic ambiguity, it is the philosophers who "have tried to mask it" by denying death and establishing a hierarchy between body and soul. They have proposed an ethics that also eliminates this ambiguity, "by making oneself pure inwardness or pure externality, by escaping from the sensible world or by being engulfed in it, by yielding to eternity or enclosing oneself in the moment."[11]

These passages are profound statements about the necessity of thinking ethics phenomenologically. Let us look the truth in the face, Beauvoir urges her reader, "let us try to assume our fundamental ambiguity. It is in the knowledge of the genuine conditions of our life that we must draw our strength to live and our reason for acting."[12] Why do we act for the good of others if we do not do so to please a God? Conversely, how can we consider a deed done in the name of pleasing a God a good act? Why would following a moral precept be considered an ethical act at all? In the search for moral templates, it seems, as Martha Nussbaum puts it in her characterization of the dominant tradition in ethical philosophy since Plato, that we struggle to eliminate all that which is "messy, needy, uncontrolled, rooted in the dirt and standing helplessly in the rain."[13] Furthermore, such a project permits us to forget the thoroughly political nature of ethics. What can "moral autonomy" mean when we never act alone, never make decisions alone, and when our actions never affect only ourselves?

Deleuze appears to echo Beauvoir's sentiment that it is the immanent conditions of life that give us our reason for acting when he writes that ethics means "not to be unworthy of what happens to us."[14] It is an enigmatic claim that unmoors our association of ethics with identity and norms, evoking instead the absolute surprise of the event, which can never be anticipated, which comes to us from the future—an unknown interruption of time. Politics is "active experimentation" then, since we never know what will come, Deleuze suggests.[15] If ethics no longer appeals to a God, if it is considered immanent, no longer based on judgment but on the creation of new ways of existing, he adds, then ethics becomes inextricably related to politics. We could say then, that *both* politics and ethics become "active experimentation." Not to be unworthy of the unpredictable, uncontrollable events that come to us out of nowhere and hold us in their powerful grip alludes to our responsibility and agency as subjects of history, and to our rejection of *ressentiment*: "To grasp whatever happens as unjust and unwarranted (it is always someone else's fault) is, on the contrary, what renders our sores repugnant—veritable *ressentiment*, resentment of the event. There is no other ill will. What is really immoral is the use of moral notions like just or unjust, merit or fault. What does it mean then to will the event? Is it to accept war, wounds, and death when they occur? It is highly probable that resignation is only one more figure of *ressentiment*, since *ressentiment* has many figures."[16]

Not resignation, then, in the face of crises, but a turning of the event into an affirmation. What will we do with our inheritances? How will the past enable a future? I will return to these questions later.

These ideas have much in common with the later writings of Derrida, who doggedly insists on the aporetic nature of politics and ethics. We must "calculate"—make decisions, judgments, laws—yet these must always remain open to the "incalculable," those "messy" contingencies impossible to contain or prescribe away, without which we could never act ethically or justly, only technocratically through the deployment of rules. A decision which is not made in the midst of this obligation to calculate when calculation is impossible, Derrida argues, one made neither freely nor responsibly but according to a program, is not just.[17] Hence there is a fundamental moment of undecidability required in an ethical decision, one that is a prerequisite for any action and any judgment at all.

At the phenomenological, immanent level of lived experience, I think we know this well. Both Deleuze and Derrida are criticized for ideas that necessarily lead to relativism or nihilism, but we need to ask why it is that when we are forced to rely solely on our responses to the events that enfold us—often without the luxury of time for deliberation—we fear there is no ethical component to our actions. This seems to be precisely when we are *most* ethical; when we respond to the human need that confronts us where we are standing, or when we deliberate between two impossible choices, agonizing over a paradox no rule could ever resolve, and attempt to do the right thing—*or not*—a possibility that will always exist.

Looking back over my Mennonite childhood and youth through the lens of these ideas, I see the scrupulous fuss over everyday behavior—especially that of one's neighbor—as deflecting from the events one cannot control or prevent. There is no way to account for the atrocities many members of our community once experienced, and no way to prevent future violence from occurring, hence the interest in moral minutiae, the substance of which supplied many occasions for idle gossip at best, condemnation and excommunication at worst.[18] There is some comfort in the narrative that such atrocities were allowed by God as punishment for the sins of excess; for becoming prosperous and indifferent. Self-blame is easier to deal with than the utter randomness of violence, since it permits a modicum of control; violation and repression can be prevented from happening again simply by guarding against prosperity and a faith that has lost its fervor. Is there another way? How can we accept what we inherit—the events and our collective memory of them—and turn these unanticipated, often unwelcome, legacies into an affirmation of the future?

Deleuze's insistence that ethics must deal with the event is a rejection of the question: how could I have become a victim of this or that tragedy? How do we not dwell in our "repugnant sores"? Several years ago I accompanied my mother on a "Mennonite Heritage Tour" to visit the place of her birth and the remnants of Mennonite villages in what were once the thriving Molotschna and Chortitza colonies of Ukraine, established by the Prussian Mennonite immigrants in 1789 and 1804 respectively. My interest in family history overrode the discomfort I knew I would experience being among a large group of Mennonites for the first time in many years, but I did not anticipate the force of my reaction to Mennonite ethnocentrism. One of the tour guides, an eminent scholar of Russian Mennonite history who gave frequent lectures on the tour, seemed intent on promoting a Mennonite association with victimhood. Frequent comparisons were made with the Jewish experience. There were low rumblings of resentment at the world for failing to acknowledge the history of suffering of the Mennonite people—a people in perpetual exile, we were told. While visiting the memorial for the massacre of some 34,000 Jews on September 28 and 29, 1941, at Babi Yar, I overheard an elderly member of the tour group complaining to her companion about visiting a Jewish memorial when we were here to commemorate Mennonites. Jewish suffering received more than its share of world attention; what about Mennonite suffering? When I turned to her and asked why we could not commemorate tragic histories other than our own, she simply retorted that I was too young to understand as I had not been there to experience what they had.

As I had once been surprised to discover that the world from which we had been taught to separate ourselves was full of goodness and beauty, I was shocked when I discovered as an adult that many Russian Mennonite farmers were the prosperous "kulaks" I had read about in Marx and Engels and in Russian history texts, and that some of them had exploited the Ukrainian peasants who labored for them. No one ever spoke of this racism, and although I knew of the wealth of some of my ancestors from the photographs of their estates and family stories, this economic privilege was rarely mentioned except to remark on the fact that it was taken from them brutally. Although we heard repeatedly from the pulpit that it is easier for a camel to go through the eye of a needle than for a rich man to enter the kingdom of God, this seemed not to translate into daily practice.[19]

Equally surprising was my grandmother's sudden show of emotion—rare indeed for this strong and stoic woman—one day as she talked to me of her past, describing how she had to beg for food with her starving young brothers. It was the Russian peasants who gave them bread, however, not her Mennonite neighbors. "They kicked us out!" she said repeatedly, her voice breaking; this indomitable woman under whose stalwart shadow we grew up.

None of these details detract from the inestimable gifts of a secure and happy childhood among people who loved me. Neither do they suggest that the work for which Mennonites are known and respected throughout the world is somehow less worthy, less deserving of respect. What they reveal for me is the necessity of rethinking this past and this inheritance of mine in order to understand the nature of community and the ethical relations that constitute them. I would like to ask how we should demand accountability from those who have been traumatized. History has shown us that the experience of victimization does not often lead to an increased tolerance toward others, but to the folding of a community back into itself, and to the fortification of its borders. Sometimes, and perhaps more than sometimes in the infancy of this century, this leads to ongoing expressions of grievance and retaliatory violence. How indeed, can we become worthy of the events that happen to us?

Today

It took me roughly twenty years after leaving the church and my hometown before I could return without experiencing an identity crisis. While there was never any pressure from my immediate family to return to the church, for they had (in less dramatic ways) also drifted from our religious community, there remained a veiled, residual sense of judgment that seemed to hang in the air for many years, probably in part the product of my own internalized criticism. This posed the most significant challenge for me, one that I confronted whenever I found myself in the company of Mennonites. It required a certain silencing; an encounter with who I once was and a dissociation from who I was in the present. It was not only a matter of remaining silent about my thoughts and ideas, but of betraying a profound insecurity about my voice—my agency—when I did attempt to speak up in the face of a daunting moral authority that no longer had any content for me, but nevertheless lingered and haunted.

The paradox of my inheritance has become clear: the very experiences that might lead a community to moralism and exclusivity, perhaps even hypocrisy and racism, are those that enable a revaluation of our notions of community and ethics. In other words, individuals and communities who have experienced hardship and violence have a choice: they can attempt to secure themselves from the random and unexpected events of the future by fortifying their borders, hardening an identity against another, and nurturing a melancholic attachment to past victimhood that is in danger of sabotaging any kind of political survival; or they can engage in what is no doubt a painful, seemingly impossible struggle to accept a fundamental vulnerability to violence and injury and risk the trust and openness necessary for ethical and political practices that do not in turn victimize others. I have witnessed both of these responses in the Russian Mennonite community, and in numerous other groups recovering from acts of discrimination and violence. It is the task in particular of my generation—in my time and place—and of all those whose parents once told them stories of inexplicable horror, to turn this legacy into an affirmation of an unpredictable future; to waive our right to the victim's revenge in its various guises from intolerance to extreme violence, and work tirelessly for the *prevention* of hatred, discrimination, and intolerance, not merely toward the application of emergency measures once they take hold.[20]

NOTES

1. I speak specifically of the population referred to as "Russian Mennonites," who originated in Prussia and populated Ukraine from the end of the eighteenth century to the 1930s, by which time most had emigrated or were sent to Russia, and whose ethnic identity and national allegiances remained German. I would add that my experience is very specific to a time and place—a relatively rural Mennonite community (of the branch called "United Mennonite" or "General Conference")—and I make no claims to speak for the experiences of others in my own community or elsewhere.

2. One of the best-known organizations is the Mennonite Central Committee, a development agency that works in areas such as education, health, agriculture, peace and justice issues, relief work, and job creation around the world, and in North America with issues concerning immigration, refugee assistance, offenders and victims of crime, and so on. Other organizations include the Mennonite Disaster Service, the Mennonite Coalition of Refugee Support, the Mennonite New Life Centre, and the Mennonite Economic Development Associates.

3. I would like to stress here that this is not the case for everyone. There are, of course, Christian philosophers and Mennonite intellectuals who have not rejected their faith.

4. It is worth noting that the reference to "my church" here refers to the Mennonite Brethren church I began to attend in the latter years of high school, a group more evangelical and strict in their approach to moral behavior than the United Mennonite church of my childhood. These groups originally split in Ukraine over a disagreement about how baptism is performed (and in fact, during my youth the Mennonite Brethren expected any United Mennonite who wished to join their church to get rebaptized). That my formative teenage years were spent being active in the youth group of a Mennonite Brethren church meant that I experienced my faith quite differently from that of my siblings and the children with whom I grew up.

5. Maurice Merleau-Ponty, *The Phenomenology of Perception* (New York: Routledge and Kegan Paul, 1962), 369.

6. Mechtild of Magdeburg, *The Flowing Light of the Godhead*, trans. Frank Tobin (Mahwah, N.J.: Paulist Press, 1998), 52.

7. Sigmund Freud, "Mourning and Melancholia," in *On Murder, Mourning, and Melancholia*, trans. Shaun Whiteside (New York: Penguin Books), 204–5.

8. Virginia Woolf, *To the Lighthouse* (London: Grafton Books, 1977), 38–39.

9. Simone de Beauvoir, *The Second Sex*, trans. H. M. Parshley (New York: Alfred A. Knopf, 1952), 1. See also chapter 25, "The Independent Woman," 679–715.

10. Simone de Beauvoir, *The Ethics of Ambiguity*, trans. Bernard Frechtman (New York: Carol Communications, 1948), 7.

11. Ibid., 8.

12. Ibid., 9.

13. Martha Nussbaum, *The Fragility of Goodness: Luck and Ethics in Greek Tragedy and Philosophy* (Cambridge: Cambridge University Press, 1986), 2.

14. Gilles Deleuze, *The Logic of Sense*, trans. Mark Lester and Charles Stivale, ed. Constantin V. Boundas (New York: Columbia University Press, 1990), 149.

15. Gilles Deleuze, "Many Politics," in Gilles Deleuze and Claire Parnet, *Dialogues II*, trans. Hugh Tomlinson and Barbara Habberjam (New York: Columbia University Press, 1987), 137.

16. Deleuze, *The Logic of Sense*, 149.

17. Jacques Derrida, "Ethics and Politics Today," *Negotiations: Interventions and Interviews, 1971–2001*, ed. and trans. Elizabeth Rottenberg (Stanford: Stanford University Press, 2002), 298.

18. While I did not belong to the kind of Mennonite sect that practices excommunication in the literal sense of banning, there are more subtle forms of this practice. One need not be physically exiled from family and church to feel excommunicated psychologically or emotionally.

19. Matthew 19:24.

20. I am inspired by two authors here: Frantz Fanon and Giorgio Agamben. Frantz Fanon writes in *Black Skin, White Masks* (New York: Grove Press, 1967), 228–29, that he will not accept the "amputation" of his victimization, explaining that he does not have the right to hope that the white man will feel guilt, the right to destroy white pride, to claim reparations, or to "cry out [his] hatred at the white man." The only right he does claim is "that of demanding human behavior from the other." Giorgio Agamben writes, in the context of a very different discussion on the task of democracy, "Maybe the time has come to work towards the prevention of disorder and catastrophe, and not merely towards their control. Today, there are plans for all kinds of emergencies (ecological, medical, military), but there is no politics to prevent them. . . . It is the task of democratic politics to prevent the development of conditions which lead to hatred, terror, and destruction—and not to reduce itself to attempts to control them once they occur." Agamben, "Security and Terror," trans. Carolin Emcke, *Theory and Event* 5.4 (2002): 2. I feel this is the task we face in local communities that have experienced some form of violation, and one which considerably alters our understanding of politics.

10

FINDING MY VOICE

Stefani Jones

Nothing out of the ordinary marks the day of my birth. I was born the second daughter to devoutly religious parents in a hospital in Provo, Utah. There were four similar births to come for my parents over the ten years that followed, concluding with the long-awaited son. The only thing my mother will say about my birth is that it was a very fast labor and delivery, for which she was understandably grateful. My father has never said anything to me about the day of my birth. I am certain that it was a happy event, as it would be for most parents. I am also certain that on that particular day, the eve of spring 1971, they did not expect that the daughter who came so quickly into this world would eventually challenge their desire to remain a complete family in eternal life.

But it seems that that is what I have done. Or so I've been told. And I am still unwilling to trade my voice for a family seat in whatever happens after death. I am certain that in some ways I remain a disappointment to my parents, and considering the beliefs that are important to them, a burden too. And that is all right with me. I do not feel the guilt and shame I used to. These feelings are not entirely gone, but they are not as predominant in my life now. But getting to this point took a great deal out of me, as I expect it did for my parents.

Frequently I wonder what a girl (now woman) from Utah raised strictly Mormon is doing *here*. *Here* for me is nowhere particularly notable. I am not unusually accomplished or famous, nor have I done anything that would seem remarkable to anyone but me. I am now a mother to two young daughters, a partner to a man I love—a man who was born and raised in a part of the world that as a child I did not even know existed—I have a doctorate, and I am a woman with a voice. The latter two are things I was never supposed to be. Among other things, getting *here* first took a high school English teacher who, much to my surprise, actually wanted me to speak, two female undergraduate philosophy professors who, in different ways, challenged me to think critically, and a philosophy professor in graduate school who became my mentor and friend, and among other important things, encouraged me to feel like I belonged at the university.

In this chapter I draw from my own experience of being raised in a Mormon family and a broader community dominated by Mormonism to explore how religious indoctrination may hamper a child's developing sense of autonomy. Children tend to experience parental love as simultaneous with parental approval; and when parental approval is conditioned primarily or exclusively upon their having successfully internalized the religious injunctions held by the parents, conflict often results as children become adults and develop beliefs of their own. Parental love, perhaps more than any other kind of love, is risky, since it entails a delicate balance between the responsibility to act on behalf of children and the responsibility to create the space for children to act (and think) on their own. This balance is often thrown off when parents indoctrinate children and either fail to provide that space, or exact emotional punishment when the children learn to explore alternatives and potentially come to believe otherwise.

I do not think my parents set out to indoctrinate me or my siblings, nor did they wish to harm us in any sense of the word—the thought, I believe, would have been repugnant to them. They educated us, both religiously and otherwise, in accordance to what was known and familiar to them, how they themselves were both raised and educated. There was no other way to go about it, at least not one they were willing to consider or accept. There was no need to teach us critical thinking skills, since they could conceive of no situation in which it would be necessary to question what we were being taught. Though my childhood indoctrination was unintentional, I do think it is nonetheless morally questionable. As a child, I was taught that obedience, reverence, respect, and silence were, in practice, synonymous terms imposed by God, the church, and my father. Being a female child didn't help matters—submission was that much more expected. While I doubted the beliefs I was taught as a child, I had very little space or opportunity to learn otherwise. I did not have a voice to express my doubts, nor did I have any person in particular to appeal to for understanding or encouragement. I did, however, have the curiosity and will eventually to explore my doubts and to desire something more in my life; but this was not without a great deal of pain and argument with my parents, which ultimately resulted in a rift in our relationship that to this day has not been bridged. It was through my somewhat accidental introduction to both feminism and philosophy that I was able to begin first to find that I had a voice, and second to learn that I deserved to be heard.

What follows is my story. It is a story I am sure my parents would tell differently. I will first describe the situation in which I was raised and how my parents' beliefs informed what, early on, I took to be my own possibilities. I will then describe the process of finding my own voice—a voice that did not (and still does not) fit within my parents' belief paradigm. And finally, I will discuss the morality of indoctrinating children.

Childhood Situation

My mother and father have always taken great pride in having been born into families with ties to the early days of the Church of Jesus Christ of Latter-day Saints. Nearly all of my male relatives, both living and dead, have served in some capacity of leadership in the Church: bishops, stake presidents and patriarchs, and so on. Most, if not all, of my female relatives served the church in the limited roles available to them, usually by teaching Primary or Young Women's classes, or heading up the Relief Society. With the exception of the main Sunday meeting (Sacrament meeting), men and women, and boys and girls, are separated from one another for other meetings; the lessons are tailored to topics appropriate for each gender and age group. Not having been privy to the details of teenage boys' lessons, I cannot say firsthand what they were taught, but I am fairly confident that they were not being instructed on how to set the table with the appropriate silverware and how to have dinner prepared when one's husband returns home from work in the evening as I was. Churches are located on what seems every block, and they are gathering spots for neighborhood events or socials typically held multiple times a week. Neighborhoods are divided up into sections, each designated as a ward. The members of each ward become, in effect, extended family.

As a child, I was frequently reminded of the suffering and persecution of the Mormon pioneers as they traveled West on foot and in wagon trains from Nauvoo, Illinois, to eventually settle in the Salt Lake Valley. We would often celebrate Pioneer Day (an official state holiday) by recreating the journey in the form of children's plays, dressing up in aprons and caps, carrying our dolls and walking behind makeshift wagons. I have vivid memories of hearing stories of starvation, freezing temperatures, raids on the wagon trains, and mothers having to bury their dead babies along the way. My parents encouraged me and my siblings to honor the memory of the pioneers and to remember what they endured to settle in the chosen land. We were made to feel a sense of duty to remember the suffering of the pioneers and to honor it by living righteously and serving the church. The persecution of the pioneers reinforced the idea that the world outside Provo, or more generally Utah County (which does not include Salt Lake City), was dangerous and sinful.

Images of the early prophets, Joseph Smith and Brigham Young, hung on our walls alongside pictures of God, the Lord Jesus, and the Holy Ghost. Little was said about the controversial past of the church in practicing polygamy, other than to revere it as a noble practice that eventually outgrew its utility. I was told that men were obligated to marry the widows of relatives to care for them and any children they may already have, and that one day, miraculously, the prophet received a revelation from God that it was no longer necessary. Coincidentally, shortly after that revelation, Utah was granted statehood. While I was at the university, my father and I had a disagreement on the topic of polygamy that resulted in months of not speaking to each other, not even in the usual somewhat removed but cordial way we had grown accustomed to at that time. The argument had to do with the fact that he believed in uncritically honoring, as righteous, ancestors who practiced polygamy because they were, at that time, doing what the Lord and the church asked. I disagreed and did not see the point of honoring a practice I considered demeaning to women.

Required by the church to declare one evening a week as family night, every Monday evening our family would gather in the living room, with my father at the head of the group. On most occasions, he would bring a chair from the kitchen table to the adjoining living room. Sitting on this chair would prop him up higher than sitting intermingled with us on the sofa or floor. To my eyes, as a child sitting on the floor in front of him, he, slim but broad-shouldered, standing six feet four inches, appeared magnificent and larger than life. I was aware that he was (and still is) a respected church leader and businessman, and I felt proud to be his daughter. He would more often than not read to us from the Book of Mormon, or recount an article from the official church magazine, the *Ensign*. Invariably, the sessions would involve at least one of my parents bearing testimony to the church, which was always an emotional event ending with tears shed. To this day, the only time I recall ever seeing my father cry was when speaking of God, the Lord, the Holy Spirit, Joseph Smith, or Brigham Young. My older sister frequently joined in and would bear testimony to the church too. My younger siblings would often tease each other, prompting one of my parents to scold them for not being reverent. Occasionally, I would ask my father a question about the Lord or a church leader. He would happily entertain my questions, but would quickly become irritated when I would repeatedly ask "why?" to every response he gave. His answers were calm, but when his lips would purse and his jaw would flex, I could tell that he had grown tired of my questions. It became increasingly apparent to me, in a child's way of processing the information, that questioning was disrespectful, and would result in my father's disapproval and withdrawal of affection. Silence, which he called reverence, earned his approval. My father was the spiritual head of our family, as the prophet was the spiritual head of the church. And like the prophet, his word was law, since it was through them both that the Lord's message was made available to the rest of the family.

I was baptized when I was eight years old, an expectation for all Mormon children at that age. My father spoke to me in a benevolent voice about the event weeks before, explaining that he, having priesthood authority, was able to offer me a path to eternal salvation and to official membership in the church. He continued to tell me that "families are forever" and that baptism offered me the ability to join him and the rest of our family in eternal life. As was customary, extended family and friends all gathered for the event. I was excited and embarrassed by all the attention. I expected to feel vastly different after being baptized—I thought I would then finally understand why when my father, mother, or older sister spoke of their feelings about the church they would well up with emotion. I thought I would suddenly feel these things too. Standing in a pool of water with my father, one of his hands raised over my head and the other holding on to my arms folded across my chest, I squeezed my eyes together tightly in preparation for being immersed in the holy water. He concluded by saying, "I baptize you in the name of the Father, and of the Son, and of the Holy Ghost. Amen." And into and out of the water I went. It was over just like that. I stood in the baptismal font, dripping wet and full of anticipation. And waited. Nothing miraculous happened. I kept my eyes squeezed shut until I felt my father gave me a loving pat on the shoulder; his eyes brimming with tears, he smiled softly. I felt irritated at all the heavy baptismal clothing weighed down by the water, but I didn't feel different. I returned to the dressing room and put on my Sunday dress. And I continued to wait for something to change inside me. Nothing changed. Relatives and friends offered their congratulations and told me how proud they were of me. I started to suspect that something had gone terribly awry, that maybe I had done something wrong that would account for why my baptism didn't appear to have worked.

Someone took a picture of me and my father standing outside the church doors: he in his suit and me in my dress, my hair still wet and dripping down my back. I felt the weight and heat of his hand resting on my shoulder. I clenched my hands together tightly and thought to myself: he must never know. No one must ever know. I did not want to disappoint him by admitting that nothing had changed, that I felt nothing. And, more important, I did not want to be without my family in eternal life.

When I look at that picture as an adult, I feel a sense of sadness for the girl I was: a girl who desperately wanted to fit in and be loved; a girl who was unable to articulate that she was terrified of being rejected for being different and needed someone, namely her parents, to recognize and love her for what she was and was not. I also feel both sympathy and anger toward my father: sympathy, because at that time he would have been younger than I am today and he was a father and sole provider to five young daughters; anger, because each of his five daughters, from my perspective, has lived the effects of an oppressive religious upbringing inextricably tied to an oppressive gender system. I do not feel at liberty to expand on the effects of how I believe my sisters have internalized and lived what they have been taught. I love them dearly, and am deeply grateful that they accept me for who I am now. I will, however, say that with my sisters (and at least in one case with a female cousin), intolerable things that can happen to female human beings have been brushed under the rug, with twisted blame, and in other cases ignored, or otherwise left to the church to resolve. Around the time of my baptism, I did experience a growing sense that something was not right, but I did not have the capability to express my doubts or fears. The environment was not amenable to such a thing.

Shortly after my baptism, a school friend of mine, Christina, called me to ask if it was possible for my father to baptize her. Christina was the daughter of a single mother. It was well known that Christina's mother was on welfare and was not interested in joining the church, which I now imagine was the main reason why Christina had very few friends. We frequently played at my house after school. I had become friends with Christina earlier that year and repeatedly begged my parents to let me play at her house. They were reluctant at first because, they said, Christina's mother smoked. Eventually, they gave in and allowed me to play at her house for a couple of hours after school. Christina's mom would make us treats while we played in the room she shared with her younger brother.

I do not recall talking about my baptism with Christina, but I'm sure I must have repeated something to her that I was told, most likely having to do with eternal salvation and being able to be with your family after you died. At Christina's request, I asked my father if he would baptize her too. My father's face lit up from ear to ear, and he told me that next time Christina came to play, he would talk with her about what baptism means and what would be required of her to join the church. He told me how proud he was of me for spreading the Gospel, and I later heard him tell my mother how pleased he was with me and then after that I heard him telling someone else on the phone. Although I recall feeling happy that my father was proud of me, I also felt horrible. I was being rewarded for something I had not done, and once again, I felt like a fake. I did not understand exactly what my father thought I had done, but I was pretty sure I had not done it. The next day, my paternal grandfather gave me a loving pat on the head and told me how proud of me he was for being a little missionary. I was embarrassed and figured that must have been whom my father was talking to on the phone. I ran to my room, shut the door, and threw myself on the bed, wondering why I didn't feel emotionally or spiritually connected to the church and why, unlike it seemed for everyone else, I felt nothing notable, other than a bit silly, when praying or bearing testimony. At church camp, I didn't feel the Spirit of the Holy Ghost as all the other girls my age seemed to. I asked one of my teachers how she knew the Spirit was with her. "I feel it in my heart," she said. I was disappointed with her response as I was expecting something more profound and concrete to go on, but I was not bold enough to ask additional questions for fear that she would see that I was not the same as the other girls. Once I asked my older sister what it felt like. She responded by telling me it was like a burning in her chest. And while that was something more concrete to go on, I was suspicious and thought the feeling was probably a result of something she ate.

I am ashamed now of what I did, as I expect that it hurt Christina: I refused to play with her or to talk with her again. I avoided her at all costs. When I saw her crying a couple of times on the playground at school, I would turn and walk the other way. I would not take her phone calls. I knew that she did not have many friends and that I may have been her only one at that age. Weeks later, I saw her mother at a school play; she was clearly upset. She told me how hurt Christina was that I ignored her and scolded me for not having the courtesy to tell her why I did not want to be Christina's friend.

I stared blankly at her, wanting to explain, but I had no idea how. I couldn't move. I wanted to grab hold of her legs and hug her, and tell her how sorry I was to have misled Christina and how I missed her, but my body froze and no words would come out of my mouth. She grew frustrated with my silence and walked away briskly. I had no idea how to reconcile being her friend with feeling like I was a fake. I could not stand the thought of more words of praise being lavished on me by my parents and relatives for her interest in the church. And I couldn't stand the thought of feeling like a fake in my relationship with my friend.

The Beginning of the End

I can confidently say that I was never a devout believer. And I'm fairly sure, to their dismay, my parents would agree. They have said that I was a stubborn, difficult, and determined child. Looking back, I think the appearance of belief satisfied them as much as if I actually had believed. Their view of my being difficult was probably a result of my gradual withdrawal from participation in the church. When asked to pray at dinner time, I would always recite my prayer like a script read very fast. As I grew older, I refused to bear even a scripted-style testimony or offer a prayer. I went to church on Sunday with my family and sat through all the meetings day dreaming. When the opportunity presented itself, I skipped out of Young Women's class and wandered around the cemetery just down the road from our church. Sometimes I convinced a friend to come with me for the company. As I grew older, I would beg out of any church-related activity I could, attending only the bare minimum required. In high school, I refused to attend seminary. All family gatherings and trips became increasingly uncomfortable for me because of the form that they would take: always a prayer before departing, usually one or two during the event, and conversations were always laced with the church, the Lord, and the Holy Ghost. Testimony was always borne. Camping trips became unbearable. Someone would always get hurt, which would necessitate my father laying his hands on someone's head and offering a blessing. I could not relate to the feelings of my parents or siblings. I do not doubt that common preteen and teenage issues were also in play, but the awkwardness and rebellion of that age didn't seem to hinder my siblings in their participation in these family events, which contributed to my feelings of unease.

The older I grew, the more dissatisfied with the situation I became. I felt hopeless and could not envision how things could possibly change. The world outside Utah Valley seemed totally inaccessible. I was intrigued by what was beyond the mountains that surrounded Provo and also terrified of it. At fourteen, I made a feeble attempt at suicide. I became wretchedly ill for a few days, recovered, and since I was not prone to violence, I figured suicide was not an effective option. I continued to feel tormented and helpless. My life plan had long been mapped out for me: I would be a good Mormon girl who would eventually marry a returned missionary, in the Temple of course, we would have lots of children, and our lives would be like my parents, and my parents' parents, and so on, navigated exclusively around the church. My education was never an issue, and it was hardly ever discussed. On those few occasions when it was brought up, it was determined that in the worst case I could learn a trade appropriate for women, so that if absolutely necessary I could work to help support my family.

As a teenager, I received little encouragement from my parents, extended family, or school counselors and teachers. In grade school and junior high, I excelled in math and was always allowed to attend the grade above me for that session, until one year the school counselor who helped plan my courses the following year decided that I should be taking home economics rather than any additional advanced mathematics, perhaps since both courses fulfilled the same requirement, and home economics was considered more suitable for a girl. Although I'm certain my parents were made aware of my course schedule, I imagine it never occurred to them to object. I did not resist and silently went to class, listened, and did my assignments. I continued to float unnoticed through what I now understand to be an abysmal K–12 educational system. But unexpectedly, things started to change in an English class during my junior year.

Ms. Jarmin was a petite woman, probably in her late twenties or early thirties, with short red hair cropped to her ear. She would sit on a tall wooden stool at the front of the room. It seemed that she would hop a bit to get on or off the stool. Unlike the other teachers, who were content to find me sitting at the back of the classroom silent, Ms. Jarmin actually wanted me to speak. The first time she called on me, it caught me by surprise and I felt my face flush. We were reading *To Kill a Mockingbird*, and she asked me a question about Scout. I replied, and she seemed satisfied. I do not recall her question or my answer, but I do recall feeling as if she really did want to know what I thought, and I felt exalted. As the bell rang, she asked me to stay. She told me she liked what I had to say and would like to hear more the next day. I left the room feeling a sense of purpose. And I could not wait to return the following day. The next day she called on me again and that went on day after day, until I started raising my hand to say something as opposed to being called on. It was in Ms. Jarmin's classroom that I decided I was going to college and began to suspect that my way out of my current situation resided in using what was in my head.

By the end of my junior year, I could not wait to get on with my life and found that I could attend a local community college my senior year and take classes for both high school and college credit. I spoke with the school counselor about it and was told that I would need my parents' authorization. I knew they would resist, but I was also determined that I was going to go to college the following year. As expected, my parents forbade it, asking why I would want to do such a thing, and thought it foolish since I didn't know exactly what trade I would be trained in. I insisted and told them I was moving out and would find a way to go on my own. During the summer, I moved into the apartment of a friend who was a couple of years older than me. The arrangement didn't last long, as my parents insisted I move back home, but they did finally agree to let me attend college the upcoming fall.

My parents were worried about my spiritual development, and my growing explicit disinterest in the church caused them a great deal of pain. The community was very tightly knit, and everyone knew everything everyone else was doing. People were talking about my increased absence at church functions and my sudden disappearance in high school, and they were speculating what could be the cause. None of the theories were particularly flattering, and the chatter caused my parents a great deal of embarrassment. My father and I argued endlessly. When I pushed too much, our arguments would turn physical, and on occasion would prompt him to "beat the devil out of me." My mother would disappear during these episodes. In hindsight, I imagine it was because they frightened her, although at the time I didn't understand why she would not intervene. My mother was less resistant to what I was doing, and secretly I thought she was happy that I was pursuing an education. When she married my father, she dropped out of school, where she was training to become an elementary schoolteacher. Years later, on one occasion, she told me how much she regretted not finishing.

While attending community college, I had a good deal of work to do to overcome a poor education. I stuck with it; and when I had earned enough credits, I transferred to the University of Utah. I moved into an off-campus house in Salt Lake City shared with three other girls. This worried my father, not just because he would have preferred that I attend Brigham Young University, which was within a few miles of our house, but also because he thought Salt Lake City was worldly and sinful. My father and I were hardly speaking to one another. I could see in his eyes that I had disappointed him. We had nothing at all in common. He hoped I was going through a phase and would eventually turn back to the church and to him. I hoped that he would see me for who I was and love me anyway. It started to become very clear to me that the church and my father were one and the same, if I rejected the former, I would be rejected by the latter. It also started to dawn on me that my mother was caught in the middle. As a woman, she was disempowered in the church; and in our family, she was equally disempowered to change the situation. In a way, my mother had to choose a side. Looking back now, I could not have rightfully expected her to choose me. She did, however, resist in little ways; when I would visit my parents on the weekend, she would send me back to the university with bags full of food, and she would mail me money from time to time with a little note saying to use the money to do something for myself. These gifts seemed a secret, and many of her gestures to help and to stay in contact with me seemed an attempt to mend the growing rift in our relationship. She would sign her notes with the words "I love you, Mom." And while these ordinarily would be common words used between a mother and daughter, they seemed remarkable to me and would invariably make me long for a better relationship with both of my parents. My father would occasionally send me letters, but I could hardly bear to read them as they were always a forum for him to bear testimony to the church and to offer his wish that I find the Lord. He would write about our family and his parents intertwined with religious rhetoric. I do not recall him asking about my education or inquiring about my general welfare.

Although my parents had six children to care for, they were financially secure. Their help with the cost of my tuition and school expenses was often times contingent on the state of my relationship with my father, which was contingent on the state of my activity in the church. I worked as much as I could to support myself and eventually took out Pell grants and loans when our relationship took turns for the worse. At one point, my father offered me what at the time seemed a substantial amount of money every month if I were to go to church. I declined.

Like many other students, I was not sure what I wanted to study, and I changed majors several times. Early on, succumbing to my parents' wishes that I do something they viewed as useful for a woman, I started taking the required preparatory courses for nursing school. This plan was quickly abandoned after I found that my ability and interest in introductory chemistry left a lot to be desired. I felt a great deal of guilt for causing my parents so much pain, and I often questioned whether or not I deserved to be at the university. While I didn't believe in the church the way my parents and siblings did, I did experience terrible bouts of anxiety and shame that I could not easily reason away. I sometimes wondered: What if I am wrong and the church is right? Am I condemning myself to misery for all of eternity? I learned as a child that the Lord was always watching over his children. Relatives who passed away watched over us too. Although I was taught that this was meant to be comforting, it felt eerie and reinforced my unease.

The first philosophy class I took was an introductory ethics course taught by Mendel Cohen. I did not fare particularly well in the class, but it was exciting, more so than any other class I had taken to date. Argument and disagreement were actually encouraged, if not expected. Questions were asked about the existence of God and what it would mean if God didn't exist. And in my naïveté, it felt delightfully scandalous. I had never heard a grown man talk about God's existence or nonexistence in such a religiously uncommitted and open way. Although before this time I had wondered about the possibility that maybe God did not exist, but not in a reasonably mature or lasting way: of course he exists, I would casually conclude. Until Professor Cohen's class, I had no idea what being an atheist or agnostic meant, as I had never heard the terms before. I didn't know what I was: a believer, an agnostic, or an atheist. I never thought of myself as a believer since God's existence was just a fact of life as I knew it. From that point on, however, it became increasingly more difficult to accept, and it started to dawn on me that sorting through what was morally right from wrong was far more complicated than I had previously thought. I signed up for another philosophy class, this time with a professor new to the department.

Bridget Newell was young, pretty, and dressed in such a way that she could have easily blended in with the student population. We read Plato and Aristotle, and the social contract theories of Locke, Hume, and Rousseau. Professor Newell was critical but approachable and did not hesitate to point out the implications for the status of women in our readings. Again, I performed poorly. The first paper I turned in came back to me dissected severely from beginning to end. I was humiliated and felt sure she assumed I did not belong at the university and that she might recommend that I leave. But I was also determined to learn and to stay. I never missed a class and spent hours reading and making notes about the texts. Other students in study group would always beg to make a copy of my typed and detailed notes. Professor Newell worked with me to revise and resubmit my paper, and she continued to provide valuable feedback throughout the course. On my last paper, she congratulated me for making so much progress. It was the encouragement I needed to continue with my studies.

At that age, I did not know what it meant to be a feminist, but whatever it was, that's what other students were calling Professor Newell. And based on what I had heard from her during class, I was not convinced it was a terrible thing. A couple of male students seated behind me were talking one day and dismissing her as "just a feminist." I turned to them and abruptly asked why that mattered. Did it make her arguments less credible? If they were blind and somehow unable to decipher gender based on the sound of her voice, would her points be more palatable? Neither one responded. I turned away and fumed. What I had long felt in the pit of my stomach, but was unable to articulate, started to become clear: that being a female mattered in ways that both confused and angered me. Being my father's daughter suddenly doubled in significance. This knowledge felt sharp and cutting.

My thoughts at the time were muddled and unrefined. In my childhood world, silence masked as reverence to my father and the Father was different for me, my sisters, and my mother. Silence as reverence was a sign of respect and honor. God spoke through men. And men spoke to or on behalf of women. Where is their voice? What about my voice? It started to dawn on me that women are not supposed to have one. I had no idea how to change the situation for myself, but I was sure that I would not accept it.

I continued to enroll in as many philosophy classes as I could. I took more classes with Professor Newell and enrolled in my first class with Leslie Francis. At the same time, I was taking courses in political science and had enrolled in political theory. Margaret Sanger was the only female author on the list of assigned readings, and I decided to ask the professor if there were other female authors of the time that I might read. I had heard about Simone de Beauvoir but knew nothing about her work and if it was compatible with the topic of the class. I went to his office during office hours and posed the question. He responded by asking me what I was accusing him of. Not being cognizant of what might have been happening in the university with respect to more robust and gender-friendly syllabi, I responded, flush faced, with apologies and promptly exited his office. I recall feeling both embarrassment that I had probed in an area that was obviously inappropriate and a sense of growing discontent with the fact that it seemed women everywhere were being brushed under the rug. I later recounted this incident to Professor Newell, who reassured me that I had done nothing wrong. I also bought myself a copy of Beauvoir's *The Second Sex*. I skimmed the book many times, reading a few pages here or there, but it would be years before I took it in cover to cover.

I feel indebted to both Professor Newell and Professor Francis in similar but different ways, and I sometimes wonder about the coincidence that both happen to be philosophy professors: a profession where questioning and argument is not just allowed, but expected. This stands in stark contrast to my childhood world, where questioning was discouraged, if not prohibited as disrespectful. Meaning. Mattering. Truth. Consequences. This is one of the first things I recall hearing Peter Caws tell a group of students while explaining how philosophical questioning gets started: What does it mean? Does it matter? Is it true? What are its consequences? But I am getting ahead of myself. One point worth calling out now is that it was not just philosophy as a subject that helped me to confront and work out my childhood indoctrination, but it was also, and perhaps more important, the people who taught the subject and were committed to it, who personalized it and gave me the support and encouragement I needed to ultimately feel at home with myself.

While my confidence and ability was cultivated by Professor Newell, it was Professor Francis who first introduced me to feminist philosophy. I read Catharine MacKinnon and Andrea Dworkin in her class and learned what it meant to critically question what it means to be a woman in a patriarchal culture. My voice was growing stronger and was decidedly feminist. I started to dissect the beliefs of the church and how I was raised and became increasingly aware that neither supported me as a woman who thinks. I scored high marks on exams and papers, and Professor Francis would frequently encourage me to go to law school or graduate school.

After graduation, I continued working and saved up enough money to move. I stayed in my parents' house for a couple of days before leaving for the East Coast. My father and I spoke very little to one another. Hours before I drove off, I sat with my mother on the sofa and put my head on her lap. Few words were spoken. She stroked my head as I cried. I knew I would not be coming back. She left the house before I did. None of my siblings or parents were home when I pulled out of the driveway, and there was nothing and nobody left to say goodbye to. But there was much to look forward to, and at that moment, the future seemed more up to me than it ever had before.

After arriving in the Washington metropolitan area, I worked at various jobs, and for a while worked as a volunteer in the White House during the Clinton administration. Walking through the Old Executive Building, I felt a sense of disbelief that I had made it from Utah Valley to the White House (figuratively speaking, of course). I applied for graduate school at universities in the area, and luckily, I had more than one acceptance to choose from. Although I felt more confident in my academic ability than when I was an undergraduate, the residue of my upbringing lingered. I remained terribly shy and had difficultly speaking in the presence of authority for fear of it being discovered that I shouldn't be there. I was lucky enough to find professors who encouraged me to pursue my studies and one, in particular, who believed in me and encouraged me to feel a sense of belonging.

I am pretty sure that early on what I felt to be encouragement was a result of his passion for philosophy, which was, from a student's perspective, contagious. Over the years that followed, I learned that that passion and his generosity are part of who he is as a philosopher and professor, and as a mentor, a friend, and a human being. Prior to enrolling in courses with Peter Caws, I had heard from fellow students that he was a remarkable professor. With his grayish-white hair, glasses, and a suit with no tie effortlessly thrown together, upon first meeting him I thought he fulfilled the quintessential image of a philosopher: eyes gleaming, and overflowing with ideas and responses in any situation. He always spoke to students in a very excited and approachable manner. Over time, Professor Caws and I developed an ongoing conversation about the similarities of our childhood upbringings. We discussed the moral issues of religious indoctrination and our own (albeit different) experiences of being alienated by our parents in the process of questioning and, ultimately, rejecting our childhood belief systems. I read Beauvoir's *The Second Sex* and *The Ethics of Ambiguity*, and gradually I came to the conclusion that religious indoctrination is incompatible with the idea of children as free. It is their status as free that is often ignored and neglected. Beauvoir is not usually someone referenced when talking about the situation of children, but she actually has a lot to say about children, their moral status, and relationships with others. I think in a significant sense, Beauvoir can be read as an advocate for children—not an advocate against particular abuses or an advocate for a particular issue, but an advocate for situating children's dependency and their need for help from others to have a full future that is worth living; a future where children learn to make choices and decisions that are more their own, and where they recognize the effects of their choices and decisions on others and assume responsibility for them.

My voice was starting to take shape. I was able to more clearly articulate what had caused me so much pain and sadness. I was coming to understand why my childhood indoctrination was morally suspect. For the first time, I was starting to feel at peace with myself.

Moral Issues

It has been well over a decade since I left Utah and more than that since I left the church. The miles between me and my parents, in particular my father, have done some good. My relationship with him is not as hostile as it once was, and we have learned to more or less avoid topics that will cause argument. On occasion, I will receive letters from him with the same religious tone as before. They still strike the wrong chord in me, but I don't feel the anxiety I would have felt years ago; I can bear to read them, I just don't particularly care to personalize them. My father rarely calls and has taken very little interest in getting to know my children. Although he has traveled to Illinois and New York on church excursions, he has never come to visit me. My relationship with my mother has improved. We talk frequently, though mostly through pictures and gifts that arrive by mail; my older daughter knows who I mean when I say Grandma Jones is on the phone or that a package is from her. I have taken both of my children to visit their grandparents in Utah, and I am hopeful that my younger daughter will also get to know them as she grows older.

What saddens me the most is thinking about how different things could have been if, early on, we had figured out a way to set religious disagreements aside and relate to one another as parents and child. It might not have resolved the issue of equipping me with the skills and space to deconstruct the belief system in which I was raised and then construct one in its place I could call my own, but it would have enabled us all to avoid a great deal of pain. Given the vulnerability and dependence of children, this strikes me as a misfortune that could easily be avoided, given a little parental understanding or even toleration.

While I do think a good argument can be made against Mormonism, that is not my purpose here. In spite of the fact that the church tries to appear outwardly inclusive (arguably for image and recruiting purposes), its tenets easily lend themselves to exclusion. By not accepting and living according to what the church dictates, I remain more or less excluded from family: in theory, for eternal life; in practice, in this one. The former matters more to my parents. The latter matters more to me.

There are at least two related points that need to be called out as moral issues. The first has to do with parents closing off alternatives. A child can only choose or earnestly consider alternatives she is made aware of and, ideally, encouraged to explore. The second has to do with a selective giving or withholding of parental love in the face of considering and choosing alternatives. Long before I was capable of intellectually understanding that there were alternatives I could examine or consider, I absorbed my parents' love and affection and their disappointment and irritation, slowly gaining a sense of what met or did not meet their approval. The emotional stakes of making choices were laid down at an age of vulnerability.

A parent-child relationship is one clear case in which one person impinges, for better or worse, upon the future of another. The dependency and vulnerability of children makes a good deal of parental impinging absolutely necessary. Impinging can open children's future. I draw from Beauvoir's use of the word "impinge" for my purposes because it captures not only the meaning of the verb "to impose" but also the sense of impacting and affecting others in significant ways.[1] One reason I find the word "impinge" helpful here is because it tends to more accurately account for the fact that we do modify the situations of others and it is indicative of a responsibility we have for others. But where do we draw the line between justified and unjustified impinging in parent-child relationships, how might this impingement be characterized, and under what conditions is the line to be drawn?

On the one hand, an answer seems quite clear. Parents can legitimately dictate a good deal about what children can and cannot do, and do and do not have access to, including, for instance, the food they eat (or ought not to eat), that they must attend school and play nicely with siblings and friends, the number of hours spent watching television, or playing on the Internet, and what children can watch and the sites they can visit. On the other hand, parents cannot legitimately dictate who and what children will become, nor can they dictate what children will believe. Parents do inform who and what children will become and what they believe, but when children's possibilities are unreasonably cut off or interfered with as a result of what parents believe to fall within their legitimate range of authority, I claim that they are relating to their children in unjustified and irresponsible ways. The degree to which parental impinging is justifiable is directly correlated to whether or not the impinging is aimed toward opening future possibilities for children or shutting them off. The challenge is to find a way of impinging while simultaneously offering children what is needed to become free in relation to others. This is a challenge my parents failed.

Surely parents might be justified in attempts to shut off potentially destructive possibilities or alternatives. Children who have stolen candy from the corner store, or a toy from a friend, may need to be taught dogmatically that stealing is wrong and that growing up to be a thief is not moral or acceptable. But closing off or interfering with children's ability to learn to consider alternatives and to make informed choices on their own cannot be justified. In *The Ethics of Ambiguity*, Beauvoir is attuned to this and explains that even though a child's situation necessitates that others assume authority over him, that "even in this situation the child has a right to his freedom and must be respected as a human person."[2]

Situated within an ethical background not of their own choice, children's sense of self is modified by others. Attributes of our situation, while not always chosen, become vital to who we are, believe ourselves to be, and sometimes even believe ourselves to be capable of becoming. These attributes include not only the social, religious, economic, and political features of the community into which we are born, but are also attributes related to how others recognize and relate to us. Children's relationships with others, notably parents, are not merely incidental. They are absolutely primary. Children's open future is contingent upon others recognizing their ability to inhabit their own future, and moreover, encouraging them to do so. Once children have matured and discovered their freedom, it is up to them to make the best of their circumstances. Parents' responsibility is to ensure that those circumstances are the best they can be and to provide children the encouragement, confidence, and self-esteem to forge futures of their own.

In *The Ethics of Ambiguity*, Beauvoir poses the question "Just what is meant by the expression 'to love others'?"[3] Her question does not arise from a philosophical inquiry specifically on the topic of love, but from an inquiry concerning freedom and the association of love with willing freedom. Beauvoir is clear in this text, as well as in *The Second Sex*, that for love to be genuine (for it to be moral), it must be based upon a robust notion of freedom.[4] In loving another morally, one must be attentive to how love situates the loved one. Does it enhance or detract from the other's ability to be morally free? Beauvoir's work suggests that in order to interrogate the concept of love one must concurrently interrogate the concept of freedom, and because freedom incites the risk of violence,[5] an inquiry about the ethics of love is also an inquiry about the risk of violence. Love is a risky venture—freedom makes it so. There are a whole host of unpleasant side-effects associated with the motion of love, such as domination, disappointment, grief, and pain. But love also holds the promise of affection, joy, and the pleasure of seeing loved ones flourish in their freedom.

Feelings of love cannot be brought about by command or magically summoned for particular others at the appropriate time and situation. The issue I am concerned with is when parental love for children is present and becomes caught up in their motivation to respond to children. I do not think that my parents would ever say that they did not, or do not, love me. I know they do. But it is how they chose to express the love they feel that is the problem. Expressions of love do not escape the demands of freedom, nor is love the only way to address the demands. It does, however, intensify the need for the demands of freedom to be met. In loving others we may want to protect them from harm and shelter them from unpleasant life experiences. We may also be too protective, wanting for them what we want for ourselves, and attempting to rob them of the fullness of their own experiences.

Beauvoir tells us that the interdependence of freedoms creates a bond between human subjects that makes each subject responsible for the freedom of the other. While children are not entirely free in a moral sense, and early on are not equipped to take responsibility for their own freedom or the freedom of others, others—particularly parents—are responsible to create a situation within which children can choose to live up to the demands of their own freedom. Although we are responsible for the other's freedom, Beauvoir recognizes that we cannot possibly be expected to take responsibility for the situation of every individual in the world. But that there is a bond opens up possibilities for responsibility, love, and violence. Love is not required to sustain freedom, but freedom is required to sustain love within a moral relationship.

Simply put, violence, for Beauvoir, boils down to acts that affect, interfere with, or thwart the freedom or the concrete possibilities of freedom for the other. Violence is not inherently good or bad. Like freedom, it is ambiguous. Beauvoir recognizes that not all violence functions on the same moral plane; some forms of violence offer no hope for freedom but only seek to erase the possibilities of freedom. Beauvoir's description of violence is indeed broad, perhaps too much so to describe everyday situations. She is right, however, to point out that because there will likely never be the perfect affirmation of freedom, the risk of violence will always remain present. For those who are dependent and most vulnerable to the effects of violence—children—it is important, from a moral perspective, to interrogate the way in which others—parents—relate to them, teach them or fail to teach them to practice freedom, particularly when love functions as a reason for doing so. There is a degree of psychic violence that occurs when parents indoctrinate children. Forced belief systems can incite self-inflicted torture (in many cases that is the likely goal) by means of shame, sin, guilt, bodily hatred, and so on. In such cases, parental love is often withheld depending on how well children assimilate the belief system. This is a form of violence that is, too often, disguised beneath the veil of love.

Then how are we justified, or under what conditions are we justified, in responding violently toward another under the pretext of love? It is not that love offers justification for violence that other ways of relating cannot, but that love can make us more willing to take risks. We are more inclined to respond to those we love, and the response is likely to be different from responses based solely on care or other emotions. The feeling of love itself is not a matter of ethics or morality, but it becomes one by what we chose to do with the love we feel. One cannot be justifiably held morally accountable for loving or not loving another person, but one can be held morally accountable for how one chooses to express love. Feelings of love do not mediate relationships; it is when love is combined with commitments, beliefs, and practices that function as intermediaries between subjects that love's ethical force is set in motion.

Violence, for Beauvoir, is a mark of the unavoidable failure of being human. It is a condition of being human, of being free. What Beauvoir makes clear is that assuming the responsibility of love means accepting the responsibility to preserve the loved one's freedom, and when violence becomes necessary, love entails the responsibility to justify the violence one has invoked in the name of love. Clearly, for Beauvoir, there will never be the perfect affirmation of freedom; there will always be the violence of conflicts and disagreements. One might question how useful or appropriate it is to explore parent-child relationships in terms of violence. Admittedly, it does seem to produce a dismal picture. But Beauvoir does introduce a parent-child relationship into her discussion and says that the freedom of parents can be "the ruin of their sons."[6] When children are introduced into the picture, she continues, it is their freedom and future that takes precedence over the freedom of parents.[7]

Most parents do not oppress their children in ways that might be called violent. What Beauvoir's work does offer is a way to understand the dynamics of freedom within the interaction of parents and children, and how inculcating a belief system might be a moral problem when children's own freedom and future is not taken into consideration. In effect, what her work suggests is that for parents to morally interfere in the freedom of children, they must simultaneously offer that interference as a route to freedom for the children. Loving responsibly means that one must recognize that the emotion of love produces a risk, a risk that parents are responsible to ensure does not result in violence, and if it does, that the violence is aimed at expanding children's freedom to become. Parents may teach children a belief system that is the same as what their parents taught, and it might never have occurred to them or seemed feasible to question it, but imposing a belief system on children, leaving little to no room for them to explore and experiment with other possibilities, is a moral offense. It is a form of violence. And ignorance, as Beauvoir suggests, is not a justifiable excuse.[8]

Conclusion

Shortly after realizing that I was going to become a mother, I started to wonder if I would soon figure out that all of what I had come to learn about children as free was nonsense. I thought perhaps it is easier to argue for children's autonomy and freedom when one is not directly tasked with what I imagined to be an overwhelming responsibility to actually care for them. Beauvoir didn't have any children. It occurred to me that maybe this fact would have made it easier for her to argue for children as free. But now the mother of two young daughters, I am more convinced than ever that it is not nonsense, that children do deserve the opportunity to make the best of their futures, which includes being encouraged and allowed to take an active role in making their futures their own. And as a parent, I am on the hook to ensure that my children have the opportunity to explore alternatives and to chose futures they can call their own. I am certain that, like my parents, I will make mistakes. But I am confident that they will not be the same ones.

In *The Philosophy of Simone de Beauvoir*, Debra Bergoffen writes something I find particularly compelling and descriptive of what I think it means to understand children in terms of freedom. She captures an important aspect of what children need from parents, that is, to give them a point of departure and something to return to. She says, "It is not as a disinterested subject seeking to transcend my immanence that I offer the gift of love to my child. It is as an engaged mother who feels my child's pain in the pit of my stomach that *I encourage this child to become the fullness of her otherness and wait to find her there*" (my emphasis).[9] This seems to me to be the challenge and responsibility of being a parent and it is incompatible with indoctrination. A child's opportunity to engage in the process of living his or her own future is something worth arguing for.

NOTES

1. In *The Prime of Life*, Beauvoir links the effects of the inevitability of impinging with responsibility by saying that "whether we like it or not, we do impinge on other people's destinies,

and must face up to the responsibility which this implies." Beauvoir, *The Prime of Life*, trans. Peter Green (New York: Harper and Row, 1962), 479.

2. Simone de Beauvoir, *The Ethics of Ambiguity*, trans. Bernard Frechtman (New York: Citadel Press, 1996), 141.

3. Ibid., 136.

4. Simone de Beauvoir, *The Second Sex*, trans. H. M. Parshley (New York: Vintage Books, 1989), 473.

5. Beauvoir explains that "in the rearing of the child, as in any relationship with others, the ambiguity of freedom implies the outrage of violence." Beauvoir, *The Ethics of Ambiguity*, 142.

6. Ibid., 143.

7. Ibid., 143–44.

8. Ibid., 138.

9. Debra B. Bergoffen, *The Philosophy of Simone de Beauvoir: Gendered Phenomenologies, Erotic Generosities* (Albany: SUNY Press, 1997), 209.

11

TRAGEDIES OF BELIEF

Peter Caws

Introduction

I begin with a caveat. In this chapter I shall be speaking of my own indoctrination and how I got free of it. The primary agents of this indoctrination were my parents. In telling the story I shall attribute to them thoughts and feelings that, if they were living and could read what I write, they might not recognize as their own. Perhaps I did not know them well enough. But perhaps they did not know themselves well enough. Both views are plausible—as I remember them they were not open or articulate about personal matters, and they were probably not given to self-examination except on questions of conscience, before God. But I shall tell the story as well as I can recall it, roughly in chronological order. The first part deals with my upbringing, and how it was guided by their hopes and beliefs. They were members of a small and intolerant but self-satisfied sect, the Exclusive Brethren, a nineteenth-century offshoot of the Church of England whose basic tenets were two: strict separation from the world, and unquestioning obedience to the rules promulgated by the leading "ministering brother," later called the Elect Vessel, the Man of God, or the Minister of the Lord in the Recovery. I lived my early years against a background of biblical doctrines and sectarian practices, which I took to be the normal human condition.

The second part describes the gradual awakening of a critical intelligence, through teachers and reading and observation and reflection; the realization of an irreconcilable dissonance between what seemed manifest facts about the world and the beliefs with which I had been indoctrinated; and the eventual rejection of those beliefs and the structure of authority that upheld them. The third part details the tragic cleavage between parents who would not consider the possibility that they might be mistaken, and a son who could not pretend to believe doctrines that did not satisfy what he took to be essential criteria for honest and authentic belief. And the fourth part reflects on the moral issues that were at play in this standoff between parents and child: the requirement that beliefs be held for good reasons, the consequences of parental indoctrination for the freedom of children, the desire to protect as against the duty to enlighten, and most particularly the toxic nature of disagreements about belief for family affection and stability.

I write as a philosopher, as a parent—and as a former child. As a parent I take myself to have, and to have had, specific moral obligations to some particular others (among others), namely my own children. As a philosopher I am professionally interested in the structure and grounds of these obligations, and indeed of obligations in general. Not all parents are philosophers, although Plato's celebrated (and often misunderstood) point about philosophers and kings deserves generalization. Not just kings but parents too—who in the microcosm of the family have analogous powers and responsibilities—could profit from sharing in "the spirit and power of philosophy," as he puts it.[1] This means being reflectively and self-reflectively aware, inquiring, and careful in argument. Plato's point was less that people who were already philosophers should become kings than that people who were already kings should become philosophers, or as he later came to think, should at least consult with philosophers. His own success at being a consultant to kings—in particular to the tyrant Dion of Syracuse—was less than brilliant, but that is no argument against the principle, articulated repeatedly by Socrates throughout the Platonic corpus, that it is always worthwhile to keep trying (as he puts it in book 10 of the *Republic*) "to distinguish the life that is good from that which is bad, and always and everywhere to choose the best that the conditions allow."[2] That effort is one of the marks of the spirit of philosophy, whether on the philosophers' own behalf or on behalf of those who come to them for guidance.

Doesn't everyone want the good rather than the bad, the best that conditions allow? Don't all parents want the best for their children? The short answer here is, unfortunately, no—too many people enter into parenthood unthinkingly, even by accident, not inquiring about the best at all (though no doubt the act that resulted in the conception of the child seemed like the best thing at the time, for one of the partners at least). The weight of the responsibility of bringing into the world a new individual, a new feeling and knowing subject, equal in value and importance to the parents who produced it, often seems hardly to be noticed, much less acknowledged. Even when children are planned and wanted (as opposed to being merely the unintended, and often enough unwelcome, result of purely animal lust), they may be regarded first as miraculous playthings, then as sources of pride and status and as excuses for conspicuous consumption, later on as ornaments, as heirs, as carriers of the family name and tradition. Occasionally, as must surely have been true in my own case, there may in addition to the natural unreflective drive to procreate be an element of duty or devotion, to raise up offspring for God or (in another variant) for country. All too rarely are children seen primarily as new beginnings of lives that are to be their own. Perhaps they are no longer thought of mainly as property, as sources of family income or as insurance against old age, but it is still by and large the parents' desires and interests and convictions that count. Many parents, it must surely be said, do genuinely want the best for their children. Unfortunately, wanting the best, and knowing what *is* best (and for whom exactly) do not necessarily go together. This is where the tragedy begins.

The Gift of a Son

As a former child I wonder about the things that were done to me that helped to determine what I was to become. How did my own parents think of me, what did they think their obligations were toward me? I'll give them credit for wanting the best, but how did they arrive at their view of what it was? I have before me an old photograph, taken I think during their engagement in the mid-1920s. They make an attractive couple, serious and full of hope. She is pretty and shy, he is handsome and in a quiet way proud: of her, of himself for being hers—not just for having won her affection, but for having claimed her in spite of a social difference, one that had no doubt been commented on by his family. She is the daughter of a railway signalman, he is the son of an army officer. He has been to a minor public school (as that term was understood in England—in other words, an exclusive private school), she to one of the local county schools established in the early years of the century as education began to be extended more and more to the less affluent classes. He is conscious, though, not so much of having defied a convention as of having lived up to a principle: the principle that in Christ there are no distinctions of wealth or rank, that all are equal before the Lord. They are very young. Both of them have clear eyes, looking at something in the distance, off to the left of the photographer—their future, perhaps. A few years into that future, already no doubt an object of anticipation, is the child I once was, the son I still am and will always be, in spite of estrangement and death.

I was named Peter for my father's uncle, James for my mother's father, but the fact that both are apostolic names cannot have been insignificant for my parents. They may not have realized what a burden the name of Peter might be to a boy nourished on the Scriptures, what a terrible possibility of betrayal it carried in the Gospel account of the thrice-repeated denial of Jesus, the subsequent weeping. From the point of view of my mother's hopes it might have been better to call me Samuel, a son to be dedicated to the service of God. We read together the story of Hannah, who vowed: "O lord of hosts, if thou wilt give unto thine handmaid a man child, then I will give him unto the LORD all the days of his life."[3] When God did indeed give her a son, she named him Samuel and took him to Eli the priest: "For this child I prayed; and the lord hath given me my petition which I asked of him; therefore also I have lent him to the LORD; as long as he liveth he shall be lent to the LORD."[4] Samuel's own wishes in the matter did not form part of the story. The idea was that I too should be alert for the word of the LORD; he would call me, "Peter, Peter," and I would answer as Eli instructed Samuel to answer: "Speak: for thy servant heareth."[5]

No doubt this story, and my mother's investment in it, made me feel special, but probably not in the way she would have wished. Now that I look back on them, I realize that many of the Bible stories of unexpected recognition—Samuel being called by God, David slaying Goliath and being anointed (by Samuel) as king, Jesus confounding the elders in the Temple—were vehicles for identification, just like the boys' adventure stories I consumed in a very different context. In those cases too I was the hero—the boy who saves the day, the boy who wins the prize (or later on, the girl) to the amazement of his more popular classmates, the boy who discovers that he is the lost son of the nobleman, and so on. But Bible texts also had doctrinal content, which I accepted at its face value. In that sense I was thoroughly *indoctrinated*, that is, unwittingly programmed to hold a certain set of beliefs that amounted to a doctrine—something taught, passed down from teacher to pupil, from elder to neophyte, from parent to child. So I grew up believing that Jesus loved me, whatever that meant, that he had given his life to save me (or been sent by his Father to do so—as in the case of Samuel, or for that matter Isaac, it was not clear whether the son's private desires counted for anything independently of the parent's), that I had been washed in his blood, that he was to be remembered on the Lord's Day in the Breaking of Bread, that any deviation from the path of righteousness would grieve him, and that I was to expect to be raptured into his presence at the Second Coming.

These doctrines were so pervasive that I never for a moment, as a boy, dreamed of questioning them. They were kept present not only by daily morning prayer and scripture reading in the family but also by big framed calligraphed texts on the walls of the main rooms of the house. I don't remember them all, but opposite the place where I sat at the dining-room table hung Proverbs 18:10, in black Gothic lettering on a stark white background: "The name of the Lord is a strong tower; the righteous runneth into it and is safe." I imagined the tower as square, in heavy grey stone; it had a big doorway but no door, and I could run into it and stand in a dark corner, safe from what? from playmates in a game of hide and seek?—nothing more threatening than that, but it was reassuring just the same. The texts and their archaic language were so familiar that it did not occur to me to think of their meanings in context—that the righteous, for example, might have actually needed a place to take refuge in, from persecution. We were not persecuted; the closest thing was something called "reproach," which we were supposed to welcome. Another frequent choice for outsized calligraphy, whose context also escaped me, was from Genesis 16:13: "Thou God seest me." I did not know at the time that this was in fact not a statement but a name, the name Hagar gave to God when he promised to multiply the seed of Ishmael. Nor in my innocence did I know why it sometimes hung in bathrooms. The principle of divine omniscience was certainly accepted and familiar, but somehow it did not seem to imply divine surveillance.

I was, or wanted to be, a good son. I acquiesced in domestic piety, not rebelling against family prayers or incessant attendance at the meetings of the Brethren (three times every Sunday, every Monday and Thursday night, twice a month on Tuesday night, very often on Saturday afternoon and evening), running the errands and performing the duties required by the family and the assembly (the Brethren's name for the local church). In due time— I must have been about sixteen—I asked, as was expected, to be admitted to the Breaking of Bread (their name for holy communion). Although I already had another life—at school, in the privacy of my room, on walks and bicycle rides, in trains—it did not compete with the meetings. While I would have liked to go to the cinema, the fact that this was forbidden, along with comic books and the radio and dances and sporting events, did not seem like a deprivation. I learned enough about these worldly entertainments from my schoolmates not to appear ignorant, and my friendships at school did not extend to social involvements after hours or on weekends.

When I say that this "other life" did not compete with life among the Brethren, what I mean is that the latter had a sort of practical priority: I was always willing to drop secular enjoyments in order to meet sectarian requirements. However, I knew very early on, if in an inarticulate way, that they were, respectively, happy enjoyments and tedious requirements. I read books, talked and joked with my friends, and explored the countryside and the railways because I wanted to, but I read the Bible, knelt at family devotions, and sat through the meetings because I had to. No doubt there was a sense in which I wanted to fulfill the requirements because that was expected of me as the son of my parents; I wanted their approval, and the approval of their fellow believers. For approval, however, observance was enough—it did not require conviction. I think I also wanted to be convinced, like the father of the afflicted youth in Mark's Gospel: "Lord, I believe; help thou mine unbelief";[6] perhaps I sometimes thought that I was. But when put to the test conviction failed me. It was expected that I would confess the name of the Lord, to my schoolfellows, to all and sundry—that was one of the marks of salvation. But it was one thing to acquiesce in belief among believers, quite another to affirm it to unbelievers. I agonized over my reluctance to do this, putting it down to cowardice. I had been taught to expect the world's reproach, to run into the strong tower, to enjoy the attendant blessing, as in the Sermon on the Mount: "Blessed are ye, when men shall revile you, and persecute you, . . . for my sake,"[7] and refusing to embrace these things felt like another case of the betrayal my name had set me up for.

Given, however, that I was quite prepared later on to take principled but unpopular stands, I came to think that what had really been going on at this time was the emergence of a natural—and wholly convincing—skepticism. The stories that were reiterated in the meetings, and set forth in evangelical tracts (I resisted also the practice of handing these to unsaved strangers, and was uncomfortably embarrassed when my mother did so, approaching unwary fellow passengers on buses with stumpers like "Where will you spend eternity?") came to seem implausible and simple-minded. All this happened gradually, but could not be altogether concealed, and when eventually I could not be persuaded to take any part in the preaching of the Gospel—I shrank in alarm from the prospect of standing up and proclaiming to others what barely commanded my own assent—my parents must have begun to admit to themselves that this was not the son they had bargained for.

Awakening

Along with my unwillingness to be drawn further into the spiritual practices of the Brethren—even though for some years I continued to participate practically in their affairs, buying the communion wine, setting up an amplifier system, managing the food service at regional meetings, and so on—went an extension and enlargement of the life of the mind. I had been a voracious reader since childhood, and there was a good public library about a mile from the house; children's books and boys' books were given as presents, and I also read the girls' books belonging to my sisters. My father was something of a bibliophile, haunting the secondhand bookshops in Paternoster Row in London (all of which burned in the Blitz during World War II), though most of what he bought was sent to his father, the grandfather I never met who lived in Jamaica. Major Caws was a local figure and newspaper columnist in Kingston and an object of veneration on my father's part; he appeared to live the normal life of a military retiree in the colonies, in spite of having belonged to the Brethren, and I became aware of some dissonance between the restrictions my father imposed on us and the worldliness he tolerated in his own father.

And yet, now that I think of it, the restrictions did not extend to control of my reading, and I can be grateful for that. One memory that still surprises me is that of a gift from my parents, on some birthday in my teenage years, of a book by the novelist Dornford Yates called *Brother of Daphne*. Yates, whom I devoured early on, along with P. G. Wodehouse, John Buchan, Rider Haggard, Conan Doyle, and the rest, was really Captain C. W. Mercer, a snob and a conservative—perhaps that was why my parents didn't mind him. But Boy Pleydell, the brother in question, was a sentimental flirt, and the book strung together a number of stories of technically innocent but at the same time suggestive conquest. I don't think they could have realized this. Is it conceivable—surely not, and yet they were in their way astonishingly naïve—that "Brother" in the title was reassuring to them as Brethren? At all events my reading at this time was thoroughly worldly, as well as being widely eclectic, and in a hundred ways it began to undermine the simple certainties of their Christian beliefs.

It would take a full-fledged autobiography to do justice to this development; one or two salient cases will have to suffice. On some other birthday my elder sister gave me a copy of one of the truly great stories of heroism and endurance, Apsley Cherry-Garrard's *The Worst Journey in the World*, an account of an excursion—a secondary mission of Scott's expedition to the South Pole (by whose tragic ending it was eclipsed in the popular mind)—to the emperor penguin colony at Cape Crozier, undertaken in the depth of the Antarctic winter. Cherry-Garrard and his companions came near to losing their lives on more than one occasion, and in recounting such an episode he observes, almost in passing, "Men do not fear death—they fear the pain of dying." This remark, buried hundreds of pages into the book, had a profound effect on me. It seemed obviously true, and that meant—though I didn't formulate this thought at the time—that somehow the doctrine of the fear of death and of the judgment to follow as the worst things, from which we needed to be saved by the blood of Christ, had simply not taken hold.

That doctrine, along with all its associated baggage, from the Pauline epistles to the Revelation of St. John the Divine, gradually lost its dominance and took on the neutral coloring of other mythologies and fictions. That it might itself have elements of fiction was brought home to me by a short text of R. L. Stevenson, one of the authors who most profoundly influenced my thought (and my writing), not because of his popular stories (like *Treasure Island*) but because of his essays. It helped that Stevenson came in an elegant series of small volumes, collectible by a student of limited means. My collection was started with *Virginibus Puerisque*, half a dozen texts of near-perfect style (as I then judged of style) and surprising wisdom. I soon acquired *The Strange Case of Dr. Jekyll and Mr. Hyde*, and this came bound with some minor pieces including a number of fables, one of which, "The Yellow Paint," was a brilliant send-up of evangelical belief and its nostrums. It is hard to stick to a conviction once you have learned to laugh at it, and Stevenson had an exquisite and subtle humor that I still admire, along with an understated tolerance that was the very opposite of the shrill and worried preoccupations of the Brethren. "Mr. Utterson the lawyer," with whom the story of Jekyll and Hyde opens, embodied that tolerance, and Stevenson has him say, "I incline to Cain's heresy.... I let my brother go to the devil in his own way." This is perhaps not accurately biblical, but I found it a refreshing sentiment in contrast to the solemn moralizing I was used to.

Two other kinds of reading deserve mention as contributing to the opening up of my horizons. My father had an appetite for poetry, and he communicated it to me (later on, as I understand it, he reproached himself for this on the grounds that it must have helped to sow the seeds of my defection, just as my mother—a modestly talented pianist—reproached herself for having given me a taste for classical music: poignant forms of self-flagellation that I find terribly sad). He would recite Milton's "Lycidas" at his morning toilet, and the long narratives of Barham's "Ingoldsby Legends" during bicycle rides. In school we were introduced to the warhorses of the English canon—Milton's "L'Allegro," Gray's "Elegy in a Country Churchyard," and the rest—but also to Yeats and the early Eliot and Auden. I liked to immerse myself in these texts just for the pleasure of the language. Later I acquired a pocket edition of Palgrave's *Golden Treasury*, in which a once-popular long poem, FitzGerald's "Rubáiyát of Omar Khayyám of Naishápúr," met my situation exactly—my appetite for experience, my deep disinterest in religious practices:

> Myself when young did eagerly frequent
> Doctor and Saint, and heard great Argument
> About it and about: but evermore
> Came out by the same Door as in I went.

This captured to a T the repetitive futility of the Brethren's meetings.

The other decisive form of reading I also owed to my father's interests, though I came to it with an attitude very different from his. He was in his way an amateur astronomer, for whom the heavens declared the glory of God and the firmament shewed his handiwork, as the Psalmist has it. He read Sir James Jeans (*The Mysterious Universe*) and Sir Arthur Eddington (*The Nature of the Physical World*)—and so did I. But where he was awed by the mystery of it all, I saw only an extension of what my crusty old physics teacher, Mr. Shingler, had drummed into my head: that the world is there to be observed, to be taken apart and pieced together thoughtfully, with care and with persistence; it is not there to exclaim about or swoon over. One of Mr. Shingler's lessons was typical: I had derived some result in my notebook and written the formula triumphantly in big letters, underlined in red and surrounded by a neat box; Mr. Shingler struck it all through and made me rewrite it in the same ink, and the same size, as all the rest—no valid statement took precedence over any other, none deserved more serious attention than another. I saw his point, and it reflected back on those big texts, taken out of their scriptural contexts. Giving the rest of the Bible, with its primitive violence and sexuality, equal weight with the snippets on which doctrine rested put the whole sacred enterprise in a new light. I also read at this time A. N. Whitehead's *Science and the Modern World*, lent to me by the scholarly father of my best friend—a rebel, like me—among the Brethren. There were then a few brothers with genuinely intellectual interests; I do not think there are many now.

Finally, but perhaps in the long run most important of all, there was the influence of the headmaster of my school, C. G. Vernon, who spent the mandatory hour a week officially devoted to Scripture in the sixth form curriculum first on Egyptology and then, during the second half of the year, on philosophy. He didn't assign philosophical texts but talked through simply—

and, as I came to realize later, with great fidelity—the main points of the doctrines of Locke, Berkeley, Kant, and others. Mr. Vernon had been trained as a science teacher; he was a learned, gentle, and ironic man, one of a class of schoolmasters at that time who later on would probably have had university appointments, and he showed by example a strictness and lucidity in argument that, when applied to the beliefs I was fed at home, tended to dissolve them away. He wasn't the only teacher with that gift—now that I think of it the staff of the school, collectively, set a standard that would be hard to match in public education today. The result of all this was that I went up to university thoroughly split between critical engagement in my intellectual life and passive acquiescence in my life among the Brethren.

Conflict and Rupture

School work did not bring me into open conflict with my parents, but extracurricular activities sometimes did. Movies were prohibited, but I was allowed to see *The Great Mr. Handel* at the local Odeon with my school class, because of *The Messiah*; so was theater, but again I went with a school outing to see *Much Ado About Nothing* at the Aldwych, with Robert Donat and Renée Asherson as Benedick and Beatrice. I don't remember much about the Handel film, except for the mystery and luxury and darkness of the cinema and the comfort of the seats, but I remember quite lot about the Shakespeare, most particularly Renée Asherson's performance and her stunning, heart-stopping beauty—makeup and lighting to be sure, but I'd never encountered anything like it. I didn't see how any of this could be wicked, as my parents seemed to think it must be. No doubt the events were made especially vivid for me because of their rarity in my life, but there was another side to the experience that turned what for any other child would have been ordinary, if exciting (not too many people from our dormitory suburb went to West End plays), into something momentous. In both cases there was a long period of preliminary negotiations, with pleadings (on my part) and tears (on my mother's), before leave was granted for me to accompany my class to these entertainments. What were the permissible limits of contact with the world? What would be the consequences of going beyond those limits? Such agonizing, such soul-searching!—and all because of what seemed to me easy and innocuous. I knew the Scripture passage about the broad and narrow ways, but I also knew the one about the easy yoke and the light burden, and the fuss and near-hysteria provoked by these episodes showed that the burden of the Brethren's doctrine was far from light.

I did not often openly test the limits of approved behavior—the family stress was not worth it. But one of the damaging effects of being brought up in what are now called "high-demand organizations" is that people look for surreptitious ways around the demands while still appearing to meet them, and learn to be furtive if not actually dishonest. This is not good for character. Parental watchfulness extended into my university years (the age of majority at the time was twenty-one, and I lived at home and commuted to South Kensington). Next door to the Royal College of Science was the Royal College of Music, where on some weekday afternoons were held the "concerto trials" of diploma candidates. Serious live music entranced me. Apart from my mother's piano playing—limited to relatively simple works like Clementi's sonatinas—some records at the after-school music society, and the occasional brass band in the park, I hadn't heard any classical music, indeed any music (the lugubrious hymn singing of the Brethren, with no instrumental accompaniment, didn't count). While I had some idea of what was going on from having taken out from the local library, and tried out haltingly at home, piano reductions of Bach concerti, the real thing was something else again; to hear and watch professionals, even in training, took me to another level of admiration and enjoyment. But if I was home an hour late my mother would be waiting for me with the sad reproach that dominates my memory of her: I'd been to another concert, hadn't I? and how grieved the Lord must be at such worldly behavior! I would say something evasive, and half-true, about time spent in the lab, but the reproachful look would follow me. It permeated the house, and my life.

The argument about grieving the Lord seemed simply absurd—he had after all been a friendly sort of chap, consorting with publicans and sinners, and might, *mutatis mutandis*, have appreciated the talent (and appeal) of the young people who played the oboe or the viola as much as I did. I still believed in him, but I did not think he would mind my enjoying myself in this innocent way. (It did not occur to me to take the line that, given the depth of my parents' disapproval, I might as well be hung for a sheep as for a lamb—crossing the threshold of the concert hall being in their eyes as spiritually fatal as actual drunkenness and debauchery, delights I was too naïve even to envisage.)

Liberation at a deeper level followed from my university studies. I read physics, but a dominant figure in the history of Royal College of Science was the biologist Thomas Henry Huxley, "Darwin's bulldog," and one of my predecessors as a student was the writer H. G. Wells. Wells was bracing and iconoclastic, but it was Huxley who took on the greatest importance for me, because of his straightforward treatment of credulous believers who stood in the way of the acceptance of the theory of evolution. One of the most sentimentally pious of these was the writer Charles Kingsley, who was ill-advised enough to try Christian consolation on Huxley after the death of the latter's young son. Huxley's letter in response is a masterpiece, and makes clear the possibility of deep feeling and intellectual honesty in the complete absence of anything like traditional belief. He speaks as a representative of the class of scientists for whom the Royal College of Science was founded, thinkers who had calmly transcended the old arguments about faith: ". . . all the younger men of science whom I know intimately are *essentially* of my way of thinking. (I know not a scoffer or an irreligious or an immoral man among them, but they all regard orthodoxy as you do Brahmanism.)"[8]

The preoccupations of the Brethren thus came gradually to seem beside the point—not just the narrow doctrinal differences that marked them off from other Christians but, with time, the basic creed of Christianity itself, and with it the competing creeds of the other great faiths. A basic point in logic came into play here: if there are two inconsistent accounts of some matter, such as the creation of the world or the destiny of mankind, one of them must be false—but so might the other. So might all competing accounts—and why, in any case, was it necessary to have such accounts in the first place? Was it not better to remain provisionally at least in ignorance, holding in reserve (and in resolve) the possibility of future knowledge, rather than rushing to choose one implausible story among all the other implausible stories and raise it to the status of revelation? The one story was just too simple to take account of the complexities of natural history and psychological experience, although it was easily gilded with literary or academic assurance, as for example by G. K. Chesterton or that smug romantic C. S. Lewis. Reading Lewis did briefly give me pause, partly I think because I discovered to my alarm that the name of his diabolical apprentice-master, Screwtape, was a perfect anagram of my own. Could that be a message? Could Lewis's imagination, and all the apparatus of writing and publishing and bookselling that put *The Screwtape Letters* into my hands, have been manipulated by God to deliver it to me? Implausibility on implausibility! I stared them down and kept going.

The dire alternative to the creation story was the theory of evolution, anathema to the Brethren, though I cannot help thinking that it might have had some appeal to my father, to the extent at least of requiring serious attention rather than just dismissal, if he had allowed himself to become familiar with it. At all events he immersed himself in the paleontological problem, and the saving alternatives to evolutionary theory. In particular he had a number of old bindings (from Paternoster Row) of the nineteenth-century Scottish geologist Hugh Miller, a self-taught scholar who was already thinking in terms of a very long history of the earth even though he was critical of pre-Darwinian development theories. Miller committed suicide in 1856, three years before the publication of Darwin's *On the Origin of Species*—it would be interesting to know what he would have made of that careful and exhaustive book. My father did not mention Miller's suicide, and as far as I know he did not read Darwin—that would have meant touching the unclean thing, so thoroughly had evolution become demonized in the evangelical community.

Nor did he mention Philip Henry Gosse, F.R.S., though there may have been another reason for that. Gosse was a remarkable naturalist, one of the staunchest defenders of the literal truth of the Bible as against the evolutionary view. He advocated an ingenious theory of his own, which held that geological strata and their fossils had been created in place along with Adam and Eve and the rest, thus giving the (false) impression that the earth was millions of years old, when in fact it was only six thousand or so. His point was that any creation of a natural thing would inevitably give a false impression of a nonexistent past—a newly created tree would have rings, for example, because that is what trees consist of. So it wasn't possible to figure out the age of the earth from the evidence, any more than it would have been possible to figure out the age of that miraculous tree from its rings. It couldn't, therefore, have been God's intention to deceive (which is what some critics said the theory amounted to)—on the contrary, he had given us in the Bible the true account of what really happened and when, thus undercutting the whole enterprise of dating geological ages.[9]

It still astonishes me that evangelicals don't take more advantage of this argument, which is foolproof, if entirely implausible—though no more implausible than the rest of what they believe. But Gosse was an awkward case on other grounds. He had also been a member of the Plymouth Brethren, of which the Exclusives were an offshoot, and his son Edmund, a minor Victorian writer, had published a memoir called *Father and Son*, giving his own account of a Brethren upbringing and of his escape from it. He describes in sometimes hilarious detail the extraordinary beliefs about Old Testament prophecy and New Testament practice that were mandatory in the sect. These were mainly the brainchild of a passionately opinionated Anglo-Irish ex-priest called John Nelson Darby, who, through his influence on the American theologian Cyrus Scofield and the latter's annotated version of the Bible, is even at this late date largely responsible for some of the wilder excesses of the Christian right in the United States. What made Edmund Gosse's book dangerous, however, was not so much his dismissal of doctrine as his respectful and poignant treatment of his relationship to his father. Here was a man essentially in my situation, unable to conform to parental expectations (his mother had died, and left the son's spiritual welfare to her husband as a sacred trust), but reasonable, dutiful, affectionate even, while at the same time adamant in his resolve to go his own way. He impressed me as an ally and as an exemplar: escape was both reasonable and possible.

Father and Son became underground reading, but the argument about evolution broke out into the open, along with other heated discussions—about the innocence of music, about the reality of eternal torment, about my spiritual and academic future (unpromising at the time, on both counts). What I remember of these verbal battles is less their content than their atmosphere, the tension and recrimination and anguish that marked them, the building-up to a kind of desperate standoff. My mother would be silent, her mouth turned down in a mixture of sadness and disapproval; my father would throw up his hands. We were at hopeless cross-purposes. They knew what was right (they'd been told) and wanted submission; I didn't believe them, and wanted argument. They were the sanctified; I was the rebel and apostate. And they were prepared to cut me off if I threatened the austerity of their separation from the world—which happened eventually, when the rules of the Brethren tightened. In Edmund Gosse's day things were less draconian. He describes the growing distance between himself and his father:

> There came a time when neither spoke the same language as the other, or encompassed the same hopes, or was fortified by the same desires. But, at least, it is some consolation to the survivor, that neither, to the very last hour, ceased to respect the other, or to regard him with a sad indulgence. The affection of these two persons was assailed by forces in comparison with which the changes that health or fortune or place introduce are as nothing. It is a mournful satisfaction, but yet a satisfaction, that they were both of them able to obey the law which says that ties of close family relationship must be honoured and sustained.[10]

My parents obeyed no such law, and were willing—against my own wishes in the matter—to break those ties. Nor, I think, did they ever really respect me as an independent person in my own right. No doubt they thought they were answering to a higher law. But the forces that assailed the family were every bit as strong as Gosse had claimed.

All this time I was still nominally in fellowship with the Brethren, though my failure to conform was beginning to be noticed. There was, however, one other contentious issue that could not be discussed without hastening the impending break, which was softened in the end by geographical distance. Like all young British males I was required to register for military service at the age of eighteen, and like all young Exclusive brothers I registered as a conscientious objector. Not to do so was unthinkable. But my heart and my conviction were not in it, and I did not see how I could face the tribunal that ruled on that status and ask to be excused, according to the formula that I loved the Lord Jesus and that accepting combatant status would be grievous to him. I wasn't really so sure about either proposition. I was lucky, if I had to belong to the Brethren at all, to belong when I did, because what they called "the recovery of the truth" was a progressive matter, and came to involve a prohibition of university studies. (At this epoch the recovery consisted largely of petty tyrannies on the part of the leading brother of the moment, an alcoholic from Brooklyn named James Taylor Jr.) As a student, before this axe fell, I was entitled to deferment of military service, and then as a graduate in physics I was eligible for a short service commission as an instructor in navigation in the Royal Navy. So in due course I revoked my conscientious objection and began the process of application for the commission.

I knew that when this became known new trouble would break out. But at about this time I also became aware of academic opportunities in the United States, and left for a year—and this became fifty-odd years, which fall outside the scope of this account. Three footnotes: first, I gave up the navy for philosophy, which took over my intellectual life and has been my companion and vocation ever since. Second, my mother was inconsolable, and wrote to me that she thought she had damaged her eyes by crying over my abandonment of the faith. Third, my father responded to the gift of my first book with the observation that it must have taken a lot of work, and what a pity it was that that work had not been devoted to bringing souls to Christ. Neither of them, as far as I know, ever took the slightest satisfaction in anything I was able to accomplish.

I left the Brethren for good during my first year in the United States. The process was not completed in their minds until they had "withdrawn from" me, that is, true to their name, excluded me. The image is that of a recoil from, and an expulsion of, something evil. When complete, and with the further progress of the "recovery of the truth," it became final, and absolute. I was not allowed to visit my mother, or have any direct contact with her, for the last eighteen years of her life. My father outlived her by nine years, and I did manage to see him in his latter days, on two occasions of five minutes each, supervised by the disapproving relatives with whom he lived. He was blind and infirm and, as it seemed to me, profoundly sad. No handshake was permitted, no hug. My heart went out to him; his, to all appearances, remained closed to me. When my parents died, no one told me for weeks.

A Question of Morality

The cardinal principle of philosophy, as I practice and teach it, is this: that men and women should have reasons for doing what they do and believing what they believe, and that these reasons should be good reasons—not merely good as supporting the beliefs and practices in question but good as meeting standards of rigor and adequacy no matter what they are intended to justify. This may seem like a high standard to set for the everyday behavior of ordinary people—yet even to put the matter in that way is to risk an accusation of elitism: who am I to talk of "ordinary people" as if their standards are necessarily low? The thing about being human at this late stage in the history of culture is that the reflective powers and techniques thoughtful people have cultivated are in principle available to everyone, out of no one's reach. Being a philosopher doesn't take exceptional talents—according to Plato, anyone qualifies "who has a taste for every sort of knowledge and who is curious to learn and is never satisfied." So it was not limited to kings (or parents). Now everybody can—and we might say should—aspire to it.

Why does it matter what people believe and what they do? Why does it matter what their reasons are? Of course, below a certain level of significance it doesn't—things can be done, and even believed, casually and unreflectively, and within limits people have total discretion about how they think and how they behave. The limits are encountered when acts, or indirectly the beliefs that lead to them, have consequences for others. Not all beliefs are of the same kind. I distinguish three main varieties—things people aren't sure of that can be decided by evidence (I believe we're having waffles for breakfast), things they are sure of that can't be decided by evidence (he believes human life begins at conception), and things people are committed to and will therefore work for (she believes in a woman's right to terminate a pregnancy). The first category is unproblematic—it's just a matter of everyday ordinary usage. But the last two categories involve values, which may or may not be moral values, that determine behavior toward others.

Values are things that people aim for and protect. There are *end values*, which don't require justifications beyond themselves, and *instrumental values*, which are entertained because they serve end values.[1] I claim that there is no such thing as a universal end value—nobody can legislate other people's ultimate desires. But there is a universal instrumental value, namely freedom. If I really want anything, I must, on pain of inconsistency, want to be free to pursue it (which doesn't mean I am or will actually be free to pursue it, it only means that if whatever it is is a value for me, then being free to pursue it will also necessarily be a value—and this is true for everyone always). Freedom, however, is not a simple concept—to enjoy what I call "complex freedom" an agent, in performing an act, must (a) understand it and mean to do it, (b) not be prevented from doing it (which includes not being coerced into doing something else), (c) have the resources of energy and material required in order to do it, (d) be adequately informed of the context in which it is done, and (e) know enough about how the world works to be able to foresee its probable consequences.

So I can offend against the freedom of others by misleading or confusing them, by restraining or constraining them, by weakening or depriving them, by deceiving them, or by keeping them in ignorance. If my beliefs contribute to any of these offenses, then acting on them becomes immoral. Working out the specifics here is a large task. Some elements of "not being prevented" and "having the resources" include not being brainwashed into thinking something wrong or impossible, not being fed unrealistic apprehensions about the consequences of doing it, having the confidence required to undertake it, and so on. Some aspects of "weakening or depriving" include undercutting self-esteem and failing to provide a loving and protected environment. These are all conditions to which the children of controlling parents, or parents who devote all their emotion and affection to otherworldly objects, are especially vulnerable.

One more detail, and the argument can proceed. Who are the "others" against whose freedom I am liable to offend? To put it differently, what are the boundaries of the moral community to which I belong, to whose other members I owe consideration and from whom I can, as a rule, expect it? (The qualification is necessary because I have obligations to weak or helpless members—small children, for example—but cannot hold them to similar obligations toward me *while* they are weak or helpless.) Different people may have different answers to this question—for example, some will include animals and fetuses, some won't—but two things would seem to command general assent, namely that parents and their children belong to the same moral community, and that once the boundaries of the community are established justice requires that those included within them are entitled, other things being equal, to similar consideration. This amounts to saying that no member's freedom is to be privileged over any other's. "Other things being equal": there are subcommunities, families for example, within which preferential or differential treatment is reasonable, but the modifications to general moral principles warranted by such special cases are limited. It is permissible to override children's freedom when they are too young to make wise use of it, but only until they have acquired the necessary wisdom (which it is the moral obligation of parents to nurture), and never to serve the parents' personal interests, such as for example their standing with coreligionists. It is permissible to make things better for family members, but not at the expense of making things worse for strangers. Also—a stipulation it seems hardly necessary to make, and yet one that is systematically violated in too many families—family members should be treated at least as well as strangers.

With all this apparatus in hand we can now look directly at the question of the morality of indoctrination—in particular the indoctrination of children by believing parents, beginning with the beliefs of the parents. What are their reasons for holding their beliefs? How good are these reasons? There is obviously not room here for a complete analysis of the concept of a good reason, but it may be enough to cite some obviously inadequate reasons that are often offered for belief. The fact that a lot of other people believe something is not in itself a good reason to follow their example. (The argument that "all those people can't be wrong" holds no water at all. They can be, and frequently have been—in fact it is probably not too much to say that most of what most people have believed for most of history, away from the simple certainties of the moment, and what they have passed on as beliefs to the next generation, has been false.) The fact that some belief is of great antiquity is not in itself a good reason to subscribe to it—in fact the more venerable a belief, as a general rule, the more likely it is to be wrong, a matter of prejudice or superstition rather than confirmed reliability. In a similar way the fact that something is recorded or stated in some sacred text, no matter how ancient, is not in itself a good reason for believing it. The fact that one's parents hold, or held, a belief is not in itself a good reason for following in their footsteps. The fact that holding a belief provides comfort is not in itself a good reason for doing so—nor is the fact that it helps to control behavior.

This begins to sound intolerant. There are so many believers, in so many varieties, and these and other similar strictures would put nearly all of them in the wrong. In fact that would probably be justified—I think it is a bad idea to entertain unnecessary beliefs, and most of the beliefs in my second category are unnecessary—but some compassion is due to well-intentioned and sincere belief on the part of those to whom the thought of questioning it, or the need for it, has never occurred. I think this is culpable on their part, but understandable given the cultural prejudice in favor of belief and the lamentable state of education in self-knowledge and critical reflection. It is possible to entertain a belief with good (if selfish) intentions but for bad reasons, and if it affords reassurance in the face of loss, for example, or helps the believer to be a better person, it would seem cruel to try to refute it. All this, however, assumes that no one else is affected negatively by the beliefs in question—as soon as someone is, benign tolerance becomes unacceptable.

What counts as a negative effect? Who judges? I do not doubt that my parents believed quite sincerely that my eternal welfare was at stake in our arguments about belief; they wished to keep me out of Satan's hands and assure my eventual salvation, my place in glory with Christ. The impoverishment of my mind was a small price to pay for this. Human reason in any case was corrupt—"the mind of man" was dismissed as a snare, the thing was to know the mind of God and obey it. Human beings were in themselves worthless, they could do nothing good: "We are as an unclean thing, and all our righteousnesses are as filthy rags."[12] The whole armamentarium of primitive belief was regularly brought to bear on the most trivial of offenses as I was growing up, so that a venial lie would provoke solemn lectures about being cast into outer darkness, where would be weeping and gnashing of teeth. These things make a powerful impression, and forcing them on children is an abuse as damaging, in the long run, as anything physical—possibly more so, because the body heals itself and anger at unjust punishment can be cleansing, but the mind carries its scars into a long future, along with the conviction that they are deserved.

Should my parents not have believed what they did? Why did they believe it? Primarily for reasons I have already judged as inadequate: in my father's case because his father had led the way (even if he himself eventually departed from it), in my mother's because she had been saved from some late adolescent crisis, whose details I never knew, by the reassurance of the

Brethren in the person of a father figure to whom she was introduced by her oldest sister and under whose influence, as I understood it, she abandoned a teachers' college career. Illness played a role, I think, in some form or other, but salvation from the crisis came (as so often) in personal abnegation and grateful commitment. If asked why they believed what they did, they responded in one of several ways: because it was in the Bible (in the translation, and with the interpolations, of J. N. Darby); because it was true; because their belief was in a Person, the Lord Jesus Christ, whom they had accepted as their Savior. If asked why they believed what was in the Bible, they would quote from the Bible itself: "All scripture is given by inspiration of God, and is profitable for doctrine,"[1] to challenge which could only be the work of Satan. If it was pointed out that "because it is true" cannot be a reason for belief (because *that it is true* is just what is believed), they would take refuge in the denunciation of human reasoning. This last point was connected to the personal belief, since Jesus had said, "I am the Way, the Truth, and the Life,"[14] and no logical questioning of truth could hold against that. And indeed, to the extent that it is authentic (and who is in a position to tell?), nothing counters the immediacy and intimacy of religious experience. (But such experience was precisely what immersion in my parents' religiosity had immunized me against. And I must say that there was very little evidence that they enjoyed anything of the sort themselves.)

Still, given their convictions, what were they to do with a son who refused to be convinced, or whose childish trust (which had been real enough) was being eaten away by doubt and argument? Can I blame them for trying to keep their faith and restore mine? For me truth was becoming a matter of evidence and consistency, and I came, long before reading W. K. Clifford,[15] to his view that holding a belief is a solemn responsibility, not to be concluded lightly or for insufficient reasons. I simply could not believe just because they wanted me to; I could not have believed just because I wanted to, if I had wanted to (and sometimes I still did). At the same time I was probably brash and opinionated and unsympathetic—I am sorry about that now and wish I could tell them so. My brashness as a young man, on this very point of belief, drew a gentle reproach from Brand Blanshard, a wise professor at Yale, for whom I wrote a paper on "authority" in which I argued that a believer could not count a belief's proclamation of its own rightness as a reason for accepting it. In red ink, in his meticulous minuscule script, Blanshard wrote laconically at the bottom of the page "unless, indeed, he happened to be right." For all my criticism of their failure to be self-critical, then, I cannot directly fault my parents' fidelity to their own persuasion.

But then what sustains the indictment that I have indirectly been building throughout this account, and which I mean to hold generally against parents who behave as mine did?

Three things, I think, all three major, all implicit in what has been said so far, all needing to be held up as culpably immoral. One is the abdication of their own judgment in the face of doctrinal leadership from others, themselves fallible men (all men) with venal interests, more and more transparent as events unfolded. Both my parents were educated individuals in their way, both had been exposed to literature and history and in my father's case at least to science. They were capable of intelligent judgment, but they were sucked into a pattern of tyranny and dogmatic conformity from which it would have become progressively more difficult for them to escape even if they had wanted to. But they didn't want to. Pressure from fellow believers, whose common willingness to report each other's infractions to the assembly gave the community of the Exclusive Brethren the structure of a demagogic police state, meant that any gesture of kindness or reconciliation to one who had been withdrawn from had to be ruthlessly suppressed—even if the excluded person was a presumably beloved child.

Here is the second major moral offense—the disposition to use the withholding of love and loving association as a disincentive to apostasy, if not actually as a punishment for it. The charge of manipulation may seem harsh, but that was the practical effect of their behavior, whether voluntary or coerced. The brutality of the Brethren in this regard has become notorious, and the psychological damage it has done has been deep and often irreparable. Their doctrines and the enforcement of those doctrines have been responsible for the splitting apart of many families, the estrangement of parents from children and of siblings and other relatives from one another. The need for connectedness usually supplied by familial relations can of course be satisfied in other ways, and this often happens when illness or disaster strike, but there is a special poignancy in knowing that the relationships are there but are deliberately ruptured, for the essentially selfish protection of an imagined purity. The withdrawal of natural affection on the part of insiders, and its rejection when tendered by outsiders, can produce a sense of loss that inhibits the exercise of affective and creative powers, and this inhibition counts as an impairment of freedom. The obligation upon parents to supply a loving environment in which their children can flourish and develop as autonomous agents is beginning to be recognized as a basic moral imperative, but my parents would not even have understood this way of putting it: their obligations had a different basis and a different aim.

The third offense is related to the second, and it consists in the inculcation in children of a sense of worthlessness, not just the personal rejection of their individuality or family belonging—that came later—but a systematic and generic belittlement of the human, an active discouragement of the cultivation of human values and talents. My parents were momentarily pleased by my achievements in school, though not in college (the latter were considered unnecessary, and were in any case less brilliant), but this satisfaction was soon succeeded by a kind of disparagement, accompanied by warnings that I should not attach importance to worldly successes, since after all the only true value lay in the things of God. This did not encourage self-esteem. It is difficult for me even now, as I conclude this reflection on the beliefs with which I grew up, to be fully reassured of the value of the enterprise, not in the narrow context of this book but in the wider context of philosophical work in general. Professor Blanshard's quiet reservation still haunts me: "unless, indeed, they happened to be right." I have no difficulty in dealing with this cognitively, but it touches an old affective wound, kept open by an undeserved but apparently ineradicable sense of guilt, that will never, perhaps, be entirely healed. I struggle against what sometimes seems like the simultaneous arrogance and futility of my work as a philosopher; I envy those who were brought up in more humane and more supportive settings, with families who were proud of them and valued what they accomplished. I think I am entitled to be indignant at having been shaped in this way against my will, at carrying a legacy which still enacts what I now see, with some detachment at this late stage, as a personal tragedy. But indignation does no good; it is undignified; and in any case this is not the tragedy of belief with which I started out. That belongs to the hopes and dreams of the simple, innocent, timid, deluded, selfish, and irresponsible couple in the old photograph, my parents. May they rest in peace. This cliché betrays no concession to belief, but it corresponds to a filial feeling: part sympathy, part regret, part affection—and part forgiveness.

NOTES

1. Plato *Republic* 473d.
2. Plato *Republic* 618c.
3. First Samuel 1:11.
4. First Samuel 1:27–28.
5. First Samuel 3:10.
6. Mark 9:24.
7. Matthew 5:11.
8. Leonard Huxley, *Life and Letters of Thomas Henry Huxley* (New York: D. Appleton, 1901), 1:238.

9. For a fuller account of Gosse's work, see "Gosse's Omphalos Theory and the Eccentricity of Belief," in Peter Caws, *Yorick's World: Science and the Knowing Subject* (Berkeley and Los Angeles: University of California Press, 1993), 45–73.

10. [Edmund Gosse], *Father and Son: A Study of Two Temperaments* (London: William Heinemann, 1907), 1. This book was originally published anonymously. Its epigraph, from Schopenhauer, is strikingly appropriate to the present text—translated from the German, it reads, "Belief is like love: it does not allow itself to be forced."

11. What follows is a highly compressed version of some arguments worked out in Peter Caws, *Ethics from Experience* (Boston: Jones and Bartlett, 1996), especially chaps. 11 and 12.

12. Isaiah 64:6.

13. Second Timothy 3:16.

14. John 14:6.

15. W. K. Clifford, *The Ethics of Belief* (London: Macmillan, 1879).

About the Contributors

Raymond D. Bradley is Emeritus Professor of Philosophy at Simon Fraser University. His books include *Possible Worlds: An Introduction to Logic and Its Philosophy*, co-authored with Norman Swartz (1979), and *The Nature of All Being: A Study of Wittgenstein's Modal Atomism* (1992). He also edited *Environmental Ethics*, vol. 2 (1989). He has published numerous articles in journals such as *Mind*, the *Australasian Journal of Philosophy*, the *Philosophical Review*, the *British Journal for Philosophy of Science*, *Nous*, the *Canadian Journal of Philosophy*, *Dialogue*, *Sophia*, *Open Society*, and *Free Inquiry*. His recent projects include work in philosophy of religion, with nine articles published on the Secular Web; articles on philosophy of science, especially on Einstein's philosophy; and five articles on issues associated with time for a forthcoming Sage Publications encyclopedia.

Peter Caws is University Professor of Philosophy and Professor of Human Sciences at the George Washington University. His eight books and more than 150 articles include work on the philosophy of the natural sciences, on ethics and continental philosophy (Sartre and the structuralists), and more recently on psychoanalysis and the human sciences.

Damien Alexander Dupont earned his PhD in philosophy at the Graduate Center of CUNY. His current research interests include ethics, especially moral psychology and applied ethics; ancient Greek philosophy, especially Plato and Aristotle; and seventeenth-century rationalism. He wrote his dissertation on the role of the emotions in moral judgment and action.

Diane Enns is Assistant Professor of Philosophy and Women's Studies and Associate Director of the Institute on Globalization and the Human Condition at McMaster University, Canada. She is the author of *Speaking of Freedom: Philosophy, Politics, and the Struggle for Liberation* (2007). Her current project investigates the condition and status of the victim in contemporary political thought and practice through an exploration of the effects of ethnopolitical violence and the work of reconciliation.

Paul H. Hirst is Emeritus Professor of Education at the University of Cambridge. He was educated at Huddersfield College and Trinity College, Cambridge. His books include *Moral Education in a Secular Society* (1974); *Knowledge and the Curriculum* (1974); and *The Logic of Education*, co-authored with R. S. Peters (1970). He contributed substantially to, and co-edited with P. A. White, the four-volume collection *Philosophy of Education—Major Themes in the Analytic Tradition* (1998). He has published approximately one hundred papers in journals of philosophy and philosophy of education. His current research interests include the nature of educational theory and practice, school curriculum planning, and moral and religious education.

Amalia Jiva earned her master's in applied linguistics at Boston University (2001), where she wrote her thesis on the role of Protestant fundamentalist discourse in establishing and maintaining group identity. Currently, she is a doctoral candidate at Boston University, writing her dissertation on linguistic topographies of interior space as represented in speaking of the divine. She is also Assistant Director of Writing Resources at Tufts University. Her interests include hermeneutics, linguistics, and divine expressibility in theological and literary texts from within the Christian tradition.

Stefani Jones earned her master's in philosophy and her doctorate in the human sciences at the George Washington University. Her dissertation was titled "The Becoming of a Moral Agent: Autonomy, Recognition, and the Parent-Child Relation." She currently works in the IT industry, and her interests include feminist ethics, the ethics of care, women in the workplace, and business ethics.

Irfan Khawaja is Adjunct Assistant Professor of Philosophy at Felician College in Lodi, New Jersey, and, with Carrie-Ann Biondi, managing editor of *Reason Papers: A Journal of Interdisciplinary Normative Studies*. Recently published work includes "Celebrating Arabs and Grateful Terrorists: Rumor and the Politics of Plausibility," co-written with Gary Alan Fine, in *Rumor Mills: The Social Impact of Rumor and Legend* (2005), and "Essentialism, Consistency, and Islam: A Critique of Edward Said's *Orientalism*," *Israel Affairs* 13 (October 2007). He is currently at work on a book manuscript with the tentative title *What Days Are For: Ethical Egoism and the Foundations of Ethics*.

Christine Overall is Professor of Philosophy and Queen's University Research Chair at Queen's University in Kingston, Ontario, Canada, and is an elected Fellow of the Royal Society of Canada. She co-edited *Feminist Perspectives: Philosophical Essays on Method and Morals* with Lorraine Code and Sheila Mullett (1988), and *Perspectives on AIDS: Ethical and Social Issues* with William Zion (1991). She is the editor of *The Future of Human Reproduction* (1989). Her books include *Ethics and Human Reproduction: A Feminist Analysis* (1987), *Human Reproduction: Principles, Practices, Policies* (1993), *A Feminist I: Reflections from Academia* (1998), *Thinking Like a Woman: Personal Life and Political Ideas* (2001), and *Aging, Death, and Human Longevity: A Philosophical Inquiry* (2003). *Aging, Death, and Human Longevity* won both the Canadian Philosophical Association 2005 Book Prize and the Abbyann D. Lynch Medal in Bioethics from the Royal Society of Canada in 2006. Her current research interests are in the areas of feminist philosophy, social philosophy, applied ethics, and philosophy of religion.

Tasia R. Persson earned her master's in philosophy and is a doctoral candidate at the University of Wisconsin–Madison. She is writing her dissertation on evil and moral responsibility in dirty-hands conflicts.

Glen Pettigrove is a lecturer in philosophy at the University of Auckland, New Zealand. He earned his doctorate from the University of California, Riverside, in 2003. His recent work includes "Understanding, Excusing, Forgiving," *Philosophy and Phenomenological Research* 74, no. 1 (January 2007), and "Ambitions," *Ethical Theory and Moral Practice* 10, no. 1 (February 2007). His current research is focused on the role of emotions in normative assessment, the moral responsibility of collective agents, and religion in public life.

Index

abortion, 104, 105, 107
Adam and Eve, 12, 58, 60, 67, 226
Aeneid (Virgil), 47
afterlife, 45
After Virtue (MacIntyre), 166
Agamben, Giorgio, 191 n. 20
agnosticism, 170, 203
Aldwych Theater, 223
L'Allegro (Milton), 221
Allen, Woody, 54
Anabaptists, 148
Androcles and the Lion (Shaw), 61
Anglicans, 4, 12ff., 20, 22, 24, 25, 150 n. 24, 156
Arabic, 30
Aristotle, 203
Armstrong, Karen, 133 n. 33
Asherson, Renée, 223
atheism, 18, 19, 22, 23, 26 n. 2, 50, 53ff., 70, 71, 76, 124, 135, 203
atonement, 13, 111
Attar, Farad al-Din, 109
Auden, W. H., 221
Augustine, Saint, 64
Augustus Caesar, 66
Austin, J. L., 163
authenticity, 6, 126, 141, 146ff., 151 nn. 28, 35, 37
Autonomy and Self-Respect (Hill), 120
Ayer, A. J., 162

Baal, 54
Babha, Homi, 185
Babi Yar, 188
Baby Boomer generation, 15
Bach, Johann Sebastian, 224
Baier, Annette, 138, 149 n. 12
baptism, 57, 102, 107, 148, 190 n. 4, 196ff.
Baptists, 5, 17, 18, 51ff., 64, 65, 71, 75, 97ff., 103ff., 123, 132 n. 30, 134, 135, 150 n. 24
Beauvoir, Simone de, 183ff., 204, 206, 208, 210ff.
Benhabib, Seyla, 151 n. 31
Bergoffen, Debra, 212
Berkeley, George, 19, 223
Bible Belt, American, 5, 74

Bible Stories for Children, 58, 59, 61
biblical discernment, 119
Bill and Ted's Excellent Adventure, 82
Blaiklock, E. M., 5, 65ff.
Blanshard, Brand, 233, 235
Blavatsky, Madam, 70
Bloesch, Donald G., 132 n. 31
Bob Jones University, 74
Book of Mormon, 195
Boston College, 135
Brigham Young University, 201
Brooklyn, NY, 228
Brother of Daphne (Yates), 220
Brown, Stuart, 25 n. 12
Buchan, John, 220
Buddhists, 70, 135
Bundy, Ted, 117
Bunyan, John, 56, 59, 60
Butyrka, 179

Cambridge University, 6, 7, 159, 161ff., 166
Canada, 4, 24, 176, 179
Canadian Air Force, 14
Capaldi, Nicholas, 49 n. 15
Cape Crozier, 220
Carroll, Lewis, 60
Carter, Jimmy, 97, 105
Catherine the Great, 176
Catholics. *See* Roman Catholics
Caws, B. F., 220
Caws, Peter, 205, 206
Chalcedon, 62
Chapman, Val, 69
Charleston, S.C., 77
Cherry-Garrard, Apsley, 220
Chesterton, G. K., 225
Children's Encyclopedia (Mee), 59, 60
Chortitza colony, 187
Christ, Carol P., 26 n. 15
Christadelphians, 155, 156, 158, 159
Christian Union (Cambridge), 161
Cixous, Hélène, 185
Clementi, Muzio, 224
Clifford, W. K., 233
Cohen, Mendel, 203
communism, 98, 102, 104, 112, 116, 176, 179

Conan Doyle, Arthur, 220
Concept of Mind, The (Ryle), 163
confirmation, 13
Confraternity of Christian Doctrine, 77
Congregationalists, 135, 150 n. 24
Conly, Sarah, 136–37
Cook, Michael, 49 n. 10
Corinthians, 50, 106, 118
Cosby, Michael R., 124
cosmological argument, 19, 71
Craig, William L., 72
Critique of Practical Reason (Kant), 164
Critique of Pure Reason (Kant), 164
Cyrenius, 65, 66

Dalai Lama, 183
Dante Alighieri, 109
Darby, John Nelson, 156, 227, 233
Darwin, Charles, 224, 226
Darwinism, 135, 226
David, 12, 58, 217
Day of Judgment, 36, 37, 48 n. 1
Deleuze, Gilles, 179, 185ff., 191 n. 15
Derrida, Jacques, 184ff.
Descartes, Réne, 19
descriptive metaphysics, 164
Dialogues on Natural Religion (Hume), 83
Dion of Syracuse, 215
Dionysius, 109
dirty hands, 129, 130
Dobson, James, 115ff.
Docetists, 62
Donat, Robert, 223
doxastic voluntarism, 35
dualism, 110
Duncan, Mary, 25 n. 4
Dworkin, Andrea, 205

Eddington, Arthur, 222
Elect Vessel, 214
Elegy in a Country Churchyard (Gray), 221
Eliot, T. S., 40, 221
Eli the Priest, 217
Engels, Friedrich, 188
Ensign, the, 195
Episcopalians, 12, 135
eternal life, 43, 197
Ethics of Ambiguity, The (de Beauvoir), 185, 206, 209
Eusebius, 66
Euthyphro (Plato), 82
evangelical Christianity, 5, 58, 74, 77ff., 111ff., 219, 221, 226
evolution, 69, 70, 72, 118, 145, 170, 225ff.

Exclusive Brethren, 2, 6, 214, 226, 228, 234
existential dread, 20
explanation, 3, 4, 13, 122, 144

Faith and Reason, On, 114
Falwell, Jerry, 5, 97, 104
fanaticism, 1, 27, 40
Fanon, Franz, 185, 191 n. 20
fascism, 185
Father and Son (Gosse), 226, 227
feminism, 2, 6, 21ff., 123, 184, 185, 194, 204, 205
Fiorenza, Francis Schüssler, 150 n. 31
FitzGerald, Edward, 222
Flew, Anthony, 72, 141
Florida, 100, 102
Focus on the Family, 115
Foucault, Michel, 184, 185
Francis, Leslie, 204, 205
Frankfurt, Harry, 150 n. 25
freedom, complex, 230
free will, 62, 63, 67, 68, 138
Freud, Sigmund, 184

Gadamer, Hans-Georg, 109, 143, 151 n. 31
Genesis, 51, 53, 62, 102, 218
genocide, 60, 185
George Washington University, vii, 2
Glanton Brethren, 6, 155, 156, 160, 161, 163ff., 168, 170, 171
Gnostic scriptures, 82
Golden Treasury of the Best Songs and Lyrical Poems in the English Language, The (Palgrave, ed.), 222
Goliath, 58, 217
Gordon-Conwell Theological Seminary, 135
Gosse, Edmund, 226ff.
Gosse, Philip Henry, 226
Göttingen, 179
Gray, Thomas, 221
Great Depression, 16
Great Mr. Handel, The, 223
Greenspan, Patricia, 138
Greenville, S.C., 74
Greenville Senior High School, 76, 78
Gutmann, Amy, 127

Habermas, Jürgen, 166
Hagar, 218
Haggard, Rider, 220
Hampshire, Stuart, 163
Hannah, 217
Hare, R. M., 163
headship, 123

heaven, 16, 20, 32, 34, 54ff., 61, 63, 70, 74, 86, 99, 102, 122, 125, 126, 132
hell, 32, 37, 40, 42, 47, 50, 51, 56, 59, 60, 63, 66, 70, 71, 83, 96, 99, 116, 118ff., 122, 126, 131
hermeneutics, 105, 107
high-demand organizations, 1, 224
Hildegard of Bingen, 183
Hill, Thomas, 120, 121, 127
History of Western Philosophy (Russell), 162
Hitler, Adolf, 67, 68
Hodge, Charles, 135
homosexuality, 84, 104, 105
Horner, Michael, 72
human sciences, vii, 2
Hume, David, 19, 54, 83, 135, 139, 203
Hutchings, Maurice, 69, 70
Huxley, Leonard, 235 n. 8
Huxley, Thomas Henry, 224, 225
Hyun, Insu, 151 n. 33

Imitation of Christ, The (Thomas à Kempis), 82–83
indoctrination, indirect, 4, 11
indoctrination, self-, 5, 27ff.
Inferno, The (Dante), 47
Ingoldsby Legends, The (Barham), 221
Institute of Education (London), 164
intelligent design, 72
intuitionism, 162
Iowa, 182
Isis, 54

James, William, 141
Jantzen, Grace M., 26 n. 15
Jarmin, Ms., 200, 201
Jeans, James, 222
Jehovah's Witnesses, 17, 25 n. 8
Jesus, 12, 13, 14, 19, 50, 51, 55ff., 61ff., 65, 66, 70, 71, 77, 78, 86, 87, 90, 99, 102, 105, 106, 111, 135, 195, 217, 228, 233
Jews, 18, 23, 40, 52, 54, 135, 148, 150 n. 24, 188
jihad, 29
John of the Cross, Saint, 109
Jonah, 30, 58, 106
Josephus, 66
justice, 30, 43ff., 50, 55, 120, 126, 134, 166, 177, 178, 192 n. 2, 231

Kant, Immanuel, 43, 44, 149 n. 6, 163, 165, 166, 223
Kazepides, Tasos, 141
Kelsay, John, 150 n. 31

King James version, 13, 15, 23, 66, 135, 155
Kingsley, Charles, 225
Kingston, Jamaica, 220
Knowledge and Human Interests (Habermas), 166
Koenig, Don, 132 n. 25
Kollbocker, Ray, 132 n. 15
Koresh, David, 138
kulaks, 188

Language, Truth and Logic (Ayer), 162
Language of Morals, The (Hare), 163
Latter-day Saints. *See* Mormons
Letter Concerning Toleration, A (Locke), 138
Levinas, Emmanuel, 184
Lewis, Bernard, 48 n. 2
Lewis, C. S., 69, 180, 225
Liberty University, 5, 97, 98, 102, 103
Lindbeck, George, 141
Liszt, Franz, 101
Livingstone, David, 51
Locke, John, 19, 138, 203, 223
logical positivism, 162
Lourdes, 57
love, 3, 4, 17, 22, 24, 25, 43, 44, 60, 76, 77, 90, 103, 157, 183, 184, 193, 207, 209ff., 217, 234, 236 n. 10
Lubyanka, 179
Luke, 65
Luther, Martin, 97
Lutherans, 135, 150 n. 24
Lutzer, Erwin W., 132 n. 10
Lycidas (Milton), 221
Lynchburg, Va., 104

MacIntyre, Alasdair, 166ff.
MacKinnon, Catherine, 205
Macmillan, C. J. B., 149 n. 16
madrasas, madrassas, 1, 27
Makhno, 176
Manitoba, 181
Man of God, 214
Mark, 219
marriage, 44, 101, 123, 124, 128, 161, 177
Martin, Michael, 26 n. 14
Martin, Sam, 52
Marty, Martin, 108
Marx, Karl, 188
materialism, 110
mathematics, 6, 159, 160, 162ff., 200
Matthew, 52, 65, 100, 106, 191 n. 19, 235 n. 7
McDowell, Josh, 114, 125
Mead, George, 143
meaning of life, 20ff., 24

Mecca, 29
Mechtild of Magdeburg, 183
Mee, Arthur, 59
Mennonites, 6, 176ff.
Meno (Plato), 19, 93 n. 1
Mercer, C. W., 220
Merleau-Ponty, Maurice, 183, 185
Messiah, The (Handel), 223
Methodists, 17, 80, 134, 135, 150 n. 24
Mill, John Stuart, 151 nn. 38, 39
Miller, Hugh, 226
Milton, John, 221
Minister of the Lord in the Recovery, 214
modernism, 107
Moffatt, Robert and Mary, 51
Molotschna colony, 187
Monnier, Ricki, 26 n. 14
Moody Blues, 100
Moore, G. E., 162
moral drift, 128
Mormons, 2, 6, 192ff.
Moses, 12, 30, 55, 56, 58, 61
Moyers, Bill, 114
Much Ado About Nothing (Shakespeare), 223
Muhammad, 28, 29
Muslims, 1, 5, 18, 27ff., 48 n. 2, 54, 135
Mysterious Universe, The (Jeans), 222

Nagel, Thomas, 67
naturalism, 43, 44, 107
Nature of the Physical World, The (Eddington), 222
Nauvoo, Illinois, 194
Newell, Bridget, 203, 205
New Testament, 12, 23, 50, 58, 87, 105, 107, 110, 155, 156, 165, 226
New Zealand, 5, 50, 51
noble lies, 89
Northumberland, 6
numinous, the, 141
Nussbaum, Martha, 186

Odyssey (Homer), 47
Ohms, Peter, 71
Old Testament, 12, 23, 50, 58, 105, 107, 110, 226
Ontario, 6, 176
ontological argument, 19, 71
Origen, 66
Origin of Species, On the (Darwin), 226
Orthodox, 99, 101, 102
Osiris, 54
Otto, Rudolf, 141

Out to Win (Thornton), 59
Oxford University, 7, 163

Palgrave, Francis Turner, 222
pantheism, 23
Paraguay, 176
Pascal, Blaise, 25 n. 6
Pascal's Wager, 16, 38, 131
Paternoster Row, 220, 226
Paul, Saint, 50, 58, 72, 182, 221
Pell grants, 202
Peter, Saint, 102
Peters, Richard, 164
Pharisees, 45
philosopher-king, 215
Philosophical Investigations (Wittgenstein), 163, 164
Philosophy and the Mirror of Nature (Rorty), 166
philosophy of education, 164, 165
philosophy of religion, 23
Philosophy of Simone de Beauvoir, The (Bergoffen), 212
Pilgrim's Progress (Bunyan), 59, 60
Pioneer Day, 194
Plantinga, Alvin, 48 n. 9
Plato, 19, 60, 82, 83, 93 n. 1, 186, 203, 215
Plymouth Brethren, 6, 155, 226
postmodernism, 107
Potala Palace, 183
Presbyterians, 17, 104, 135, 136, 150 n. 24
Principia Ethica (Moore), 162
private language argument, 164
Problem of Pain, The (Lewis), 69
Problems of Philosophy (Russell), 162
Proverbs, 218
Provo, Utah, 192, 200
psychiatry, 21
punishment, 20, 30, 36, 37, 39, 43ff., 48 n. 10, 76, 116, 119, 120, 121, 125, 157, 187, 193, 232, 234
purges, 179

Quakers, 165
Quest for the Historical Jesus (Schweitzer), 61
Qur'an, 27ff., 109, 151 n. 31
Qur'anic promise, 40, 42, 44
Qur'anic ultimatum, 32, 33, 38

Ramadan, 29
Ramsay, Mrs., 184
Rand, Ayn, 48 n. 8, 49 n. 16
relativism, 108, 114, 125, 187
Republic, The (Plato), 215

Revelation, 68, 221
Robertson, Pat, 132 n. 1
Roman Catholics, 5, 17, 18, 22, 25 n. 5, 51, 54, 57, 72, 73ff., 93 n. 10, 113, 115, 122, 148, 150 n. 24
Romania, 5, 97, 98, 100, 103, 104
Romans, 62
Rorty, Richard, 166
Rousseau, Jean-Jacques, 145, 203
Royal College of Music, 224
Royal College of Science, 224, 225
Royal Navy, 228
"Rubáiyát of Omar Khayyám of Naishápúr" (FitzGerald), 222
Rushdie, Salman, 29
Russell, Bertrand, 83, 162
Ryle, Gilbert, 163

Sabini, John, 128, 129
Said, Edward, 185
Salt Lake City, Utah, 195, 201, 202
Samson, 12
Samuel, 217
Sanger, Margaret, 204
Santa Claus, 23, 25 n. 11, 56, 57, 71
Sartre, Jean-Paul, 183
Satan, 48 n. 10, 67, 68, 116, 122, 180, 232, 233
Saussure, Ferdinand de, 109
Sawyer, Tom, 138
Scandal of the Evangelical Conscience, The (Sider), 122
Schleiermacher, Friedrich, 109, 141
Schopenhauer, Arthur, 236 n. 10
Schweitzer, Albert, 61
Science and the Modern World (Whitehead), 222
Scofield, Cyrus, 227
Scott, Robert Falcon, 220
Scottish Common Sense philosophy, 135
Screwtape Letters (Lewis), 69, 180, 225
Second Coming, 217
Second Sex, The (Beauvoir), 204, 206, 209
Sells, Michael, 109
Seneca, 66, 149 n. 6
Sermon on the Mount, 70, 151 n. 31, 219
Seventh Day Adventists, 69
sex, 1, 6, 12, 29, 30, 48 n. 7, 76, 80, 117, 118, 123, 124, 128, 161, 177, 180, 184, 222
sexism, 21, 22, 30
sexual abuse, 21, 181
sexual orientation, 107, 163
Shakespeare, William, 159, 223
shame, 72, 75, 83, 89, 180, 192, 198, 203, 210

Shaw, George Bernard, 61
shehada, 28, 29, 30
Shingler, S. V., 222
Shoah, 185
Shroud of Turin, 106
Siberia, 176
Sider, Ronald J., 122
Silver, Maury, 128, 129
sin, 12, 37, 50, 52, 60, 67, 75, 97, 101, 105, 114, 119, 122ff., 122, 129, 156ff., 172, 173, 187, 195, 202, 210, 224
skepticism, 14, 15, 18, 20, 22, 63, 101, 145, 170, 219
Smith, John, 97
Smith, Joseph, 195, 196
Smithouser, Bob, 132 n. 18
Socrates, 82, 215
Solomon, 12
Solovetsky, 179
Southern Baptists, 75, 87, 107, 123
South Kensington, 224
Soviet Union, 176
spirituals, 13
Spivak, Gayatri, 185
Stace, W. T., 23
Stalin, Joseph, 176
Stevens, Wallace, 46, 47
Stevenson, Robert Louis, 221
Stocker, Michael, 130
Strange Case of Dr. Jekyll and Mr. Hyde, The (Stevenson), 221
Strawson, P. F., 163, 164
Strong, A. H., 62, 63
Student Christian Movement, 69
Sunday School, 1, 12, 15, 17, 52, 58, 180
Systematic Theology (Hodge), 135
Systematic Theology (Strong), 62

Tacitus, 66
Tart, Charles T., 25 n. 10
Taylor, Charles, 143, 148
Taylor, James, Jr., 228
teleological argument, 19, 71
Ten Brave Boys, 59
Teresa of Avila, Saint, 109
Texas, 80
theism, 19, 23, 54
theoretical entities, 30
theosophy, 70
Thomas Aquinas, Saint, 49 n. 18
Thomas Road Baptist Church, 104
Thornton, Guy D., 51, 59
Tiberius, 66
Tibet, 183

Tillich, Paul, 141
To Kill a Mockingbird (Lee), 200
Toronto, 16, 19
totalitarianism, 33, 177, 185
Tracy, David, 150 n. 31
Trinity College, Cambridge, 159

Ukraine, 176, 178, 187
United Church, 17
United States, 176, 228
University of California at Riverside, 135
University of London, 164
University of Michigan, 135
University of Utah, 201
Utah, 2, 6, 192
utilitarianism, 162

values, 4, 15, 20, 22, 24, 28, 42, 43, 45, 49 n. 16, 50, 63, 101, 112ff., 116, 119, 124, 127, 140ff., 165, 230, 235
Vanderbilt University, 80
Vernon, C. G., 222, 223
Virgin Mary, 57

Wang, Thomas, 132 n. 9
Warner, Anna B., 25 n. 1
Wells, David F., 113
Wells, H. G., 225
Wesley, John, 134
Wesleyans, 5, 134, 135
Westminster Confession, 63

White, John, 25 n. 10
Whitehead, Alfred North, 222
White House, 205
Whose Virtue? (MacIntyre), 166
Why I Am Not a Christian (Russell), 83
Williams, Bernard, 133 n. 39
Williams, Rowan, 151 n. 31
Wilson, John, 141
With the Anzacs in Cairo (Thornton), 59
Wittgenstein, Ludwig, 143, 163, 164, 166
Wodehouse, P. G., 220
Wolterstorff, Nicholas, 48 n. 9
women's liberation, 179
Women's Studies, 184, 194
Woolf, Virginia, 184
World War II, 160, 220
Worst Journey in the World, The (Cherry-Garrard), 220
Wowser, The (Thornton), 59

Xian, 183

Yaffe, Gideon, 138
Yahweh, 55
Yambulakang, 183
Yates, Dornford, 220
Yeats, W. B., 221
Young, Brigham, 195, 196

Zeus, 54

www.ingramcontent.com/pod-product-compliance
Lightning Source LLC
Chambersburg PA
CBHW021400290426
44108CB00010B/319